Lab Manual for
A+ Guide to Hardware
Managing, Maintaining, and
Troubleshooting
FOURTH EDITION

Jean Andrews, Ph.D.

Todd Verge

THOMSON

COURSE TECHNOLOGY ™

Australia • Canada • Mexico • Singapore • Spain • United Kingdom • United States

Lab Manual for A+ Guide to Hardware
Managing, Maintaining, and Troubleshooting
FOURTH EDITION
is published by Thomson Course Technology

Managing Editor:
Larry Main

Senior Product Manager:
Michelle Ruelos Cannistraci

Editorial Assistant:
Jessica Reed

Marketing Manager:
Guy Baskaran

Development Editor:
Lisa M. Lord

Content Project Manager:
Summer Hughes

Executive Editor:
Stephen Helba

Acquisitions Editor:
Nick Lombardi

Manuscript Quality Assurance:
Christian Kunciw

Senior Manufacturing Coordinator:
Justin Palmeiro

Compositor:
Integra—Pondicherry, India

Cover Designer:
Betsy Young

Text Designer:
Betsy Young

ISBN-13: 978-0-619-21766-2

ISBN-10: 0-619-21766-9

Table of Contents

Preface

This lab manual is designed to be the best tool on the market to enable you to get the hands-on practical experience you need to learn to troubleshoot and repair personal computers. It contains 71 labs, each of which targets a practical problem you're likely to face in the real world when troubleshooting PCs. Every attempt has been made to write labs that allow you to use generic hardware devices. A specific hardware configuration isn't necessary to complete the labs. Each chapter contains labs designed to provide the structure novices need, as well as labs that challenge experienced and inquisitive students.

This book helps prepare you for the new A+ Certification exams offered through the Computer Technology Industry Association (CompTIA): A+ Essentials, 220–602, 220–603, and 220–604 as well as the previous A+ Core Hardware examination. Because the popularity of this certification credential is quickly growing among employers, becoming certified increases your ability to gain employment, improve your salary, and enhance your career. To find more information about A+ Upgrade Certification and its sponsoring organization, CompTIA, go to the CompTIA Web site at *www.comptia.org*.

Whether your goal is to become an A+ certified technician or a PC support technician, the *Lab Manual for A+ Guide to Hardware Fourth Edition*, along with Jean Andrews's textbooks, will take you there!

FEATURES

To ensure a successful experience for both instructors and students, this book includes the following pedagogical features:

- ◢ **Objectives**—Every lab opens with learning objectives that set the stage for students to absorb the lab's lessons.
- ◢ **Materials Required**—This feature outlines all the materials students need to complete the lab successfully.
- ◢ **Lab Preparation**—This feature alerts instructors and lab assistants to items to check or set up before the lab begins.
- ◢ **Activity Background**—A brief discussion at the beginning of each lab provides important background information.
- ◢ **Estimated Completion Time**—To help students plan their work, each lab includes an estimate of the total amount of time required to complete it.
- ◢ **Activity**—Detailed, numbered steps walk students through the lab. These steps are divided into manageable sections, with explanatory material between each section.
- ◢ **Figures**—Where appropriate, photographs of hardware or screenshots of software are provided to increase student mastery of the lab topic.
- ◢ **Review Questions**—Questions at the end of each lab help students test their understanding of the lab material.
- ◢ **Web Site**—For updates to this book and information about other A+ and PC Repair products, go to *www.course.com/pcrepair*.

ACKNOWLEDGMENTS

Jean would like to thank Nadine Schreiter of Lakeshore Technical College and Michael Lehrfeld of Brevard Community College, who served as technical editors of previous editions of the manual and still had an impact on this edition, and Walt Dundore of North Georgia Technical College, Scott Johns, and Jill West for their invaluable experience and help developing many of the labs.

Todd would like to give special thanks to Lisa Lord, whose encouragement and commitment to excellence guided him through the editorial process. He would also like to extend his sincere appreciation to Michelle Ruelos Cannistraci, Danielle Chouhan, and all the Thomson Course Technology staff for their instrumental roles in developing this lab manual. Most of all, he would like to thank Jean Andrews for her generosity in giving him this opportunity.

Many thanks to the peer reviewers: Gus Chang of Heald College, San Jose/Milpitas; Dennis Lewis of Colorado Technical University; Don Stroup of Ivy Tech Communication College, Fort Wayne; and Keith Conn of the Cleveland Institute of Electronics.

CLASSROOM SETUP

Lab activities have been designed to explore many different hardware setup and troubleshooting problems while attempting to keep the requirements for specific hardware to a minimum. Most labs can be done alone, although a few ask you to work with a partner. If you prefer to work alone, simply do all the steps yourself.

Most labs take 30 to 45 minutes; a few might take a little longer. For several of the labs, your classroom should be networked and provide access to the Internet. When access to Windows setup files is required, these files can be provided on the Windows installation CD, a network drive made available to the PC, or some other type of removable storage media.

When the OS isn't of concern, the minimum hardware requirements are as follows:

- 90 MHz or better Pentium-compatible computer
- 24 MB of RAM
- 540 MB hard drive
- A PC toolkit with an antistatic ground bracelet (ESD strap)

These are the minimum hardware requirements for Windows XP Professional:

- 233 MHz or better Pentium-compatible computer (300 MHz preferred)
- 64 MB of RAM (128 MB preferred)
- 1.5 GB hard drive (2 GB preferred)
- An NTFS partition that can be the partition where Windows XP is installed
- A user account with administrative privileges

These are the minimum hardware requirements for Windows 2000 Professional:

- 133 MHz or better Pentium-compatible computer
- 64 MB of RAM
- 650 MB hard drive
- An NTFS partition that can be the partition where Windows 2000 is installed
- A user account with administrative privileges

Here are the requirements for Windows 9x:

- ◢ 90 MHz or better Pentium-compatible computer
- ◢ 24 MB of RAM
- ◢ 195 MB hard drive

A few labs focus on special hardware. For example, one lab requires installing a CD-ROM drive, sound card, and speakers, and another lab uses a PC camera, a sound card, microphone, and speakers. Two labs require a multimeter, one lab requires a modem and a working phone line, and one lab requires a wireless card and router.

LAB SETUP INSTRUCTIONS

CONFIGURATION TYPE AND OPERATING SYSTEMS

Each lab begins with a list of required materials. Before beginning a lab activity, verify that each student workgroup or individual has access to these materials. Then make sure the correct operating system is installed and in good health. Note that in some cases, installing an operating system isn't necessary. When needed, the Windows setup files can be made available on the Windows CD, a network drive, or some type of removable media storage. In some labs, device drivers are needed. Students can work more efficiently if these drivers are available before beginning the lab.

PROTECT DATA

In several labs, data on the hard drive might get lost or corrupted. For this reason, it's important that valuable data stored on the hard drive is backed up to another medium.

ACCESS TO THE INTERNET

Several labs require access to the Internet. If necessary, you can use one computer to search the Internet to download software or documentation and another computer for performing the lab procedures. If the lab doesn't have Internet access, you can download the required software or documentation before the lab and bring the files to lab on some sort of storage medium.

THE TECHNICIAN'S WORK AREA

When opening a computer case, it's important to have the right tools and be properly grounded to ensure that you don't cause more damage than you repair. Take a look at the components of an ideal technician's work area:

- ◢ Grounding mat (with grounding wire properly grounded)
- ◢ Grounding wrist strap (attached to the grounding mat)
- ◢ Non-carpet flooring
- ◢ A clean work area (no clutter)
- ◢ A set of screwdrivers
- ◢ 1/4-inch Torx bit screwdriver
- ◢ 1/8-inch Torx bit screwdriver
- ◢ Needlenose pliers
- ◢ A PLCC (plastic leadless chip carrier)

◢ Pen light (flashlight)

◢ Several new antistatic bags (for transporting and storing hardware)

At minimum, you must have at least two key items. The first is a grounding strap. If a grounding mat isn't available, you can attach the grounding strap to the computer's chassis and, in most cases, provide sufficient grounding for handling hardware components inside the computer case. The second key item is, of course, a screwdriver. You won't be able to open most cases without some type of screwdriver.

PROTECT YOURSELF, YOUR HARDWARE, AND YOUR SOFTWARE

When you work on a computer, harming both the computer and yourself is possible. The most common accident when attempting to fix a computer problem is erasing software or data. Experimenting without knowing what you're doing can cause damage. To prevent these sorts of accidents as well as physically dangerous ones, take a few safety precautions. The following sections describe potential sources of damage to computers and explain how to protect against them.

POWER TO THE COMPUTER

To protect yourself and the equipment when working inside a computer, turn off the power, unplug the computer, and always use an antistatic grounding strap. Consider the monitor and the power supply to be "black boxes." Never remove the cover or put your hands inside this equipment unless you know the hazards of charged capacitors. Both the power supply and the monitor can hold a dangerous level of electricity even after they're turned off and disconnected from a power source.

STATIC ELECTRICITY OR ESD

Electrostatic discharge (ESD), commonly known as static electricity, is an electrical charge at rest. A static charge can build up on the surface of a nongrounded conductor and on non-conductive surfaces, such as clothing or plastic. When two objects with dissimilar electrical charges touch, static electricity passes between them until the dissimilar charges are made equal. To see how this works, turn off the lights in a room, scuff your feet on the carpet, and touch another person. Occasionally you see and feel the charge in your fingers. If you can feel the charge, you discharged at least 3000 volts of static electricity. If you hear the discharge, you released at least 6000 volts. If you see the discharge, you released at least 8000 volts of ESD. A charge of less than 3000 volts can damage most electronic components. You can touch a chip on an expansion card or system board and damage the chip with ESD and never feel, hear, or see the discharge.

ESD can cause two types of damage in an electronic component: catastrophic failures and upset failures. A catastrophic failure destroys the component beyond use. An upset failure damages the component so that it doesn't perform well, even though it might still function to some degree. Upset failures are the most difficult to detect because they aren't easily observed.

PROTECT AGAINST ESD

To protect the computer against ESD, always ground yourself before touching electronic components, including the hard drive, system board, expansion cards, processors, and memory modules. Ground yourself and the computer parts, using one or more of the following static control devices or methods:

- ▲ *Grounding strap or antistatic strap:* A grounding strap is a bracelet you wear around your wrist. The other end is attached to a grounded conductor, such as the computer case or a ground mat, or it can plug into a wall outlet. (Only the ground prong makes a connection!)
- ▲ *Grounding mats:* Grounding mats can come equipped with a cord to plug into a wall outlet to provide a grounded surface on which to work. Remember, if you lift the component off the mat, it's no longer grounded and is susceptible to ESD.
- ▲ *Static shielding bags:* New components come shipped in static shielding bags. Save the bags to store other devices that aren't currently installed in a PC.

The best way to protect against ESD is to use a grounding strap with a grounding mat. You should consider a grounding strap essential equipment when working on a computer. However, if you're in a situation where you must work without one, touch the computer case before you touch a component. When passing a chip to another person, ground yourself. Leave components inside their protective bags until you're ready to use them. Work on hard floors, not carpet, or use antistatic spray on carpets.

There's an exception to the ground-yourself rule. Inside a monitor case, the electricity stored in capacitors poses a substantial danger. When working inside a monitor, you *don't* want to be grounded, as you would provide a conduit for the voltage to discharge through your body. In this situation, be careful *not* to ground yourself.

When handling system boards and expansion cards, don't touch the chips on the boards. Don't stack boards on top of each other, which could accidentally dislodge a chip. Hold cards by the edges, but don't touch the edge connections on the card.

After you unpack a new device or software that has been wrapped in cellophane, remove the cellophane from the work area quickly. Don't allow anyone who's not properly grounded to touch components. Don't store expansion cards within one foot of a monitor because the monitor can discharge as much as 29,000 volts of ESD onto the screen.

Hold an expansion card by the edges. Don't touch any of the soldered components on a card. If you need to put an electronic device down, place it on a grounding mat or a static shielding bag. Keep components away from your hair and clothing.

PROTECT HARD DRIVES AND DISKS

Always turn off a computer before moving it to protect the hard drive, which is always spinning when the computer is turned on (unless the drive has a sleep mode). Never jar a computer while the hard disk is running. Avoid placing a PC on the floor, where users could accidentally kick it.

Follow the usual precautions to protect CDs and floppy disks. Protect the bottom of CDs from scratches and keep them away from heat and direct sunlight. Keep floppies away from magnetic fields, heat, and extreme cold. Don't open the floppy shuttle window or touch the surface of the disk inside the housing. Treat disks with care, and they'll usually last for years.

CHAPTER 1

Introducing Hardware

Labs included in this chapter:

LAB 1.1 GATHER AND RECORD SYSTEM INFORMATION

OBJECTIVES

The goal of this lab is to use a system's physical characteristics and other sources to determine how the system is configured. After completing this lab, you will be able to:

◢ Gather system information by observing a system

◢ Use available tools to access specific system information

MATERIALS REQUIRED

This lab requires the following:

◢ Windows 2000/XP or Windows 98 operating system

◢ Individuals or a workgroup of 2 to 4 students

LAB PREPARATION

Before the lab begins, the instructor or lab assistant needs to do the following:

◢ Verify that Windows starts with no errors.

ACTIVITY BACKGROUND

When working with a computer system, it's a good idea to know what components are installed on the system. This lab helps you identify some of these components as you gather information by observing the system and by using system tools.

ESTIMATED COMPLETION TIME: 15 minutes

 Activity

Observe the physical characteristics of your system and answer the following questions:

1. Does the system have any identification on it indicating manufacturer, model, or component information? If so, list this information:

   _____

   _____

2. How many CD or DVD drives does your system have?

   _____

3. Describe the shape of the connection your mouse uses. How many pins does the connection have?

   _____

4. How many floppy drives does your system have?

   _____

5. How many internal hard drives does your system have? Explain how you got your answer:

   _____

Like other versions of Windows, users can customize Windows XP to behave and to display information to suit their tastes. Windows XP can also mimic the way previous versions of Windows presented menus and settings for users who are more comfortable with those methods. If the OS you're using in this lab is Windows XP, to help ensure that the step-by-step instructions are easy for you to follow, complete these steps to restore Windows XP defaults to your system:

1. Boot your system and log on, if necessary, and then click **Start, Control Panel** to open the Control Panel window.

2. Under the Control Panel heading at the left, click **Switch to Category View** if Classic view has been enabled. Figure 1-1 shows Control Panel in Category view.

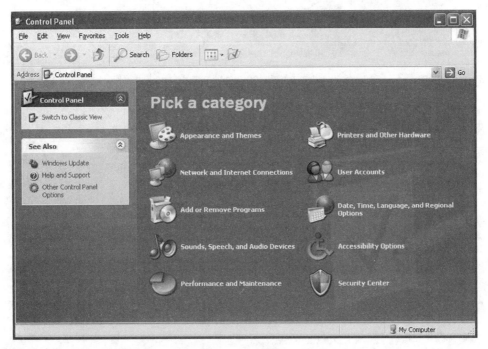

Figure 1-1 Windows XP Control Panel in Category view

3. With Category view enabled, click the **Appearance and Themes** category. The Appearance and Themes window opens.

4. In the Appearance and Themes window, click **Folder Options** in the Control Panel icons list to open the Folder Options dialog box.

5. In the General tab of the Folder Options dialog box, click the **Restore Defaults** button (see Figure 1-2), and then click **Apply**.

6. Click the **View** tab in the Folder Options dialog box (see Figure 1-3). Click the **Restore Defaults** button, and then click **OK** to apply the settings and close the dialog box.

7. In the Appearance and Themes window, click the **Taskbar and Start Menu** icon. The Taskbar and Start Menu dialog box opens.

Figure 1-2 Use the Folder Options dialog box to restore Windows XP defaults to a folder

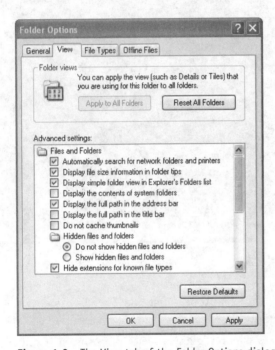

Figure 1-3 The View tab of the Folder Options dialog box

8. In the Taskbar tab, verify that all check boxes in the Taskbar appearance section are selected except for Auto-hide the taskbar and Show Quick Launch, as shown in Figure 1-4. Click **Apply** if any changes were made.

Figure 1-4   Use the Taskbar and Start Menu Properties dialog box to control
how the taskbar appears and functions

9. Click the **Start Menu** tab in the Taskbar and Start Menu dialog box. Verify that the
   Start menu option button is selected, as shown in Figure 1-5. Click **OK** to apply the settings and close the dialog box. Close the Appearance and Themes window.

Figure 1-5   The Start Menu tab of the Taskbar and Start Menu Properties dialog box

Regardless of the Windows OS you're using, from the Start menu, open Control Panel and click
the **Performance and Maintenance** category. The Performance and Maintenance window opens.

In the Performance and Maintenance window, click the **System** icon to open the System Properties dialog box. With the General tab visible as shown in Figure 1-6, record the following:

Figure 1-6   The System Properties dialog box

1. Which OS is installed?

_____

2. What is the version number of your operating system?

_____

3. Who is the system registered to?

_____

4. According to the System Properties dialog box, what type of CPU is your system built around?

_____

5. How much RAM is installed in your system?

_____

Close the System Properties dialog box and the Performance and Maintenance window.

Click **Start, My Computer** and locate the following information in the My Computer window:

1. How many floppy disk drives are listed, and which drive letters are assigned to them?

_____

2. How many other local drives are listed, and which drive letters are assigned to them?

_____

3. How many network drives are listed, and what are their names?

_____

4. What items are listed under System Tasks at the left of the My Computer window?

_____

_____

_____

REVIEW QUESTIONS

1. List two other ways to get to the System Properties dialog box besides using Control Panel:

_____

_____

2. What's one other place, not in Windows or any documentation, where you could determine the CPU, CPU speed, and amount of RAM installed on your system?

_____

_____

3. What differences, if any, are there between a list of components derived from a physical inspection versus a list of components derived from My Computer and System Properties?

_____

_____

LAB 1.2 IDENTIFY COMPUTER PARTS

OBJECTIVES

The goal of this lab is to examine your computer to identify the parts inside and outside the case. After completing this lab, you will be able to:

◢ Identify computer components outside the case

◢ Identify computer components inside the case

MATERIALS REQUIRED

This lab requires the following:

◢ A working computer

◢ A Phillips head screwdriver

◢ An antistatic ground strap

◢ Workgroup of 2 to 4 students

◢ A display of four or more computer parts to be identified by students

LAB PREPARATION

Before the lab begins, the instructor or lab assistant needs to do the following:

◢ Provide a computer that can have the cover removed for each student workgroup.

◢ Gather up four or more computer parts for display in each student workgroup or area of the lab.

ACTIVITY BACKGROUND

When working with a computer system, you must be able to identify the hardware components, both inside and outside the case. Components are not always labeled adequately, especially those inside the case. This lab helps you learn to recognize these components.

ESTIMATED COMPLETION TIME: 30 minutes

Activity

Observe the physical characteristics of your system and answer the following questions:

1. Is the monitor a CRT or an LCD monitor? What size monitor do you have? Measure from the upper-left corner to the lower-right corner (the diagonal) on the monitor screen. Is the measurement what you expected for the size of the monitor?

   _____

2. If you're using a CRT, also measure the diagonal on an LCD monitor if possible. If you're using an LCD monitor, also measure the diagonal on a CRT. What size is the second monitor?

   _____

3. How many keys are on your keyboard?

   _____

4. Are there any switches on the sides or bottom of the keyboard? If so, how are these switches labeled?

   _____

5. What other external components does your PC have (speakers, printer, and so forth)? Describe each component with as much detail as you can:

   _____

   _____

   _____

6. Look at the back of your PC and list all cables and cords connected to ports and other connections. Fill in the following chart:

Describe the port or connector the cable or cord is connected to	Purpose of the cable or cord
1.	
2.	
3.	
4.	
5.	
6.	

7. What other ports on the PC are not being used? List them:

_____

_____

_____

_____

Next, you'll open the PC case and examine the components inside. As you work, make sure you do *not* touch anything inside the case unless you're wearing an antistatic ground strap that's clipped to the case so that any electrical charge between you and the case is dissipated.

To remove the cover from a desktop PC, follow these steps:

1. Power down the PC and unplug it. Next, unplug the monitor, printer, and any other device that has its own external power supply. Do not disconnect any cables or cords (other than the power supply cord) connected to the back of the PC case.

2. Case manufacturers use slightly different methods to open the case. Many newer cases require that you remove the faceplate on the front of the case first. Other cases require removing a side panel first, and very old cases require removing the entire sides and top as a single unit first. Study your case for the correct approach.

3. If you find screws on the rear of the case along the edges, such as those in Figure 1-7, start by removing these screws. For a desktop or tower case, locate and remove the screws on the back of the case. For a desktop case, such as the one in Figure 1-7, look for screws in each corner and one in the top. Be careful not to unscrew any screws besides these. The other screws are probably holding the power supply in place (see Figure 1-8).

Figure 1-7   Locate the screws that hold the cover in place

Figure 1-8   Power supply mounting screws

4. After you remove the cover screws, slide the cover forward and up to remove it from the case, as shown in Figure 1-9.

Figure 1-9   Removing the cover

To remove the cover from an older tower PC with case screws on the rear of the case, follow these steps:

1. Power down the PC and unplug it from its power outlet. Next, unplug the monitor and any other device with an external power source from the power outlet.

2. Some cases are a solid piece of metal and come apart in one piece; others come in pieces and the sides or top can be removed separately. Look for screws in all four corners and down the sides. For one-piece covers, remove the screws and then slide the cover back slightly before lifting it up to remove it, as shown in Figure 1-10.

Figure 1-10   Removing a tower cover

For cases with panels on either side of the case held in place with screws on the back of the case, remove the screws and slide each panel toward the rear and then lift it off the case (see Figure 1-11).

Figure 1-11   Slide a side panel to the rear and then lift it off the case

To remove the cover from a newer tower PC with no visible case screws, follow these steps:

1. Power down the PC and unplug it from its power outlet. Next, unplug the monitor and any other device with an external power source from the power outlet.

2. On newer cases, you must pop the front panel off the case before removing the side panels. Look for a lever on the bottom of the panel and hinges at the top. Squeeze the lever to release the front panel and lift it off the case (see Figure 1-12). Then remove any screws holding the side panel in place, as shown in Figure 1-13, and slide the side panel to the front and then off the case.

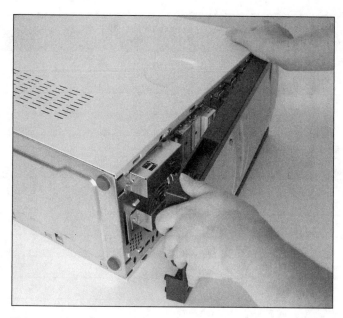

Figure 1-12   Newer cases require removing the front panel before removing the side panels of a computer case

Figure 1-13 One screw holds the side panel in place

Some case panels don't use screws; these side panels simply pop up and out with a little prying and pulling.

With the cover removed, you're ready to look for some components. As you complete the following, refer to drawings and photos in Chapters 3, 4, and 5 of *A+ Guide to Hardware* or Chapters 4, 5, and 6 of *A+ Guide to Managing and Maintaining Your PC*, if necessary.

1. Put on your antistatic ground strap and connect the clip to the side of the computer case.

2. Identify and describe the following major components. List any other components you find inside the case. Fill in the following chart:

Component	Description (include size, location, what it connects to, and what's connected to it in the system)
Power supply	
Floppy disk drive	
Hard drive	
CD-ROM drive	
Motherboard	
CPU	
Cooling fan (not inside the power supply)	
Video card	
Network card	
Sound card	

CHALLENGE ACTIVITY

If your instructor has prepared a display of four or more assorted computer parts, fill in the following chart:

Identify the part	Describe how you determined your answer
1.	
2.	
3.	
4.	
5.	
6.	

REVIEW QUESTIONS

1. Describe how you decided which expansion card was the video card:

2. If your system has a CD-ROM drive, describe how you determined which drive was the CD-ROM drive:

3. Describe how you identified the type of CPU you have:

4. How did you know that you were or were not connected to a network?

5. Does your system have much room for adding new components? What type of component might be added?

6. If you were adding or upgrading a component, what would it be and where would you install it in the computer case?

LAB 1.3 USE SHAREWARE TO EXAMINE A COMPUTER, PART 1

OBJECTIVES

The goal of this lab is to use Sandra, Standard version, to examine your system. After completing this lab, you will be able to:

◢ Download a file from the Internet

◢ Install Sandra

◢ Use Sandra to examine your system

MATERIALS REQUIRED

This lab requires the following:

◢ Windows 2000/XP or Windows 98 operating system

◢ Internet access

◢ If using Windows 98 or Windows 2000, software such as WinZip to uncompress a zipped file

LAB PREPARATION

Before the lab begins, the instructor or lab assistant needs to do the following:

◢ Verify that Internet access is available.

◢ For labs that don't have Internet access, download these files to a file server, flash drive, CD-R, or other media available to students in the lab:

> • Sandra executable file downloaded from *www.sisoftware.co.uk*

> • For Windows 98 or Windows 2000 systems, an uncompress utility, such as WinZip, downloaded from *www.winzip.com*

ACTIVITY BACKGROUND

Good PC support people are always good investigators. This lab is designed to help you learn how to conduct an investigation using the Internet. As you'll see, the Internet offers a wealth of resources to those who take the time to search, download, and investigate the possible uses of software available there. This lab helps you learn to be such an investigator. Follow these directions to find and download a shareware utility that you can use to diagnose PC problems. If you have a classroom printer available, you'll print a report from the downloaded software about the hardware and software on your computer.

ESTIMATED COMPLETION TIME: 30 minutes

 Activity

 Notes

If the SiSoftware Web site is unavailable, you can use a search engine to locate the shareware.

1. Open your browser and go to **www.sisoftware.co.uk**.

2. Click the **Downloads** link.

3. Follow one of the links pointing to a location for the Sandra download.

4. Follow the instructions on the site you selected to begin the download process.

5. When the File Download dialog box opens, save the file to your PC desktop. You can then disconnect from the Internet. What is the name of the downloaded file?

Next, follow these steps to install Sandra on your PC:

1. If the file has a .zip file extension, double-click it to uncompress the Sandra zip file and extract the setup file.

2. Run the setup program by double-clicking the executable file, which has an .exe file extension. (It might be the downloaded file or the extracted file.) In the installation

wizard, use English as the language selection, accept the end user license agreement (EULA), and accept the default settings throughout. The Sandra installation creates a new item in your Programs or All Programs menu and adds an icon to your desktop.

3. When you finish the installation, Sandra will start. Read the Tip of the Day, click to clear the **Show Tips on Start-up** check box, and then click **OK** to close. If you're using Windows XP, you should see a screen similar to the one in Figure 1-14.

Figure 1-14   SiSoftware Sandra main window in Windows XP

The screens for Windows 98 and Windows 2000 look similar, but, as shown in Figure 1-15, the icons aren't grouped under headings.

Figure 1-15   SiSoftware Sandra main window in Windows 2000 or Windows 98

You can run each utility by double-clicking its icon, or you can create a composite report of the results of each selection. To learn more, complete the following:

1. Double-click the **System Summary** icon (in the Information Modules group for Windows XP). The System Summary utility starts and gathers information about your system before displaying it in a format similar to Device Manager, with devices listed by type.

2. Click the red X at the bottom of the System Summary window or press **Esc** to close the System Summary utility.

3. Double-click the **Windows Information** icon (in the Information Modules group for Windows XP) to start that utility. Scroll down and note the information types that are listed. According to this utility, which version of Windows are you using?

   _____

4. What is the path to the Temporary folder on your system?

   _____

5. What is your Windows installation product key?

   _____

6. Click the red X at the bottom of the Windows Information window or press **Esc** to close the Windows Information utility.

7. Double-click the **Drives Information** icon (in the Information Modules group for Windows XP). The utility begins to gather information about your drives. Do not move the mouse or touch the keyboard while this procedure is in progress. How much total space does the hard drive contain? How much free space does the hard drive contain? What type of file system does the hard drive use?

   _____

   _____

8. Click the red X at the bottom of the Drives Information window or press **Esc** to close the Drives Information utility.

9. Double-click the **DMA Settings** icon to start that utility. Why are you unable to view the DMA Settings information?

   _____

10. Close the DMA Settings utility.

You can also use Sandra to create a composite report of your system. To learn more, follow these steps:

1. From the SiSoftware Sandra menu, click **File**, **Create a Report Wizard**.

2. In the wizard introduction window, click **Next** (right-pointing arrow in a green circle).

3. In the Step 1 of 9 window, verify that **Make choices and generate report** is selected in the drop-down list, and click **Next** to continue.

4. In the Step 2 of 9 window, click the **Clear All** (red X over a box) button. Click to select the **Mainboard Information** and **Windows Memory Information** check boxes, and then click **Next** to continue.

5. In the Step 3 of 9 window, click the **Clear All** button, and then click **Next** to continue.

6. In the Step 4 of 9 window, click the **Clear All** button, and then click **Next** to continue.

7. In the Step 5 of 9 window, click **Next** to continue.

8. In the Step 6 of 9 window, add any comments, if you like, and then click **Next** to continue.

9. In the Step 7 of 9 window, click the **Print or Fax** option in the drop-down list, and then click **Next** to continue.

10. In the Print dialog box, click **OK** for Windows 98 or **Print** for Windows 2000 and Windows XP. Click the **Exit** button (red X) to close the wizard, and then collect your report from the printer.

11. Continue to explore each utility in Sandra, and then close it. You'll use Sandra again in later chapters, so don't uninstall it.

In this lab, you downloaded Sandra from the SiSoftware Web site, but many popular utilities are available from multiple sources on the Internet. To see for yourself, follow these steps:

1. Attempt to find Sandra at *www.zdnet.com*.

2. Is the program available through this avenue as well? Print the Web page or pages to support your answer.

REVIEW QUESTIONS

1. What URL can you use to find a link to download Sandra?

2. Is Sandra capable of hardware diagnostics only?

3. Which two of the four system resources are you *not* able to view with the version of Sandra you downloaded, and why?

4. Some software is called diagnostic software and other software is called application software. Which type of software is Sandra?

LAB 1.4 USE SHAREWARE TO EXAMINE A COMPUTER, PART 2

OBJECTIVES

The goal of this lab is to use Belarc Advisor to examine your system. After completing this lab, you will be able to:

◢ Download a file from the Internet

◢ Install Belarc Advisor

◢ Use Belarc Advisor to examine your system

MATERIALS REQUIRED

This lab requires the following:

▲ Windows 2000/XP or Windows 98 operating system

▲ Internet access

LAB PREPARATION

Before the lab begins, the instructor or lab assistant needs to do the following:

▲ Verify that Internet access is available.

▲ For labs that don't have Internet access, download Belarc Advisor (Advisor.exe) from *www.belarc.com* and make the file available to students in the lab.

ACTIVITY BACKGROUND

Good PC support people know that there's always more than one way to do something. In Lab 1.3, you learned to use Sandra to investigate your system. In this lab, you use another shareware utility, Belarc Advisor, to examine your system. Follow these directions to find and download this utility that you can use to diagnose PC problems. Then you print a report from the downloaded software about the hardware and software on your computer.

If your lab doesn't have Internet access, ask your instructor for the location of files downloaded previously for you to use. Write the path to those files here:

_____

ESTIMATED COMPLETION TIME: 30 minutes

 Activity

> 🖉 **Notes**
>
> If the Belarc Web site is unavailable, you can use a search engine to locate the shareware.

1. Open your browser and go to **www.belarc.com**.

2. Click the **FREE DOWNLOAD** link.

3. Follow one of the links pointing to a location that offers Belarc Advisor for download.

4. Follow the instructions on the site you selected to begin the download process.

5. When the File Download dialog box opens, save the file to your PC desktop. You can then disconnect from the Internet. At the time I tested this lab, the downloaded file name was Advisor.exe, but sometimes Web sites and file names change. What is the name of your downloaded file?

Next, follow these steps to install Belarc Advisor on your PC:

1. Run the setup program by double-clicking the downloaded executable file, **Advisor.exe** (or the name of your downloaded file). In the installation wizard, click **Install**, and accept the EULA. The Belarc Advisor installation automatically takes a snapshot of your computer, and then creates an item in your Start menu and adds an icon to your desktop.

2. When you finish the installation, Belarc Advisor uses your default Web browser to show the results of the snapshot. If you're using Windows XP, you should see a screen similar to the one in Figure 1-16.

Figure 1-16   Belarc Advisor uses your browser to display information about your system

Answer the following questions to learn what Belarc Advisor is telling you about your system:

1. What is the name of the manufacturer and model of the motherboard installed on your system?

   _____

2. What is the version of Windows you're using?

   _____

3. What is the product key for Windows?

   _____

4. What is the speed and model of the processor for the system?

   _____

5. Are there any security updates that need to be applied?

   _____

6. How much total space does the hard drive contain? How much free space does the hard drive contain? What type of file system does the hard drive use?

   _____

   _____

7. To print the Belarc results, from your browser's menu, click **File**, **Print**.

8. In the Print dialog box, click **OK** for Windows 98 or **Print** for Windows 2000 and Windows XP.

9. Take a few minutes to explore the report that Belarc Advisor generated. List three other items of information not mentioned already in this lab that you think might be useful when troubleshooting a computer:

_____

_____

_____

You'll use Belarc Advisor again in later chapters, so don't uninstall it.

In this lab, you downloaded Belarc Advisor from the Belarc Web site, but many popular utilities are available from multiple sources on the Internet. To see for yourself, follow these steps:

1. Attempt to find Belarc Advisor at *www.zdnet.com*.

2. Is the program available through this avenue as well? Print the Web page or pages to support your answer.

_____

REVIEW QUESTIONS

1. What URL can you use to find a link to download Belarc Advisor?

_____

2. What tool do you use to get a printed report from Belarc Advisor?

_____

3. What type of software is Belarc Advisor?

_____

4. Compare Belarc Advisor to Sandra that you downloaded and used in Lab 1.3. Which utility do you think is the most useful, and why? Which is easier to use?

_____

_____

LAB 1.5 COMPARE COSTS

OBJECTIVES

The objective of this lab is to compare a preassembled system with the components that could be assembled to build a comparable system. After completing this lab, you will be able to:

◢ Identify the key components of a preassembled system

◢ Locate prices for components needed to assemble a comparable system

◢ Compare the cost of a preassembled system and a self-assembled system

MATERIALS REQUIRED

This lab requires the following:

◢ Internet access and/or access to a computer publication, such as *Computer Shopper*

LAB PREPARATION

Before the lab begins, the instructor or lab assistant needs to do the following:

◢ Verify that Internet access is available.

ACTIVITY BACKGROUND

In this lab, you compare the cost of a brand-name system with the cost of a system having similar specifications but assembled from separate components. Brand-name manufacturers typically build their systems from parts only they market, called "proprietary" parts. Therefore, it's unlikely that you'll be able to find exact matches for brand-name components. However, you can find comparable components. For example, if a Gateway computer has a 40 GB hard drive installed, find another 40 GB hard drive for your list of parts. The idea is to find a close match for each major component so that you can compare the total cost of a brand-name system and a similar system built from parts. Use the Internet and available computer-related publications as your sources for information.

ESTIMATED COMPLETION TIME: 45 minutes

 Activity

1. Find an advertisement for a complete, preassembled system similar to the one in Figure 1-17. Some manufacturers you might want to check out are Gateway (*www.gateway.com*), Dell (*www.dell.com*), and IBM (*www.ibm.com*).

Figure 1-17 Complete, preassembled system

2. Study the advertisement and list the following specifications:

  ◢ Processor/MHz _____

  ◢ RAM: _____

  ◢ OS: _____

  ◢ HDD capacity: _____

  ◢ Monitor: _____

  ◢ Video card: _____

  ◢ Sound/speakers: _____

  ◢ Other drives: _____

  ◢ Bonus items: _____

  ◢ Bundled software: _____

  ◢ Total price: _____

3. Find advertisements similar to those in Figure 1-18. Notice that the items are grouped by component type.

Figure 1-18   Components for sale

Using the following chart, list and describe the comparable components, their prices, and the source of your information. You might want to check several sources to find the best price. Remember, most mail-order or online purchases have shipping costs. If you can determine an exact shipping price for each component, include this information as part of the component's price. If you can't find the exact shipping price, include a 10% fee as part of the price for each shipped component. You might have to include tax, depending on the state-to-state taxing laws that apply. Sometimes the shipping cost is offset by not having to pay state sales tax on an item. Also, because you're early in the course, you might not know enough details about matching components inside the computer case, such as matching a processor to a motherboard. How to find correct matches is covered later in the book, but for now, a close match is all that's necessary.

Component	Description	Source	Price
Processor/MHz			
Motherboard			
RAM			
Case and power supply			
OS			
HDD capacity			
Monitor			
Sound/speakers			
CD-ROM drive			
Other drives			
Bonus items (such as video card)			
Bundled software			
TOTAL SYSTEM PRICE			

REVIEW QUESTIONS

1. Which approach to acquiring a system seems to be less expensive?

2. What is the single most expensive component of a system built from separate components?

3. What was the estimated cost of shipping (if any) for the component-built system?

4. What are some potential pitfalls of building your own PC? Rewards?

Notes

As you continue with this course, you'll be better able to answer this last question based on your own experiences.

LAB 1.6 PLAN AN IDEAL SYSTEM

OBJECTIVES

The objective of this lab is to plan and price your own ideal system within a budget. After completing this lab, you will be able to:

◢ Describe what you want your system to be able to do

◢ Pick components that best meet your goal

◢ Stay within a budget

MATERIALS REQUIRED

This lab requires the following:

◢ Internet access and/or access to a computer publication, such as *Computer Shopper*

LAB PREPARATION

Before the lab begins, the instructor or lab assistant needs to do the following:

◢ Provide Internet access in the lab or announce that students need to bring computer publications, such as *Computer Shopper*, to the lab.

ACTIVITY BACKGROUND

In the future, you might be in a position to build a system to your specifications from separate components. Within a budget of $800, what system would you put together? In this lab, you determine the answer based on your current knowledge and experience. Expect that your opinions will likely change as you continue in this course.

ESTIMATED COMPLETION TIME: 30 minutes

Activity

1. On a separate piece of paper, make a chart similar to the one used in Lab 1.5. Use it to list the components you would like to include in your system, the cost of each component, and the source for each component. To begin, list everything you want without considering price.

2. After you have determined the total price of all the components you want to include in your ideal system, add up the prices and see whether you are within your $800 budget.

3. If you are under budget, consider including additional components or better versions of components. If you're over budget, determine what components you need to exclude or whether you need to use less expensive versions of some components. Either way, record what components you choose. Also, note how you altered your ideal system to meet your budget.

REVIEW QUESTIONS

1. What is the goal of your system? In other words, how do you plan to use your system? Explain your choices for components.

_____

_____

_____

2. How would you change your choices if you were to use this computer in a corporate office as a business workstation?

_____

_____

_____

3. What single change would you make if you had an extra $200 in the budget?

_____

_____

4. How might you change your design if your budget was only $600?

_____

_____

 Tip

Keep your responses to this lab for later reference. As you learn more about PCs in this course, you can look back at these responses and see where you might change your mind based on new information you have learned.

PC Repair Fundamentals

Labs included in this chapter:

- **Lab 2.1:** Observe the Boot Process

- **Lab 2.2:** Take a Computer Apart and Put It Back Together

- **Lab 2.3:** Choose a System

- **Lab 2.4:** Determine System Requirements

- **Lab 2.5:** Compare What You Need with What You Can Afford

- **Lab 2.6:** Check System Compatibility

- **Lab 2.7:** Evaluate an Upgrade

LAB 2.1 OBSERVE THE BOOT PROCESS

OBJECTIVES

The goal of this lab is to give you the opportunity to observe the sequence of events in a PC's boot process. After completing this lab, you will be able to:

⊿ Describe the boot process in detail

⊿ Halt the boot process

⊿ Diagnose problems in the boot process

MATERIALS REQUIRED

This lab requires the following:

⊿ Windows 2000/XP or Windows 9x operating system

⊿ A blank floppy disk

⊿ A workgroup of 2 to 4 students

LAB PREPARATION

Before the lab begins, the instructor or lab assistant needs to do the following:

⊿ Verify that Windows starts with no errors.

⊿ Make sure that in CMOS setup, the boot sequence is the floppy drive first and then the hard drive.

ACTIVITY BACKGROUND

This lab familiarizes you with the boot process and gives you some practice recognizing when the boot process halts and observing the resulting information displayed on the screen. Working in teams, you begin by observing a PC booting up and noting every step, from turning on the power to the appearance of the Windows desktop. When you're familiar with all the steps in the boot process, your team then intentionally introduces problems that cause the boot process to fail on your PC and then observes the results. Next, you introduce one problem on your PC, and your team switches PCs with another team's PC and attempts to figure out why that team's PC failed to boot.

ESTIMATED COMPLETION TIME: 30 minutes

 Activity

Boot your team's PC and then, using the information on the screen as a guide, record every step in the process. (List this information on a separate piece of paper.) For example, you're looking for RAM initialization, display of CPU speed, a list of devices that are detected, what happens when the screen turns from black to another color, and other similar events. You might have to boot the PC several times to record all the steps. Also, sometimes you can use the Pause key to pause what's on the screen so that you can read it before it flies by.

Perform the following steps to introduce a problem in the boot process of your team's PC. For each problem, boot the PC and describe the problem as a user unfamiliar with PC technology might describe it. List any error messages you see.

1. Insert a blank floppy disk into the floppy drive. Describe the problem as a user sees it, including error messages:

   _____

   _____

2. Unplug the keyboard. Describe the problem. Does the computer still boot into Windows?

   _____

   _____

3. Unplug the mouse. Describe the problem. Does the computer still boot into Windows?

   _____

   _____

4. Unplug the monitor. Describe the problem:

   _____

5. After a minute, plug the monitor in. Did the system boot correctly?

   _____

6. Now cause one problem in the preceding steps and switch places with another team. Do not tell the other team what problem you caused.

7. Detect, diagnose, and remedy the problem on the other team's PC.

REVIEW QUESTIONS

1. What is the first message displayed on the screen after you turn on the power?

   _____

   _____

2. What devices are detected during the boot process?

   _____

   _____

3. Of all the problems you studied during the lab, which one halts the boot process earliest in the process?

   _____

4. Which problem results in messages about the operating system not being displayed?

   _____

5. Why do you think being familiar with all steps in the boot process is useful?

   _____

LAB 2.2 TAKE A COMPUTER APART AND PUT IT BACK TOGETHER

OBJECTIVES

The goal of this lab is to help you get comfortable working inside a computer case. After completing this lab, you will be able to:

- Take a computer apart
- Recognize components
- Reassemble the computer

MATERIALS REQUIRED

This lab requires the following:

- A computer designated for disassembly
- A PC toolkit with an antistatic ground strap and mat
- A marker and masking tape
- Small containers, such as paper cups, to hold screws as you work
- A workgroup of 2 to 4 students or individual students

LAB PREPARATION

Before the lab begins, the instructor or lab assistant needs to do the following:

- Verify that a computer designated for disassembly is available to each student or workgroup.

ACTIVITY BACKGROUND

If you follow directions and take your time, there's no reason to be intimidated by working inside a computer case. This lab takes you step by step through the process of disassembling and reassembling a PC. Follow your computer lab's posted safety procedures when disassembling and reassembling a PC, and remember to always wear your antistatic ground strap. Also, never force a component to fit into its slot.

You begin this lab by removing the cover of your PC and then removing the components inside. Next, you reassemble the components and replace the cover. This lab includes steps for working with a desktop PC and a tower PC. Follow the steps that apply to your computer.

Also, in this lab, you're instructed to disassemble your PC in this order: expansion cards, interior cables and cords, power supply, case fans, motherboard, and drives. Because some systems are designed so that the disassembly order is different from this one, your instructor might change the order. For example, you might not be able to get to the power supply to remove it until drives or the motherboard are out of the way. Be sure to follow any specific directions from your instructor.

> **Notes**
>
> In a lab environment, the instructor might consider giving a demonstration of tearing down a PC and putting it back together before students begin this lab.

As you work, when you remove a screw, place it in a paper cup or on a piece of paper so that you can keep different size screws separated. Later, when you reassemble, organizing the screws in this way makes it easier to match the right size screw to the hole.

Activity

Follow the procedure outlined in the following steps to remove the case cover and expansion cards. (If you're working with a tower case, lay it on its side so that the motherboard is on the bottom.)

1. Remove the cover from your desktop PC.

2. To make reassembly easier, take notes or make a sketch of the current placement of boards and cables and identify each board and cable. You can mark the location of a cable on an expansion card with a marker, if you like. Note the orientation of the cable on the card. Each cable for the floppy disk drive, parallel ATA hard drive, or CD-ROM drive has a colored marking on one side of the cable called the "edge color." This color marks pin 1 of the cable. On the board, pin 1 is marked with the number 1 or 2 beside the pin or with a square soldering pad on the back side of the board, as shown in Figure 2-1. You might not be able to see this soldering pad now.

Pin 1 is shown by a stencil on the circuit board.

Pin 1 is shown by square solder pads on the reverse side of the circuit board.

Figure 2-1 How to find pin 1 on an expansion card

3. Remove the cables from the expansion cards. There's no need to remove the other end of the cable from its component (floppy disk drive, hard drive, or CD-ROM drive). Lay the cable over the top of the component or case.

4. Remove the screw holding the card to the back of the case. If you aren't wearing an antistatic ground strap, touch the case before you touch the card.

5. Grasp the card with both hands and remove it by lifting straight up and rocking the card from end to end (not side to side). Rocking the card from side to side might spread the slot opening and weaken the connection. When you remove the card, be sure you don't touch the edge connectors on the card to avoid causing ESD damage.

6. If the card had a cable attached, examine the card connector for the cable. Can you identify pin 1? Lay the card aside on a flat surface.

7. Remove any other expansion cards in the same way.

8. In some proprietary systems, an expansion card assembly attaches to the motherboard, with each card attached to the assembly. If your system has this arrangement, remove it now. It's probably held in place by screws or clips and may or may not have a rail guide you can use to locate the assembly in the case.

9. To remove the power supply, first remove the power cables to the motherboard, case fans, other remaining components, and the power switch, if necessary. Make notes about which cable attaches to what hardware. After the cables are removed, support the power supply with one hand, and remove the screws attaching it to the case.

10. Remove any case fans.

In some systems, it's easier to remove the drives first and then the motherboard. In other systems, it's easier to remove the motherboard first. In these instructions, to make sure you don't risk dropping a drive on the motherboard when removing the drive, you're directed to remove the motherboard first and then the drives. Your instructor, however, might prefer that you remove the drives first and then the motherboard.

1. Begin removing the motherboard by removing any power cables connected to any case or component fans. Be sure to make notes or label the cables so that you can reinstall them correctly.

2. Finish removing the motherboard by removing the screws holding the board to the stand-offs. Usually six to nine screws attach the motherboard to the case. Be careful not to gouge the board or damage components with the screwdriver. Because the screws on the motherboard are often located between components, they can be hard to reach. Be very careful not to damage the motherboard.

3. To remove drives, remove the ribbon cable if it's still attached. Many cases have a removable drive bay. The drives are attached to this bay, and the bay can be removed with all the drives attached. This arrangement gives you easier access to drive-mounting screws than from inside the case. If your case has a removable drive bay, this removal method is preferred. Otherwise, remove each drive separately. Be careful not to jar the drive as you remove it from the case.

4. If your system has a removable drive bay, the floppy drive likely came out with the removable bay. If the floppy drive is still in the system, remove the screws holding the drive in place, and slide the drive out of the case.

5. Remove any CD-ROM, DVD, or tape drives from the case. These drives are usually in the 5-inch drive bays and are normally held in place by four to eight screws. After the screws are removed, the drive slides out the front of the case.

6. Remove any other components.

Now that you have removed all the components, you're ready to reassemble the PC. Replace each component carefully. Take care to install each component firmly without overtightening the screws. Don't force components to fit. If a component won't fit easily the way it should, look for some obstruction preventing it from falling into place. Look carefully for the reason the component won't fit correctly, and make any small adjustments as necessary. The following steps outline the required procedure, which is essentially the reverse of the disassembly procedure:

1. Install the power supply and replace the screws holding it in position.

2. Install the drives in their bays and then install the motherboard, unless your instructor prefers that you install the motherboard first.

3. Connect the power cables from the power supply to the drives and the motherboard. Double-check to make sure the power supply connectors to the motherboard are connected correctly, especially the relative positions of the P8 and P9 connectors (remember the black-to-black rule) if you're dealing with an older AT power supply.

4. Place each card in its slot (it doesn't have to be the same slot, just the same bus), and replace the screw. Don't place a PCI or an ISA video card near the power supply; otherwise, electromagnetic interference (EMI) from the power supply might affect the video picture.

5. Replace the cables, being sure to align the colored edge with pin 1. (In some cases, it might work better to connect the cable to the card before you put the card in the expansion slot.)

6. Check to make sure no cables are interfering with any fan's ability to turn. A common cause of an overheated system is a fan that can't move air because a cable is preventing it from spinning.

7. When all components are installed, you should have refitted all the screws you removed earlier. If some screws are missing, it's important to turn the case upside down and *gently* shake the case to dislodge any wayward screws. Any screw lying on a board has the potential to short out that board when power is applied. Don't use a magnet to try to find missing screws in the case because you might damage data on hard drives and floppy disks left in the floppy disk drives.

8. Plug in the keyboard, monitor, and mouse.

9. In a classroom environment, have the instructor check your work before you power up.

10. Plug in the power cord to the PC and to the power outlet or surge protector. Verify that any power switches on the rear of the case are set correctly. Some cases have a power switch to close the AC voltage, and others have an on/off switch.

11. Using the power button on the front of the case, turn on the power and check that the PC is working properly before you replace the cover. Don't touch the inside of the case while the power is on.

12. If all is well, turn off the PC and replace the cover and its screws. If the PC doesn't work, don't panic. Turn off the power, and then go back and check each cable connection and each expansion card. You probably haven't seated a card solidly in the slot. After you have double-checked everything, try again.

REVIEW QUESTIONS

1. When removing the cover, why should you take care to remove only the screws that hold the cover on?

2. How should you rock a card to remove it from its slot? Why is it important to know how to rock a card correctly?

_____

_____

3. What should you do to help you remember which components connect to which cables?

_____

4. What marking on a ribbon cable identifies pin 1?

_____

5. What component(s) defines the system's form factor?

_____

_____

6. What form factor does your PC use?

_____

7. Why would a PC technician ever have to change out a computer's motherboard?

_____

_____

LAB 2.3 CHOOSE A SYSTEM

OBJECTIVES

The goal of this lab is to help you determine what system you might purchase or build to meet your needs and desires. After completing this lab, you will be able to:

◢ List applications you want to run on your system

◢ Determine the type of system required for several types of application

MATERIALS REQUIRED

This lab requires the following:

◢ A workgroup of 2 to 4 students

ACTIVITY BACKGROUND

The goal of this chapter is to help you learn how to plan and build a new system from scratch. One of the first steps in planning and constructing your own PC is deciding what you're going to use it for and what applications you'll be running on it. After you make these decisions, you can determine what components are required to meet your needs. In this lab, you describe and discuss the kind of system you would build for particular uses. Some labs in this chapter require doing research, but in this case, all you need to do is discuss issues with your workgroup partners.

Activity

In the following steps, you plan four different systems. Each member of the workgroup should work separately, with each member planning four systems. Follow these steps:

1. Plan a system that will be used for gaming and Web surfing. Complete the following:

   ◢ Applications you are likely to install:

   _____

   _____

   ◢ Hardware needed:

   _____

   _____

   ◢ Most important hardware components needed for gaming and Web surfing:

   _____

   _____

2. Plan a system that will be used for programming. Complete the following:

   ◢ Applications you are likely to install:

   _____

   _____

   ◢ Hardware needed:

   _____

   _____

   ◢ Most important hardware components needed for programming:

   _____

   _____

3. Plan a system that will be used for office applications. Complete the following:

   ◢ Applications you are likely to install:

   _____

   _____

   ◢ Hardware needed:

   _____

   _____

◢ Most important hardware components needed for office applications:

_____

_____

4. Plan a system that will be used for a company file server. Complete the following:

   ◢ Applications you are likely to install:

_____

_____

   ◢ Hardware needed:

_____

_____

   ◢ Most important hardware components needed for a company file server:

_____

_____

5. For each type of system, discuss the differences in the systems each member of your group planned. List the major differences here:

_____

_____

_____

6. As a group, agree on a set of specifications for each system. How do the specifications your group agreed on differ from your original specifications?

_____

_____

7. Assign one type of system to each member of the group. List the assignments for each group member. In Labs 2.4 and 2.5, each member of the group will continue planning the type of system assigned here:

_____

_____

REVIEW QUESTIONS

1. What type of system was assigned to you?

_____

_____

2. What resources do you need to produce a detailed design for this system?

_____

_____

_____

3. Did you find the process of discussing different types of systems helpful? Why or why not?

_____

_____

4. On which type of system was there the most disagreement on requirements?

_____

5. If you had a budget crunch, where would you sacrifice on your system? Justify your reasoning:

_____

_____

LAB 2.4 DETERMINE SYSTEM REQUIREMENTS

OBJECTIVES

The goal of this lab is to help you determine the specific requirements for the system you plan to build. After completing this lab, you will be able to:

◢ List minimum software and hardware components required for a particular type of system

MATERIALS REQUIRED

This lab requires the following:

◢ Internet access

◢ A workgroup of 2 to 4 students (different people than in Lab 2.3)

LAB PREPARATION

Before the lab begins, the instructor or lab assistant needs to do the following:

◢ Verify that Windows starts with no errors.

◢ Verify that Internet access is available.

◢ Ask students to break into different groups from Lab 2.3.

ACTIVITY BACKGROUND

In the previous lab, you were assigned a type of system to build, and you made some preliminary plans for it. In this lab, you make more specific decisions about the required software and hardware components. For now, ignore budget constraints; you address those issues in Lab 2.5.

Activity

1. Working from the preliminary requirements you formed in Lab 2.3, use the Internet to research system requirements for your assigned type of system. Complete the following list of requirements:

   ◢ CPU speed:

   _____

   ◢ Memory:

   _____

   ◢ Hard drive size:

   _____

   ◢ Case:

   _____

   ◢ Motherboard:

   _____

   ◢ Monitor size and resolution:

   _____

   ◢ Type of printer:

   _____

   ◢ Expansion cards:

   _____

   ◢ Other peripheral hardware (such as keyboard, mouse, PC camera, speakers, and so on):

   _____

   ◢ Drives needed (for example, hard drives, CD or DVD, tape backup, or floppy):

   _____

   ◢ Operating system:

   _____

   ◢ Applications:

   _____

   ◢ Any other requirements:

   _____

2. Use the Internet or your local computer store to learn more about each component. List the description and cost of each component. If you're doing your research on the Internet, print

the Web page describing each component. (The Web page you print should include the component's price.) If you're conducting your research at a computer store, take careful notes, and be sure to note a price for each component. At this point, you're interested in evaluating your options for each component, so collect information on more than one possibility. For example, for a motherboard, gather information for two or three different motherboards that satisfy your system requirements. Although you need to list the price for each component, don't be concerned about total cost at this point in your research. The following Internet resources might be helpful in your search, although you can use others as well:

- *www.cnet.com*
- *www.tomshardware.com*
- *www.motherboards.com*
- *www.pricewatch.com*
- *www.dirtcheapdrives.com*

3. After you have finished gathering system requirements, find another student from another group who planned the same type of system you did. Compare your plans and note the differences.

REVIEW QUESTIONS

1. What sites did you use for your research besides the previously listed ones?

_____

_____

_____

2. Did you add any components to your list or remove any from it after researching the type of system you want to build? Explain:

_____

_____

_____

3. What processor manufacturer, model, and speed did you select? Why? How much would the same speed processor from another manufacturer cost?

_____

_____

_____

4. What amount of memory and hard drive size do you plan to use? How did you make your choices?

_____

_____

_____

5. What components did you decide to use in your system other than the ones listed in the lab? What purpose will they serve in the new system?

_____

_____

_____

6. List any differences between your plans and another student's plans for the same type of system:

_____

_____

_____

LAB 2.5 COMPARE WHAT YOU NEED WITH WHAT YOU CAN AFFORD

OBJECTIVES

The goal of this lab is to help you determine the cost of building your own PC. After completing this lab, you will be able to:

◢ Research and compare component prices

◢ Determine how to build a system within your budget

MATERIALS REQUIRED

This lab requires the following:

◢ Internet access

◢ A workgroup of 2 to 4 students

LAB PREPARATION

Before the lab begins, the instructor or lab assistant needs to do the following:

◢ Verify that Internet access is available.

ACTIVITY BACKGROUND

When planning a system, it's important to consider the cost of the components you want to include. You might not be able to afford everything you'd like to have in the system, or you might have to buy less expensive versions of some components to get what you want in another area. In this lab, you develop several versions of a budget for the system you want to build. You begin without a budget—that is, by figuring out what your dream system would cost. Then you prioritize your list of components and determine ways to reduce the system's total cost.

Activity

1. Use the information about specific hardware components that you compiled in Lab 2.4 to fill in Table 2-1. List the price of each component in your dream system in Table 2-1. (Note that you might not use all the rows in the table.) At the bottom of the table, list the total cost for your dream system.

Component	Manufacturer and model	Cost
Processor		
Motherboard		
Memory		
Case		
Video card		
Expansion card 1		
Expansion card 2		
Expansion card 3		
Hard drive		
CD or DVD drive		
Floppy drive		
Other drives		
Tape drive		
Monitor		
Keyboard		
Mouse		
Speakers		
Printer		
Operating system		
Application 1		
Application 2		
Application 3		
Application 4		
Other		
Other		
Other		
Total cost of the system		

Table 2-1 Dream system

2. Review your list of components in Table 2-1 and prioritize them. In Table 2-2, list the components in order of importance. In the Notes column, make notes on how much you need each component and whether you can use a lower-cost version or eliminate it altogether. Indicate which (if any) components you're most willing to sacrifice to be able to afford a better component in another area of the system.

Component	Priority	Notes
Processor		
Motherboard		
Memory		
Case		
Video card		
Expansion card 1		
Expansion card 2		
Expansion card 3		
Hard drive		
CD or DVD drive		
Floppy drive		
Other drives		
Tape drive		
Monitor		
Keyboard		
Mouse		
Speakers		
Printer		
Operating system		
Application 1		
Application 2		
Application 3		
Application 4		
Other		
Other		
Other		
Total cost of the system		

Table 2-2 Priority of system components

3. Pare down your list to the absolute minimum for the type of system you're building: the lowest amount of memory and hard drive space, the cheapest monitor, and so on. In Table 2-3, list the lowest prices available for each component, and calculate the total cost of your bare-bones system.

Component	Manufacturer and model	Cost
Processor		
Motherboard		
Memory		
Case		
Video card		
Expansion card 1		
Expansion card 2		
Expansion card 3		
Hard drive		
CD or DVD drive		
Floppy drive		
Other drives		
Tape drive		
Monitor		
Keyboard		
Mouse		
Speakers		
Printer		
Operating system		
Application 1		
Application 2		
Application 3		
Application 4		
Other		
Other		
Other		
Total cost of the system		

Table 2-3   Bare-bones system

4. In Table 2-4, list the components of a system that's a reasonable compromise between the dream system and the bare-bones system. This midrange system is the one you work with in Lab 2.6.

Component	Manufacturer and model	Cost
Processor		
Motherboard		
Memory		
Case		
Video card		
Expansion card 1		
Expansion card 2		
Expansion card 3		
Hard drive		
CD or DVD drive		
Floppy drive		
Other drives		
Tape drive		
Monitor		
Keyboard		
Mouse		
Speakers		
Printer		
Operating system		
Application 1		
Application 2		
Application 3		
Application 4		
Other		
Other		
Other		
Total cost of the system		

Table 2-4 Midrange system

5. Compare your results from Steps 1 through 4 with the results of another student planning the same type of system. Compare cost estimates and note differences in the components you both planned to include. Note how you arrived at your calculation:

_____

_____

_____

6. Repeat Step 5 with at least one student planning a different type of system.

REVIEW QUESTIONS

1. What was the cost difference between your dream system and the bare-bones version?

_____

_____

2. On which components were you willing to compromise and why?

_____

_____

_____

3. On which components were you *not* willing to compromise and why?

_____

_____

_____

4. How would the performance of your midrange system compare to the dream system? How would the performance of the midrange system compare to the bare-bones system? How would the performance of the dream system compare to the bare-bones system?

_____

_____

_____

LAB 2.6 CHECK SYSTEM COMPATIBILITY

OBJECTIVES

The goal of this lab is to help you verify that the components in a proposed system are compatible. After completing this lab, you will be able to:

◢ Find incompatibilities between components in a proposed system

◢ Suggest an alternative system of approximately the same price

MATERIALS REQUIRED

This lab requires the following:

◢ Internet access

◢ A workgroup of 2 to 4 students

LAB PREPARATION

Before the lab begins, the instructor or lab assistant needs to do the following:

◢ Verify that Internet access is available.

ACTIVITY BACKGROUND

No matter how much time you spend planning and building a PC, the system won't work correctly unless the system components are compatible. You can save yourself a lot of trouble by attempting to discover incompatibilities before you begin to build a system. In this lab, you figure out which components in your proposed system are incompatible and suggest compatible components so that the cost of building the system remains approximately the same.

ESTIMATED COMPLETION TIME: 45 minutes

 Activity

1. Alter your plan for your midrange system (from Lab 2.5) by introducing component incompatibilities. Write this altered version on a separate piece of paper or develop a new plan that incorporates incompatible components. Incompatibilities are suggested in the following list, but you can introduce a problem not listed here:

   ◢ A processor not supported by the motherboard

   ◢ Not enough space in the case for all your drives (hard drive, CD-ROM, tape drive)

   ◢ Power supply not powerful enough

   ◢ Too much RAM for the motherboard

   ◢ An incompatible mix of SCSI and IDE devices

   ◢ A type of memory not supported on the motherboard

   ◢ Five parallel ATA IDE devices on a system

   ◢ A video card that uses the wrong kind of expansion slot for the motherboard

   ◢ Expansion cards used with a motherboard that already has built-in logic

2. Calculate and record the total cost of components in the system:

   _____

   _____

   _____

3. Trade revised system plans with another student in your group. Ask the other student to find the incompatible components in your plan and suggest replacement components while keeping the price about the same. Do the same with the plan you receive, recording incompatibilities you find, the original cost of the system, replacement components, and the final cost of the altered system:

   _____

   _____

   _____

4. With the group, discuss incompatibilities found in the plans and how you fixed them. Make note of incompatibilities that were introduced but not found:

   _____

   _____

   _____

REVIEW QUESTIONS

1. Did you, or the other students in your group, introduce incompatibilities not suggested in Step 1? If so, list them here:

_____

_____

2. Were all the incompatibilities introduced in the plans discovered? If not, which ones were not, and why do you think they have been more difficult to find?

_____

_____

_____

3. List the incompatibility problems you found in the other student's plan and explain how you solved them:

_____

_____

_____

4. Did the students in your group have different ways of solving the same incompatibility problems? Explain:

_____

_____

5. For the plan you reviewed and revised, what was the difference in the original cost and the cost after you incorporated your solutions?

_____

_____

LAB 2.7 EVALUATE AN UPGRADE

OBJECTIVES

The goal of this lab is to help you determine the ease and cost of upgrading a PC. After completing this lab, you will be able to:

◢ Determine whether a system needs to be upgraded

◢ Explain why a system needs to be upgraded

◢ List the components needed to upgrade a system

MATERIALS REQUIRED

This lab requires the following:

- ◢ A lab computer
- ◢ Documentation for computer components, if available
- ◢ Internet access

LAB PREPARATION

Before the lab begins, the instructor or lab assistant needs to do the following:

- ◢ Verify that Windows starts with no errors.
- ◢ Verify that Internet access is available.
- ◢ Provide documentation or manuals that came with the system.

ACTIVITY BACKGROUND

An important factor to consider when purchasing or building a PC is how easy upgrading the system will be. You might upgrade an existing system instead of replacing it with a new system. Factors that affect the ease of upgrading include the processors supported by the motherboard, the size of the case, and the number and type of ports and expansion slots on the motherboard. In this lab, you examine a system to determine whether you can make upgrades to it and then evaluate how practical the upgrades are.

ESTIMATED COMPLETION TIME: 45 minutes

 Activity

Follow these steps to determine whether your system can be upgraded:

1. In Table 2-5, list the components currently installed on your system. Useful sources of information include Device Manager, Control Panel, and the Properties dialog boxes for drives and devices.

Device	Description
Motherboard (make and model)	
BIOS type	
Memory (type and size)	
Hard drive (type and size)	
Other drives installed (floppy, Zip, CD-ROM, and so on)	
Monitor (type and size)	
Printer	
Sound card	
Modem (or other Internet connection)	
NIC	
Other devices	
Operating system (including version number)	
Applications (including version number)	

Table 2-5 Current system components

2. Using the Internet and available documentation, select three components to upgrade. Record the following information for each component.

Component 1

▲ Replacement component:

_____

▲ Cost of the upgrade:

_____

▲ Do other components need to be upgraded for this upgrade to work? If so, what are they?

_____

Component 2

▲ Replacement component:

_____

▲ Cost of the upgrade:

_____

▲ Do other components need to be upgraded for this upgrade to work? If so, what are they?

_____

Component 3

▲ Replacement component:

_____

▲ Cost of the upgrade:

_____

▲ Do other components need to be upgraded for this upgrade to work? If so, what are they?

_____

3. Print a Web page showing the specifications and cost of each new component. What is the total cost of the upgrades?

_____

4. Suppose you had to sell the system in its current state (without the upgrades). What would be a reasonable price?

_____

5. When upgrading an existing system, the cost of the upgrade should not exceed half the value of the existing system. Will your proposed upgrade go over that limit?

_____

6. Using *www.cnet.com* (or another Web site where you can compare systems), locate a notebook computer with specifications similar to your lab PC. Compare the cost of upgrading the memory, processor, and CD-ROM drive on each system. (Substitute another component if your computer doesn't have a CD-ROM drive.) In Table 2-6, compare the cost of upgrading your lab PC with a similar upgrade for a notebook computer.

Component	Cost of upgrading on PC	Cost of upgrading on notebook
Processor		
Memory		
CD-ROM drive		

Table 2-6   PC upgrade versus notebook upgrade

REVIEW QUESTIONS

1. What components did you choose to upgrade and why?

2. Which would be cheapest to upgrade: your lab PC or a comparable notebook? Explain your answer:

3. What other resources, besides the ones you used in the lab, do you think might be helpful in planning an upgrade?

4. Among the components you selected, which upgrade was the most expensive?

5. If you were actually performing these upgrades, is there any component or any system you would *not* choose to upgrade? Explain your answer:

6. Which component is the most popular to upgrade? The easiest? The hardest?

Electricity and Power Supplies

Labs included in this chapter:

- **Lab 3.1:** Identify Form Factors
- **Lab 3.2:** Measure the Output of Your Power Supply
- **Lab 3.3:** Replace a Power Supply
- **Lab 3.4:** Find Documentation on the Internet
- **Lab 3.5:** Choose the Right Power Supply

LAB 3.1 IDENTIFY FORM FACTORS

OBJECTIVES

The goal of this lab is to give you experience in identifying form factors. After completing this lab, you will be able to:

▲ Identify the form factor of the case, motherboard, and power supply

▲ Select appropriate components to match an existing form factor

MATERIALS REQUIRED

This lab requires the following:

▲ A PC designated for this lab

▲ A PC toolkit with antistatic ground strap

▲ Internet access

LAB PREPARATION

Before the lab begins, the instructor or lab assistant needs to do the following:

▲ Verify that Windows starts with no errors.

▲ Verify that Internet access is available.

ACTIVITY BACKGROUND

The form factor is a set of specifications about the size, shape, and configuration of the components that make up a computer system. Sharing a common standard allows components such as the case, motherboard, and power supply to fit together and function properly. There are three common types of form factors: AT, ATX, and BTX. Each comes in several variations that determine characteristics such as size and shape. In this lab, you identify your system's form factor and research some identifying characteristics of common form factors.

ESTIMATED COMPLETION TIME: 30 minutes

Activity

1. Open your browser and go to your favorite search engine, such as *www.google.com*.

2. Use the Internet to research the main differences between AT and ATX and list them here:

_____

_____

3. Now explain the main differences between ATX and BTX:

_____

_____

4. Each form factor comes in several sizes. How could you tell whether a system was Regular BTX, Micro BTX, or Pico BTX?

_____

_____

5. Form factors are also available in various shapes. What slimline form factor is similar to ATX?

_____

6. Now turn the computer off and unplug the power cord.

7. Disconnect all peripherals and remove the case cover. Remove the cover from your desktop PC.

8. Examine the case, motherboard, and power supply.

9. What is the form factor of this system?

_____

10. Close the case, reattach the peripherals, and test the system to make sure it boots without errors.

REVIEW QUESTIONS

1. Why is it important that your case and motherboard share a compatible form factor?

_____

2. When might you want to use a slimline form factor?

_____

3. What advantages does ATX have over Micro ATX?

_____

4. Where is the CPU located on the BTX motherboard? Why?

_____

5. Is it possible to determine the form factor without opening the case?

_____

LAB 3.2 MEASURE THE OUTPUT OF YOUR POWER SUPPLY

OBJECTIVES

The goal of this lab is to use a multimeter to measure the voltages provided by a power supply. After completing this lab, you will be able to:

▲ Use a multimeter

▲ Measure voltage provided by a power supply

MATERIALS REQUIRED

This lab requires the following:

▲ A computer designated for this lab

▲ A PC toolkit with antistatic ground strap

⊿ A multimeter

⊿ Access to the online content "Electricity and Multimeters," downloaded from *www.course.com*

⊿ A workgroup of 2 to 4 students

LAB PREPARATION

Before the lab begins, the instructor or lab assistant needs to do the following:

⊿ Announce to students that before they come to lab, they should read the online content "Electricity and Multimeters." They might like to bring this content to class in printed form.

ACTIVITY BACKGROUND

In most situations, if you suspect a problem with a power supply, you simply exchange it for a known good one. In a few instances, however, you might want to measure your power supply's output by using a multimeter.

A multimeter is an electrical tool that performs several tests. It can typically measure continuity, resistance, amperage, and voltage. It might have a digital or an analog meter that displays output. It also has two leads used to contact the component you're testing. The various models of multimeters work slightly differently. Follow the correct procedure for your specific multimeter. In this lab, you measure the electrical voltage supplied to the motherboard and floppy drive. Follow your computer lab's posted safety procedures when completing this lab.

ESTIMATED COMPLETION TIME: 30 minutes

 Activity

 Caution

Be sure you have your multimeter set to measure voltage, not current (amps). If the multimeter is set to measure current, you might damage the power supply, the motherboard, or both.

Using your multimeter, measure the power output to your system's motherboard and to the floppy drive, and then fill in the following charts that apply to your system. Note that the column headings "Red Lead" and "Black Lead" refer to the color of the probes.

Detailed directions for using a multimeter can be found in the online content "Electricity and Multimeters" supplied with this lab manual. Be very careful as you work inside the computer case with the power on. Don't touch any components other than those described in the steps.

The following steps outline the basic procedure for using a multimeter:

1. Remove the cover from the computer case.

2. Set the multimeter to measure voltage in a range of 20 volts, and set the AC/DC switch to DC. Insert the black probe into the meter's - jack and the red probe into the meter's + jack.

3. Turn on the multimeter, and then turn on the computer.

4. Measure each circuit by placing a red probe on the lead and a black probe on ground (see Figure 3-1).

5. Figure 3-2 shows the connections for an AT power supply. If you're using an AT power supply, refer to Table 3-1 for the purposes of these 12 leads.

Figure 3-1 A multimeter measuring voltage on an AT motherboard

Figure 3-2 AT power supply connections

Connection	Lead	Description	Acceptable range
P8	1	Power good	
	2	Not used or +5 volts	+4.4 to +5.2 volts
	3	+12 volts	+10.8 to +13.2 volts
	4	-12 volts	-10.8 to -13.2 volts
	5	Black ground	
	6	Black ground	
P9	7	Black ground	
	8	Black ground	
	9	-5 volts	-4.5 to -5.5 volts
	10	+5 volts	+4.5 to +5.5 volts
	11	+5 volts	+4.5 to +5.5 volts
	12	+5 volts	+4.5 to +5.5 volts

Table 3-1   12 leads to the AT motherboard from the AT power supply

6. Complete the following chart for an AT motherboard. Write the voltage measurement for each connection in the Voltage measure column.

Red lead	Black lead	Voltage measure
3	5	
3	6	
3	7	
3	8	
4	Ground	
9	Ground	
10	Ground	
11	Ground	
12	Ground	

7. The 20-pin P1 power connector on an ATX motherboard is shown in Figure 3-3. Refer to Table 3-2 for the purpose of each pin.

Figure 3-3 Power connection on an ATX motherboard

Unnotched side			Notched side		
Lead	**Description**	**Acceptable range (Volts = V)**	**Lead**	**Description**	**Acceptable range (Volts = V)**
1	+3.3 volts	+3.1 to +3.5 V	11	+3.3 volts	+3.1 to +3.5 V
2	+3.3 volts	+3.1 to +3.5 V	12	-12 volts	-10.8 to -13.2 V
3	Black ground		13	Black ground	
4	+5 volts	+4.5 to +5.5 V	14	Power supply on	
5	Black ground		15	Black ground	
6	+5 volts	+4.5 to +5.5 V	16	Black ground	
7	Black ground		17	Black ground	
8	Power good		18	-5 volts	-4.5 to -5.5 V
9	+5 volts standby	+4.5 to +5.5 V	19	+5 volts	+4.5 to +5.5 V
10	+12 volts	+10.8 to +13.2 V	20	+5 volts	+4.5 to +5.5 V

Table 3-2 20 leads to the ATX motherboard from the ATX power supply

8. Complete the following chart for an ATX motherboard:

Red lead	Black lead	Voltage measure
10	7	
10	5	
10	3	
10	17	
10	16	
10	15	

Red lead	Black lead	Voltage measure
10	13	
9	Ground	
6	Ground	
4	Ground	
2	Ground	
1	Ground	
20	Ground	
19	Ground	
18	Ground	
12	Ground	
11	Ground	

9. The BTX motherboard and power supply are designed so that the power supply monitors the range of voltages provided to the motherboard and halts the motherboard if voltages are inadequate. Therefore, measuring voltage for a BTX system isn't usually necessary. However, in a lab environment, if you have access only to a BTX system, you can fill in the same chart you did for the previous motherboards for practice. Figure 3-4 shows the 24-pin power connector for a BTX motherboard, and the purposes of the pins are listed in Table 3-3.

Figure 3-4   BTX 24-pin power connector on the motherboard

Lead	Signal	Acceptable range (Volts = V)
1	+3.3 volts	3.2 to 3.5 V
2	+3.3 volts	3.2 to 3.5 V
3	COM	
4	+5 volts	4.75 to 5.25 V
5	COM	
6	+5 volts	4.75 to 5.25 V
7	COM	
8	Power OK	Voltages are in acceptable range
9	+5 volts	Standby voltage always on
10	+12 volts	11.4 to 12.6 V
11	+12 volts	11.4 to 12.6 V

Table 3-3   BTX 24-pin power connector

Lead	Signal	Acceptable range (Volts = V)
12	+3.3 volts	3.2 to 3.5 V
13	+3.3 volts	3.2 to 3.5 V
14	-12 volts	-10.8 to -13.2 V
15	COM	
16	PS ON	Power supply is on
17	COM	
18	COM	
19	COM	
20	NC	
21	+5 volts	4.75 to 5.25 V
22	+5 volts	4.75 to 5.25 V
23	+5 volts	4.75 to 5.25 V
24	COM	

Table 3-3   BTX 24-pin power connector (continued)

10. Complete the following chart for a BTX motherboard:

Red lead	Black lead	Voltage measure
1	Ground	
2	Ground	
4	Ground	
6	Ground	
9	Ground	
10	Ground	
11	Ground	
12	Ground	
13	Ground	
14	Ground	
21	Ground	
22	Ground	
23	Ground	

11. The power connectors for a drive power cord were shown in Figure 3-2. Complete the following chart for the floppy drive:

Red lead	Black lead	Voltage measure
1	3	
4	2	

12. Turn off the PC and replace the cover.

REVIEW QUESTIONS

1. What is the electrical voltage from the house outlet to the power supply?

   _____

2. What voltages are supplied by the power supply on your system?

   _____

3. What model of multimeter are you using?

   _____

4. List the steps to set your multimeter to measure resistance:

   _____

   _____

   _____

5. Besides voltage and resistance, what else can your multimeter measure?

   _____

LAB 3.3 REPLACE A POWER SUPPLY

OBJECTIVES

The goal of this lab is to give you experience in replacing a power supply. After completing this lab, you will be able to:

◢ Identify the power supply

◢ Remove the power supply from the case

◢ Install a new power supply and new cabling

MATERIALS REQUIRED

This lab requires the following:

◢ A PC designated for this lab

◢ A PC toolkit with antistatic ground strap

◢ A workgroup of 2 to 4 students

LAB PREPARATION

Before the lab begins, the instructor or lab assistant needs to do the following:

◢ Verify that a computer designated for disassembly is available for each workgroup.

ACTIVITY BACKGROUND

This lab tests your ability to remove and replace a power supply. Power supplies, as a rule, are considered field replaceable units (FRUs). To save time and avoid the danger of working inside power supplies, PC technicians don't repair power supplies; they replace them.

If you find that a power supply is faulty, replace it with a compatible power supply, and then send the original off to be reconditioned or recycled.

ESTIMATED COMPLETION TIME: 30 minutes

Activity

1. Turn the computer off and unplug the power cord.
2. Disconnect all peripherals and remove the case cover.
3. Examine the label on the power supply. What is the peak load rating of the power supply? A system requiring more power than the power supply provides can contribute to an early failure of the power supply.

_____

4. What type of power connectors to the motherboard does the power supply provide? Possible answers are P8, P9, P1, or auxiliary power connectors, such as the four-pin auxiliary connector for the Pentium processor.

_____

5. What is the form factor of the power supply?

_____

6. Remove the cabling and the power supply. Usually the power supply is held in place by four screws in the back of the case. Some proprietary systems might use other methods of securing the power supply.
7. Examine the power supply designated by your instructor, or swap your power supply with another workgroup.
8. What is the form factor of this new power supply?

_____

9. What is the power rating of this new power supply?

_____

10. Will this new power supply satisfy the needs of your system?

_____

11. Install the new power supply. *Ask your instructor to check your work before you close the case.* This check is crucial because some older power supplies must be connected correctly so that they aren't damaged when they're turned on.
12. Close the case, reattach the peripherals, and test the system.

REVIEW QUESTIONS

1. How many connectors linked your original power supply to the motherboard?

_____

2. How many watts of peak power could the original power supply provide?

_____

3. Why is it important to be able to calculate the peak power required for all components? (You learn how to do this in Lab 3.5.)

_____

_____

4. What are two reasons that PC technicians don't usually repair a power supply?

_____

_____

5. What term is used to refer to components that are commonly replaced but not repaired?

_____

6. What is the most efficient way to determine whether your power supply is bad?

_____

LAB 3.4 FIND DOCUMENTATION ON THE INTERNET

OBJECTIVES

The goal of this lab is to show you how to locate documentation on the Internet so that you can determine how much power a component uses. After completing this lab, you will be able to:

- Find the manufacturer and model of a component
- Search for a product's documentation or manual
- Download and view a product manual

MATERIALS REQUIRED

This lab requires the following:

- A computer designated for disassembly
- Internet access
- Adobe Acrobat Reader
- A PC toolkit with antistatic ground strap
- A workgroup of 2 or 3 students or individual students

LAB PREPARATION

Before the lab begins, the instructor or lab assistant needs to do the following:

- Verify that a computer designated for disassembly is available for each student or workgroup.
- Verify that Internet access is available.

ACTIVITY BACKGROUND

Often the power specifications for a component aren't labeled on the component itself but are included in the documentation. When working with PCs, it's common to encounter a component for which you have no documentation on hand. In this lab, you learn to find a component's make and model and, if possible, find online documentation for it.

3

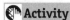 **Activity**

1. Open the PC's case and locate the component your instructor assigned to you (or select a component randomly). If you're in a workgroup, each person should be assigned a different component.

2. Examine the component until you find a sticker or stenciled label identifying its manufacturer and model number.

3. Take your notes to a computer that has Internet access.

> **Notes**
>
> The manufacturer and model aren't marked clearly on every component. If you're having trouble finding this information on a component, such as a video card, try researching based on the component's chipset. The information identifying the chip is usually stenciled on the chip. For communication devices, such as a modem or network card, look for an FCC number printed on the card and use it for your search. If you need to find out how much power an unlabeled component uses, sometimes it's helpful to consult the documentation for similar components.

4. If you already know the manufacturer's URL, go to that site and try to find documentation in these locations:

   ◢ The Support section of the site, as shown in Figure 3-5

   ◢ The Downloads section

   ◢ The Customer Service section

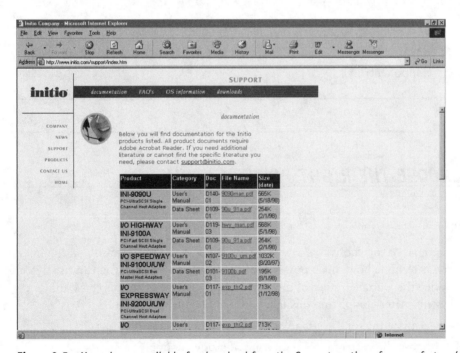

Figure 3-5 Manuals are available for download from the Support section of a manufacturer's Web site

If you're not sure of the manufacturer's URL, try searching for the manufacturer or model number with a good search engine. In fact, searching by model number can often get you to the information in the fewest steps. For example, if SD11 is imprinted on your motherboard, searching on "SD11" can take you right to the documentation you need. Keep in mind that most documentation is in PDF format, which means you might need Adobe Acrobat Reader or a browser plug-in to view the documentation.

5. Print or save the documentation, and file it as a reference for when you need information about that component.

6. What CPU does your system use?

_____

7. Go to the manufacturer's Web site, and find and print the Web page showing the power consumption of your CPU expressed in watts.

REVIEW QUESTIONS

1. How is a component commonly marked for identification?

_____

_____

2. In what sections of a Web site are manuals commonly found?

_____

3. In what format are manuals usually provided?

_____

4. What software do you need to view a PDF document?

_____

5. Why would a PC repair technician need to know the power consumption of a peripheral component?

_____

_____

LAB 3.5 CHOOSE THE RIGHT POWER SUPPLY

OBJECTIVES

The goal of this lab is to show you how to locate documentation on the Internet so that you can determine how much power a system as a whole uses. You can use this information to decide the wattage rating of the power supply you need to purchase for a new or upgraded system. After completing this lab, you will be able to:

▲ Calculate the total wattage requirements for a system

▲ Choose the correct type and rating of a power supply

MATERIALS REQUIRED

This lab requires the following:

▲ A computer designated for disassembly

▲ *Optional*: Internet access

◢ A PC toolkit with antistatic ground strap

◢ A workgroup of 2 or 3 students or individual students

LAB PREPARATION

Before the lab begins, the instructor or lab assistant needs to do the following:

◢ Verify that a computer designated for disassembly is available for each student or workgroup.

◢ *Optional*: Verify that Internet access is available.

ACTIVITY BACKGROUND

When selecting a power supply for a computer system, you must take many factors into account. It's important to look at the system's components as a whole and how the system will be used. You might be tempted to simply purchase a power supply that has a very high wattage rating, but this choice isn't always the most economical. The typical efficiency rating of a power supply is 60% to 70%. Usually, this rating means 30% to 40% of the power is blowing out of the case as wasted heat. You want to keep waste to a minimum. On the other hand, if you intend to upgrade your system, buying an overrated power supply might be wise.

Running a system with an inadequate power supply can cause the power supply to wear out faster than normal. Also, an inadequate power supply can cause a system to reboot at odd times and exhibit other types of intermittent errors. It pays to install a correctly rated power supply for a system.

> **ESTIMATED COMPLETION TIME: 45 minutes**

 Activity

1. The following chart shows the estimated power requirements for components inside a computer case. These estimates come from the Web site PC Power and Cooling, Inc. at *www.pcpowercooling.com/technology/power_usage*. Open the PC's case. Locate each component listed in the chart, and record how many components are present. Note that some entries will be zero.

Component	Wattage requirement	How many present	Total wattage
AGP video card	30 W–50 W		
PCI Express video card	50 W–100 W		
Average PCI cards	10 W		
DVD or CD drives	20 W–40 W		
Hard drives	10 W–30 W		
Case fans and CPU fans	3 W (each)		
Motherboard	50 W–100 W	1	
RAM modules	8 W per 128 MB		
Pentium 3 processor	30 W		
Pentium 4 processor	70 W–100 W		
AMD Athlon processor	70 W–100 W		
Total wattage:			

2. To fill in the Total wattage column, first check the manufacturer's Web site for each component to find the exact wattage amounts. If this information isn't available, use the estimate provided or the midpoint of the estimate. Add the wattage for all components to come up with the total wattage. Record the system's total wattage in the last row of the chart.

3. Multiply the total wattage by 1.5. This multiplier takes into account the overhead the system and a power supply need so that the system can run at about 30% to 70% of its maximum capacity. What is your calculated total wattage, taking into account the required overhead?

4. Now look at the power supply, and make sure it has the number and type of connectors needed for your system. Figure 3-6 can help you identify connectors. Many power supplies don't provide the new serial ATA (SATA) connector shown in Figure 3-7. However, you can use an adapter power cord like the one in the figure to accommodate SATA hard drives.

Figure 3-6 Power supply with connectors labeled

Figure 3-7 Adapter power cord can be used for an SATA hard drive

5. Fill in the following chart to show the available power connectors and how many are needed for your system:

Connector	Current quantity	Quantity needed
EIDE drive connectors (Molex)		
Floppy drive connectors (Berg)		
SATA connectors		
ATX connector (20 or 24 pins)		
Auxiliary power connector (P4)		
PCIe connector		

6. Look on the power supply label for the peak load rating in watts. What is this value?

_____

7. Based on what you have learned in this lab, is the power supply adequate for the job? Why or why not?

_____

_____

CRITICAL THINKING (ADDITIONAL 30 MINUTES)

Suppose your power supply stops working, and you must buy a replacement. Search the Internet for a comparable power supply. The cost of power supplies varies widely. For example, a 400-watt power supply can cost from $15 to $75. The difference in quality can be judged partly by the weight of the power supply because, in general, the heavier it is, the more transistors it has and the more heavy-duty the transistors are, which make for a better power supply. Another factor to consider is noise level; quiet power supplies can be more expensive than noisy ones. Print two Web pages showing a high-end and a low-end power supply that would meet your system's needs. Which power supply would you recommend purchasing for your system, and why?

_____

_____

REVIEW QUESTIONS

1. The estimated wattages for individual components were provided in the lab. How can you find the actual wattage for each component?

_____

2. What is the typical efficiency rating for a power supply?

_____

3. Are there any connectors your system needs that the power supply doesn't have? If so, what are they?

_____

4. Are there any connectors provided by the power supply that your system isn't using? If so, what are they?

_____

5. Why is it important to buy a power supply that's close to the requirements for your system instead of buying a higher wattage power supply?

_____

_____

Processors and Chipsets

LAB 4.1 REMOVE AND REPLACE A CPU

OBJECTIVES

The goal of this lab is to help you learn the correct procedure for removing and reinstalling a CPU. After completing this lab, you will be able to:

◢ Remove the CPU from your system

◢ Install a CPU into your system

MATERIALS REQUIRED

This lab requires the following:

◢ Flathead screwdriver

◢ An antistatic ground strap

◢ Masking tape and marker or other method of labeling parts

◢ Another computer with an active Internet connection

◢ Alcohol wipe to remove thermal compound from the CPU

LAB PREPARATION

Before the lab begins, the instructor or lab assistant needs to do the following:

◢ Verify that Windows starts with no errors.

◢ Verify that Internet access is available.

ACTIVITY BACKGROUND

Removing and installing a CPU isn't difficult after you have done it a time or two. However, in today's systems, it's fairly rare for the CPU to be the source of a problem. Instead, a CPU replacement is usually done to increase the system's operating speed. In this lab, you remove the CPU and cooling unit and then replace both. Many times, when disassembling or assembling parts to a system, you won't have step-by-step directions but must discover how to do so. Removing the heat sink for the CPU is one of these tasks. Because of the overwhelming number of models on the market, you might need to refer to the manufacturer's documentation on how to remove the unit.

When you're considering upgrading the CPU in a system, be aware that if you upgrade the CPU, you might not realize the new processor's full potential if all the other components are obsolete.

An important note on electrostatic discharge (ESD): The CPU is an intricate and complicated array of wires and transistors. When you feel a static shock, you're feeling somewhere in the neighborhood of 3000 volts or more. The CPU can be damaged by a shock of 10 to 1000 volts, a discharge you would never feel. It's important to wear your ground strap while handling the CPU and memory, or you could easily damage components and never know that you have done so.

ESTIMATED COMPLETION TIME: 45 minutes

Activity

Because the CPU is a delicate component and is easily damaged, watch your instructor demonstrate how to remove and replace one before you attempt to do so. Answer the following questions about the demonstration:

1. What CPU did the instructor remove and replace?

   _____

2. What type of heat sink or cooler was attached to the CPU?

   _____

3. What precautions did the instructor take to protect the CPU against ESD?

   _____

   _____

4. How did the instructor protect the CPU while it was out of its socket?

   _____

   _____

Do the following to remove the CPU from your system:

1. Power down the computer.

2. Unplug any cords or cables connected to it.

3. Remove the case cover.

4. Examine the inside of the case and decide what you need to remove so that you have easy access to the CPU. Next, remove and carefully label any wires or other parts that need to be removed to expose the CPU. With some system cases, the power supply needs to be removed to be able to proceed.

5. Disconnect the power cord from the heat sink and fan (HSF) to the motherboard.

6. Depending on the CPU that's installed, there are different methods for removing and installing an HSF unit. Some units can be removed by hand simply by opening the levers that attach them to the socket. Other units require using the eraser end of a pencil to carefully dislodge the unit from the retaining mechanism hooks. Typically, the HSF is latched on both sides. After the pressure is removed from the main latch, it unlatches easily from the opposite side. Rather than use a screwdriver or other metal object to unlatch a stubborn latch, the preferred method is to use the eraser end of a pencil. If you slip while releasing the latch mechanism and the motherboard is damaged, it might be beyond repair. Also, some heat sinks are permanently glued to the processor and aren't intended to be removed. In this case, leave the heat sink attached. Decide how to proceed and, if appropriate, remove the heat sink and fan unit carefully.

7. After you have removed the HSF unit, you can proceed to actually removing the CPU. Handling the CPU must be done with your full attention. The tiny pins on the bottom of socket chips can be bent easily and need to be handled with care. Typically, CPUs and motherboards are shipped with antistatic foam that's an ideal surface to set CPU pins into for protection. If you don't have this shipping container, when you remove the CPU, lay it bottom-side up so that the pins aren't sitting on your work surface. Find the CPU shipping container or plan for a way to store the CPU safely.

8. You'll see a metal bar right next to the socket of the base of the CPU. This metal bar is the lever for the zero insertion force (ZIF) socket. Pull the lever out slightly and then up 90 degrees to release the pins on the underside of the CPU. In Figure 4-1, you can see the lever about to be released from an empty LGA775 socket.

Figure 4-1 Open the socket lever

9. Carefully grasp the sides of the CPU and pull up gently to remove it from the socket.

10. Using an alcohol wipe, carefully remove any thermal grease (also called thermal compound) that's smeared on the top of the CPU. You can now safely store the CPU.

Now you're ready to install the new CPU or, for this lab, replace the CPU. If you're actually upgrading to a new CPU, you need to make several checks before installing the new CPU into a motherboard. You need to verify that the socket type, clock speed, and multiplier match the new CPU.

In this lab, you're replacing the existing CPU; however, go through the following steps to practice as though you were installing a new upgraded CPU:

1. Remember that the CPU is a delicate piece of equipment. The pins on the processor can be bent easily, and if the heat sink isn't connected properly, you run the risk of allowing the CPU to overheat. Inspect the new CPU to verify that it has no bent pins. If you suspect the CPU has been damaged or if the pins are bent, you might need to replace the CPU.

2. Visually inspect the socket on the motherboard for any indication as to what type of socket it is. Usually it's clearly marked as to the type. Double-check that the CPU was manufactured for the type of socket on the motherboard. What is the CPU socket this motherboard is using?

3. Using the manual for the CPU, determine the correct front-side bus (FSB) speed, multiplier, and voltage for the CPU. If you don't have the manual, visit the manufacturer's Web site. Although some motherboards configure this information automatically, as a technician you need to be able to determine that it was done correctly. Your CPU is

most likely manufactured by Intel (*www.intel.com*) or AMD (*www.amd.com*). Go to the manufacturer's Web site and fill in these blanks:

◢ FSB speed:

_____

◢ Multiplier:

_____

◢ Voltage:

_____

4. You might need to set the FSB speed, multiplier, and voltage on the motherboard. Again, read the manufacturer's documentation if you have it. If you don't have the documentation, visit the manufacturer's Web site and download it. Some motherboards require you to set this information by using DIP switches or jumpers, but others allow you to do so in CMOS setup. Still others detect the CPU and configure everything for you automatically. How does this motherboard recognize and configure the CPU?

_____

_____

5. Before you install the CPU in the socket, practice raising and lowering the socket lever so that you can feel how much force is necessary to close the lever.

6. Now you're ready to install the CPU. Verify that the power cable has been removed from the machine. Unlatch the ZIF lever and bring it to the up position. It should be pointing directly upward. The pins on the CPU are keyed to line up with the grid array on the socket. Gently align the CPU with the socket (see Figure 4-2) and allow it to fall into place.

Figure 4-2   Align the CPU over the socket

7. Carefully replace the socket lever so that force is applied to the top of the CPU and the CPU is installed securely in the socket. You need to place a little more pressure on the lever than you did when no CPU was present, but don't force it! If you have to force it, most likely the CPU isn't oriented in the socket correctly.

8. Now you're ready to install the heat sink. First, examine the underside of the heat sink for any foreign matter. It's common for a new heat sink to come with a thermal pad that's covered by a protective film of plastic. If this plastic isn't removed, you run the risk of damaging your CPU. If there's no thermal pad, put on latex gloves and gently apply a thin layer of thermal grease to the portion of the heat sink that will come into contact with the CPU. Be careful not to apply thermal grease so that it later comes in contact with the edges of the processor or the socket. You don't want grease to get down into the CPU socket. Figure 4-3 shows just about the right amount of thermal grease applied.

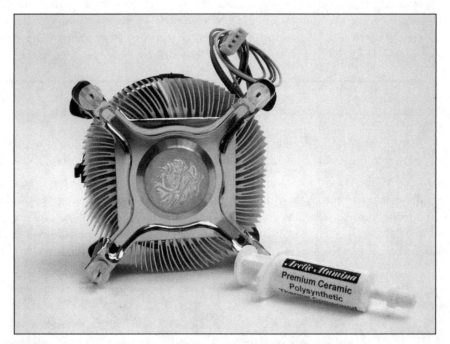

Figure 4-3   Thermal grease applied to the bottom of the heat sink assembly

9. Carefully align the bottom of the heat sink with the socket and attach the heat sink. Plug the heat sink fan's power cord into the motherboard.

10. Have your instructor inspect your work to make sure the heat sink is attached correctly. (Booting up a system with an incorrectly attached heat sink can cause damage to the processor because it will overheat.)

11. Boot your machine and test for errors.

REVIEW QUESTIONS

1. Why shouldn't you use a screwdriver to remove a heat sink?

_____

_____

2. What is the minimum voltage of an electrostatic discharge (ESD) that you can feel?

_____

3. What is the voltage range in which ESD can affect components?

_____

4. Why is it important to double-check the bottom of the heat sink before attaching it to the CPU socket?

_____

_____

LAB 4.2 INSTALL CHIPSET DRIVERS

OBJECTIVES

The goal of this lab is to learn to install the correct chipset drivers for your motherboard. After completing this lab, you will be able to:

◢ Locate the chipset drivers for your motherboard

◢ Install the chipset drivers

MATERIALS REQUIRED

This lab requires the following:

◢ Internet access

◢ A flash drive

LAB PREPARATION

Before the lab begins, the instructor or lab assistant needs to do the following:

◢ Verify that Internet access is available.

ACTIVITY BACKGROUND

Most of the time, when you install the operating system, the chipset drivers are installed automatically. However, if your motherboard is very new, drivers for your chipset might not be included with the operating system you have chosen. Also, you should know how to do install these drivers because sometimes doing so can fix problems on a system. Typically, chipset drivers for your motherboard come on a CD with the purchase of that motherboard. However, finding the original CD that came with the motherboard can be difficult. This lab assumes that the original CD for the motherboard is unavailable. If it's available, however, insert that CD into the CD-ROM drive and use the drivers on the CD.

If the motherboard becomes unstable, one thing you can do is update the chipset drivers. However, if the system is giving you problems, most likely it can't connect to a network to download drivers directly. Therefore, it's a good idea to know how to download drivers to one computer to use them on another computer. In this lab, you download the drivers and copy them to a flash drive (also called a USB thumb drive or jump drive) or burn them to a CD on one computer to be used on another computer.

Activity

1. First, you must identify your motherboard. To do that, open the computer case and look on the motherboard for the stenciled or silkscreened label printed somewhere on the board, most likely in the middle. If you need help finding this label, check out the first few steps of Lab 5.3 and Figure 5-2. What is the brand and model of your motherboard?

   _____

2. The next step is to find out what chipset this motherboard uses. You can search the documentation that came with the motherboard, or you can find the information on the motherboard manufacturer's Web site. Table 4-1 lists the URLs for major motherboard manufacturers.

   ◢ What is the motherboard manufacturer's Web site?

   _____

   ◢ What chipset does this motherboard use?

   _____

Manufacturer	URL
Motherboards.com	www.motherboards.com
American Megatrends, Inc.	www.megatrends.com
ASUS	www.asus.com
Dell	www.dell.com
Diamond Multimedia	www.diamondmm.com
First International Computer, Inc.	www.fica.com
Gateway	www.gateway.com
Giga-Byte Technology Co., Ltd.	www.giga-byte.com
IBM	www.ibm.com
Intel Corporation	www.intel.com
Supermicro Computer, Inc.	www.supermicro.com
Tyan Computer Corporation	www.tyan.com

Table 4-1   URLs for major motherboard manufacturers

3. Now you need to find the chipset drivers for this motherboard on the Internet. First, look for the drivers on the motherboard manufacturer's Web site. If you can't find the drivers there, most chipsets are made by Intel, NVidia, VIA, or SIS. Try going to the chipset manufacturer's Web site:

   ◢ *www.intel.com*

   ◢ *www.nvidia.com*

   ◢ *www.via.com.tw*

   ◢ *www.sis.com*

4. Using the Service and Support or Downloads section on the Web site, download the chipset drivers. Save this file to the desktop of the computer you're not repairing.

5. Copy the drivers to a USB thumb drive, and transport the driver to the computer you're working on. Run the installation package you downloaded to install the driver.

REVIEW QUESTIONS

1. Why would you need to install chipset drivers?

_____

_____

2. If the motherboard manufacturer doesn't have the chipset drivers available on its Web site, where else can you download the drivers?

_____

_____

3. What is the purpose of copying drivers to a thumb drive?

_____

_____

LAB 4.3 BENCHMARK AND BURN-IN A CPU

OBJECTIVES

The goal of this lab is to learn how to compare your CPU's performance in relation to other processors, to make sure the CPU is stable, and to ensure that the heat sink and fan are working correctly. After completing this lab, you will be able to:

- Benchmark a CPU
- Burn-in a CPU
- Monitor CPU temperature

MATERIALS REQUIRED

This lab requires the following:

- An active Internet connection
- SiSoftware Sandra (installed in Lab 1.3)
- A Web browser
- A computer running Windows 2000/XP or Windows 9x

LAB PREPARATION

Before the lab begins, the instructor or lab assistant needs to do the following:

- Verify that Windows starts with no errors and the Internet connection is working.
- Verify that SiSoftware Sandra is installed (see Lab 1.3).

ACTIVITY BACKGROUND

Although today's CPUs are very reliable and fast, after completing a system build, it's a good idea to test the CPU and be sure everything is working correctly. A good technician always tests a system for stability before sending it out to the owner. Although a system might boot without any errors, an unstable machine usually shows problems when a load has been placed on the system. Any time you're running a stress test, it's crucial to monitor the temperature of the CPU so that you don't damage it if there's a problem. SiSoftware Sandra (installed in Lab 1.3) allows both burn-in testing and temperature monitoring.

ESTIMATED COMPLETION TIME: 60 minutes to 24 hours

 Activity

It's best to devote 24 hours to burning in a CPU for verification that it's truly stable. In a lab environment, however, this amount of time might not always be practical. Therefore, this lab allows for one hour of testing. Follow these steps:

1. First, you'll run a short test to make sure the CPU is not overheating. Start SiSoftware Sandra. Under Wizard Modules, click the **Burn-in Wizard** link to run this module. On the opening screen, click the **forward arrow**.

2. Under the Benchmarking Modules menu, click to clear all check boxes except **CPU Arithmetic Benchmark** and **CPU Multi-Media Benchmark**. Click the **forward arrow**.

3. On the Count Down page, leave all the options at their default settings, and then click the **forward arrow**. How many times will the test run?

_____

4. On the Processor page, leave the Minimum Utilization setting at 100%, and then click the **forward arrow**.

5. On the Maximum Temperature page, enter the maximum temperature that the CPU manufacturer recommends for the processor you're using. If you don't know this temperature, leave the entry blank. Click the **forward arrow**.

6. On the Minimum Fan Speed page, leave all entries blank, and then click the **forward arrow**.

7. On the Burn, Baby, Burn! page, click the check mark to begin the burn-in test. Figure 4-4 shows the burn test in progress.

8. When the test has finished, verify that the CPU's temperature has stayed within the correct range. Are there any unusual results from this test?

_____

_____

9. If time permits, run SiSoftware Sandra again, but on the Count Down page, click to enable the **Run Continuously (Background Use)** check box. This time, when the program runs, it won't stop running until you tell it to. This way, you can allow the program to run overnight, and then come back the next day to check for errors. If there are no errors, you can assume that the system is stable.

Figure 4-4   SiSoftware Sandra Burn-in Wizard showing a burn test in progress

After you're sure the system is stable, you can see how the system compares to other systems with similar configurations. Follow these steps:

1. Open SiSoftware Sandra. Under Wizard Modules, click **Combined Performance Index Wizard** to run this module.

2. Click the green check mark to start the benchmark. The system will appear to hang while the test is running. To show you that the test is still running, an animated computer at the top-right corner continues to move.

3. When the test is complete, your computer is then compared to other systems using the coverage matrix. The red color in the graphic represents your system, and the blue color represents the reference system. Figure 4-5 shows the results for one computer. Looking at this figure, you can deduce that this computer is strong on memory performance but weakest on network performance. Based on the results of your test, which area is strongest and which area is weakest on your system?

Figure 4-5   Results of the Combined Performance Index Wizard in SiSoftware Sandra

CHALLENGE ACTIVITY (ADDITIONAL 30 MINUTES)

Sometimes updating chipset drivers on a motherboard can improve a system's overall performance. After you have used the Combined Performance Index Wizard to test performance, follow the directions in Lab 4.2 to download and install updated chipset drivers. Then retest the performance and note any improvements.

REVIEW QUESTIONS

1. Why do you place the system under a load to test for errors?

_____

_____

2. If the performance of your CPU is much lower than that of the reference comparables, how can you improve your CPU's performance?

_____

_____

3. Using the Burn-in Wizard, if you decide to run the test 10 times, can you know for certain how long it will take? Why or why not?

_____

_____

4. When using the Burn-in Wizard, if the animation hangs while the test is being performed, what does it probably mean?

_____

_____

LAB 4.4 COMPARE CPU BENCHMARKS

OBJECTIVES

The goal of this lab is to allow you to compare different CPU choices and determine which is best for a given budget. After completing this lab, you will be able to:

◢ Find CPU benchmarks

◢ Compare CPU benchmarks

◢ Compare CPU performance and price

MATERIALS REQUIRED

This lab requires the following:

◢ An active Internet connection

◢ A Web browser

LAB PREPARATION

Before the lab begins, the instructor or lab assistant needs to do the following:

◢ Verify that Windows starts with no errors and the Internet connection is working.

◢ Verify each Web site to see whether the content has changed.

ACTIVITY BACKGROUND

When purchasing or building a computer system, you need to make many choices. The CPU is one of the most critical components in your system and has a major impact on the machine's overall performance. The CPU you select must match the motherboard you plan to use. If you have already selected the motherboard or you're buying a CPU to install in an existing motherboard, you're limited in selecting a CPU that matches the motherboard. A motherboard has a socket the CPU must fit into and supports only certain ranges of CPU speed and features. However, if you haven't yet selected a motherboard, you can select the CPU first and then choose a motherboard that supports this CPU. In this lab, you begin your purchasing decisions by first selecting the CPU.

It's important to be able to choose the fastest processor your budget allows without having to give up other features. CPU manufacturers used to label their products with the chip speed, so it was easy to compare a 400 MHz AMD with a 400 MHz Intel, for example. However, as the technologies used by competing manufacturers changed, the public relations (PR) system emerged. The AMD 1800+ was clocked at 1533 MHz, but benchmarks showed it to be a comparable product to Intel's 1800 MHz chip, hence the name 1800+. Today's market is full of many different naming conventions, with names such as Pentium, Athlon, Xeon, Opteron, Celeron, and Duron. To be able to make an informed decision on which CPU to purchase, you must be able to compare CPU benchmarks.

Activity

Given a budget of $300 for a CPU, you'll compare different choices and decide on the best choice for a given situation. The first step is to see which CPUs fall into this specified price range. Follow these steps:

1. Use your Web browser to navigate to **www.pricewatch.com**. Under the heading Computer Parts, click **CPUs**. To make a valid comparison, you must look at several models. From this list of CPUs, make note of which four are closest to $300 without going over that limit:

_____

_____

2. Now click the name of each CPU you have selected. In the following chart, make note of the socket type and speed (in GHz or MHz) of each. For example, in the entry "Intel Pentium P4 660 3.6 GHz 1 MB Processor 800 MHz FSB Cache Socket LGA775 3600 MHz with 1 year warranty," the speed is 3.6 GHz and the socket type is LGA775.

CPU	Speed	Socket	Price

When choosing a benchmark for a CPU, it's important to consider the system's primary use. Different CPUs have different strengths and weaknesses, and there are several tests you can choose from to look at performance.

3. Go to Tom's Hardware Guide (THG) Web site at **www.tomshardware.com**. On the right side of the page, under the heading CPU Charts, click **Interactive CPU Charts**.

4. Examine the resulting page. When the chart is displayed, it lists CPUs from top to bottom, with the best performing models at the top of the page for the given benchmark test. Intel CPUs are listed in blue, and AMD CPUs are listed in green. The models chosen in the drop-down lists are in red. If you click a CPU in the list, an information box about the CPU is displayed.

5. From the drop-down lists, under the heading "Choose first model," click the first CPU on your list. Under the heading "Choose second model," click the second one on your list. Now you're ready to see how these two models compare in performance.

6. Assuming you're building a computer for gaming purposes, the tests that are going to interest you most are the game-related tests. This will give you the best possible comparison for how you'll be using the system. In the Choose benchmark drop-down list, click **Doom III**, and then click **Go**. Wait until the screen refreshes, which might take a few minutes.

7. The chart changes to reflect the scores for the benchmark test you selected. Note the red benchmarks in the chart. They should now be the ones for the first and second CPUs you chose earlier. What are the scores for these CPUs?

   ◢ CPU 1: _____

   ◢ CPU 2: _____

8. Look at the price for CPU 1 from the previous chart, and then look at the price for CPU 2. Based on the performance in this test, which one is a better buy?

   _____

9. You should make this type of comparison for each processor you're considering. Also, it's important to choose a benchmark that's closest to the actual type of work you'll be performing on the system. Using what you've learned in the preceding steps, make comparisons for the Doom III and Quake III benchmarks for the four CPUs you're considering. Complete the following chart with the information from the comparison charts and the two benchmark tests:

CPU	Doom III benchmark	Quake III benchmark	Price

After you have compared the CPUs based on performance and price, you should be able to choose a winner. Sometimes you must make trade-offs to stay within your budget range. Unfortunately, making trade-offs isn't an exact science and is a source of major debate among enthusiasts.

CHALLENGE ACTIVITY (ADDITIONAL 20 MINUTES)

In this lab, you used Tom's Hardware Guide (THG) Web site (*www.tomshardware.com*), a long-standing and reliable Web site, to find reviews and comparisons of computer components. However, many other similar sites exist on the Web. Using a good search engine, locate three more Web sites that offer technical reviews of computer parts. Complete the following chart:

Web site	Products reviewed

REVIEW QUESTIONS

1. How would the results change if you were using the computer system for encoding DivX 5.2 home movies instead of for gaming? (Note that DivX 5.2 is the benchmark initially displayed in the chart.)

_____

_____

2. Why shouldn't a technician simply put the lowest price CPU into a machine to save costs?

_____

_____

3. What is the purpose of choosing four models of CPUs for comparison?

_____

_____

4. It seems that for the best performance, you could simply look at the chart and choose the fastest model in each category. Why isn't this method a good way to choose a CPU?

_____

_____

_____

5. How would you predict that the benchmark test results would change if you were given only a $100 budget to work with?

_____

_____

LAB 4.5 CHOOSE A CPU COOLING SOLUTION

OBJECTIVES

Years ago, you could run your 25 MHz computer all day long without a heat sink. Not so today. Because users continue to demand more speed from their CPUs and many hobbyists overclock their CPUs, their systems must constantly battle high temperatures. The most common solution for cooling a CPU is an air-cooled solution: a heat sink and fan (HSF). Although water cooling is effective and extremely quiet, it's still not a mature enough technology to be considered safe for a system's internals. The heat sink is a metal unit that conducts heat away from the CPU and dissipates that heat into the air, typically with a fan forcing air over the top. Some fans are variable-speed fans that adjust their speeds according to the CPU's temperature. Varying the fan speed must be supported by the motherboard chipset.

If you purchase a retail CPU, odds are the HSF will be included. However, most system builders choose to purchase an original equipment manufacturer (OEM) CPU to save money, so they must purchase the HSF separately. Another reason to purchase the HSF separately is that the HSF that comes with the CPU isn't adequate if the builder intends to overclock the CPU. After completing this lab, you will be able to:

⊿ Choose a heat sink and fan

MATERIALS REQUIRED

This lab requires the following:

⊿ An active Internet connection

LAB PREPARATION

Before the lab begins, the instructor or lab assistant needs to do the following:

⊿ Verify that Windows starts with no errors and the Internet connection is working.

ACTIVITY BACKGROUND

There are several things to look for when choosing an HSF. First and foremost, the unit must fit the CPU and socket you're using. Next, the unit must provide adequate cooling at an acceptable noise level. Finally, the preferred unit should be easy to mount. In a perfect world, you would be able to test all these cooling units and make an educated decision based on performance, but it's not practical in a lab environment. The most common model of CPU that's purchased OEM is the AMD Athlon series; therefore, you'll look at the tests Tom's Hardware has run on 55 coolers and make a decision based on those results. AMD's weight limit for the HSF is 300 grams, which is a good idea because an HSF that's too heavy can damage the CPU, CPU socket, or motherboard components.

ESTIMATED COMPLETION TIME: 45 minutes

 Activity

It's essential to choose an HSF made specifically for the processor you're using. Just because a unit fits doesn't mean it will cool the CPU sufficiently. Follow these steps:

1. Go to the Tom's Hardware Guide (THG) Web site at **www.tomshardware.com,** where you need to search the site for articles about coolers. To do that, in the SITE SEARCH box on the right side of the home page, click **Tom's Hardware** in the drop-down list and type **Coolers** in the text box. Click **Search** to search the site for articles about coolers.

2. Look for the article "Cool Stuff: How THG Tests Coolers." After reading it, answer these questions:

    ⊿ How did THG measure the performance level of coolers?

    _____

    _____

    ⊿ How did THG test the noise level of coolers?

    _____

    _____

◢ Why is it important to know the weight of a cooler when comparing coolers?

_____

_____

◢ What type of guarantee should you look for when comparing coolers?

_____

_____

◢ What are some factors to consider about the ease of installation and size of coolers?

_____

_____

_____

3. Now look for the article "A Cool Bunch: How To Put a Lid on the Die Temperature of Your Athlon." After reading it, answer these questions:

◢ Click page 59 of the article and look at the performance ratings of the heat sinks that were tested. What are the top three units in keeping the lowest temperature?

_____

_____

_____

◢ Click page 58 of the article. What are the top three units in terms of noise? They will be the units with the lowest decibel (dB(A)) rating.

_____

_____

_____

◢ Click page 60 of the article. One cooler listed on this page is the Alpha PAL8045, which has a good blend of performance and noise level. What is its weight in grams?

_____

CHALLENGE ACTIVITY (ADDITIONAL 20 MINUTES)

Based on what you've learned in this lab, do the following to select a cooler for an AMD processor you plan to use in a computer for gaming:

1. Using the AMD Web site (*www.amd.com*), select a processor for gaming, and then answer these questions:

◢ Which processor did you select?

_____

◢ Describe the processor:

_____

_____

◢ Why did you select this processor?

_____

_____

2. Using other Web sites that sell or manufacturer coolers, select the best cooler for the processor. Answer these questions:

◢ What is the cooler manufacturer and model?

_____

_____

◢ Why did you select this cooler?

_____

_____

_____

REVIEW QUESTIONS

1. List five factors mentioned in this lab that you should consider when selecting a cooler:

_____

_____

2. If you were in an office building and needed a very quiet system, which of the coolers tested would be a good choice?

_____

_____

3. If you have a CPU that gets very hot and will be used in a noisy industrial building, what effect would these conditions have on your choice of coolers? Would you choose a different cooler than the one you selected in Question 2? Which cooler would you choose?

_____

_____

4. When you purchase a boxed CPU with a cooler, the cooler is usually one with a blend of cooling performance and low noise level. Which of the units that you see in the charts would be a good unit for the manufacturer to include?

_____

_____

5. Can you see any reason that AMD wouldn't recommend the Alpha PAL8045 cooler?

_____

Motherboards

Labs included in this chapter:

- **Lab 5.1:** Examine and Adjust CMOS Settings

- **Lab 5.2:** Use a Hardware Information Utility

- **Lab 5.3:** Identify a Motherboard and Find Documentation on the Internet

- **Lab 5.4:** Identify Motherboard Components and Form Factors

- **Lab 5.5:** Remove and Replace a Motherboard

- **Lab 5.6:** Flash BIOS

LAB 5.1 EXAMINE AND ADJUST CMOS SETTINGS

OBJECTIVES

The goal of this lab is to help you explore and modify CMOS settings. After completing this lab, you will be able to:

◢ Enter the CMOS setup utility

◢ Navigate the CMOS setup utility

◢ Examine some setup options

◢ Save changes to setup options

MATERIALS REQUIRED

This lab requires the following:

◢ A computer designated for this lab

◢ SiSoftware Sandra, installed in Lab 1.3

LAB PREPARATION

Before the lab begins, the instructor or lab assistant needs to do the following:

◢ Verify that Windows starts with no errors.

◢ Verify that SiSoftware Sandra has been installed (see Lab 1.3).

ACTIVITY BACKGROUND

When a system is powered up, the startup process is managed by a set of instructions called the BIOS. The BIOS, in turn, relies on a set of configuration information stored in CMOS that's refreshed continuously by battery power when the system is off. You can access and modify CMOS setup information via the CMOS setup utility in the BIOS. In this lab, you examine the CMOS setup utility, make some changes, and observe the effects of your changes.

Setup utilities vary slightly in appearance and function, depending on the manufacturer and version. The steps in this lab are based on the CMOS setup program for Award BIOS, which is a common BIOS. You might have to perform different steps to access and use the CMOS utility on your computer.

For most computers today, you seldom need to make changes in CMOS setup except to set the date and time for a new system or perhaps to change the boot sequence. The exception is if you're attempting to overclock a system, which is done by changing the default frequencies of the processor and/or motherboard. Overclocking isn't a recommended best practice, however, because of problems with overheating and possibly causing the system to become unstable.

ESTIMATED COMPLETION TIME: 30 minutes

 Activity

Before you access the BIOS on your computer, you need to record the exact date and time indicated by your computer's internal clock. (You use this information later to confirm that you have indeed changed some CMOS settings.) After you record the date and time, you use the Sandra utility (installed in Lab 1.3) to determine which version of BIOS is installed on your computer. Follow these steps:

1. In Windows, double-click the clock on the taskbar, and record the time and date:

_____

2. Close the Date and Time Properties dialog box.

3. Start Sandra, and then double-click the **CPU & BIOS Information** icon (under the Information Modules heading in Windows XP).

4. Click **System BIOS** in the Device drop-down list.

5. Record the manufacturer and version information for your BIOS:

_____

6. Close Sandra.

Now that you know what BIOS your computer runs, you can determine how to enter the setup utility. In general, to start the setup utility, you need to press a key or key combination as the computer is booting. Some CMOS utilities are password protected with a supervisor password and a user password (also called a power-on password). The supervisor password allows full access to CMOS setup, and the user password allows you to view CMOS setup screens, but you won't be able to change any settings

or sometimes you can change only certain settings. In addition, if the user password is also set to be a power-on password and you don't know this password, you won't be able to boot the system. When you attempt to access CMOS setup, if password protection has been enabled, you're asked for a password, and you must enter a valid password to continue.

 Notes

CMOS setup supervisor, user, and power-on passwords are different from the Windows password required to log on to Windows. Also, if you're responsible for a computer and have forgotten the supervisor password, you can remove a jumper on the motherboard to return all CMOS settings to their default values, which erases any CMOS passwords. Lab 6.5 covers how to find this jumper.

To learn more about entering the setup utility on your computer, follow these steps:

1. Using the information you recorded previously in Step 5, consult Table 5-1 to find out how to enter your system's setup utility. (Alternatively, when you first turn on your PC, look for a message on your screen, which might read something like "Press F2 to access setup.")

BIOS	Method for entering CMOS setup utility
AMI BIOS	Boot the computer, and then press the Delete key.
Award BIOS	Boot the computer, and then press the Delete key.
Older Phoenix BIOS	Boot the computer, and then press the Ctrl+Alt+Esc or Ctrl+Alt+S key combination.
Newer Phoenix BIOS	Boot the computer, and then press the F2 or F1 key.
Dell Computers with Phoenix BIOS	Boot the computer, and then press the Ctrl+Alt+Enter key combination.
Some older Compaq computers, such as Deskpro 286 or 386	Place the diagnostics disk in the drive, reboot the system, and choose Computer Setup from the menu.
Some newer Compaq computers, such as Prolinea, Deskpro, DeskproXL, Deskpro LE, or Presario	Boot the computer, wait for two beeps, and when the cursor is in the upper-right corner of the screen, press the F10 key.
All other older computers	Use the setup program on the floppy disk that came with the PC. If the floppy disk is lost, contact the motherboard manufacturer to get a replacement.

Table 5-1 Methods for entering CMOS setup utilities by BIOS

Notes

For Compaq computers, the CMOS setup program is stored on the hard drive in a small, non-DOS partition of about 3 MB. If this partition becomes corrupted or the computer is an older model, you must run setup from a diagnostic disk. If you can't run setup by pressing F10 at startup, a damaged partition or virus is likely taking up space in conventional memory.

Now you're ready to enter the CMOS setup utility included in your BIOS. Follow these steps:

1. If a floppy disk is necessary to enter the CMOS setup utility, insert it now.

2. Restart the computer.

3. When the system restarts, enter the setup utility using the correct method for your computer.

4. Notice that the CMOS utility groups settings by function. For example, all the power management features are grouped together in a Power Management section.

5. The main screen usually has a Help section that describes how to make selections and exit the utility. Typically, you can use the arrow keys or Tab key to highlight options. After you have highlighted your selection, usually you need to press Enter, Page Down, or the spacebar. The main screen might display a short summary of the highlighted category. Look for and select a category called something like **Standard CMOS Setup**.

6. In the Standard CMOS Setup screen, you should see some or all of the following settings. List the current setting for each of the following:

   ◢ Date: _____

   ◢ Time: _____

   ◢ For IDE hard drives, a table listing drive size, mode of operation, and cylinder, head, and sector information:

   _____

   _____

   ◢ Floppy drive setup information, including drive letter and type:

   _____

   ◢ Halt on error setup (the type of error that halts the boot process):

   _____

   ◢ Memory summary (summary of system memory divisions):

   _____

   ◢ Boot sequence (drives the BIOS searches for an OS):

   _____

7. Exit the Standard CMOS setup screen and return to the main page. Select a section called something like **Chipset Features Setup**.

8. Record settings for the following as well as any other settings in this section:

   ◢ RAM setup options:

   _____

   _____

◢ AGP setup options:

_____

_____

◢ CPU-specific setup options:

_____

_____

◢ Settings for serial and parallel ports:

_____

_____

◢ Provisions for enabling and disabling onboard drive controllers and other embedded devices:

_____

_____

_____

_____

9. Exit to the CMOS setup main screen. Explore the menus and submenus of the CMOS setup utility and answer these questions:

> ✐ **Notes**
>
> Most of the CMOS settings never need changing, so understanding every setting isn't necessary.

◢ Does CMOS setup offer the option to set a supervisor password? If so, what's the name of the screen where the password is set?

_____

_____

◢ Does CMOS setup offer the option to set a user password? Is so, what options can affect the way users can access and use CMOS setup?

_____

_____

_____

10. Exit to the CMOS setup main screen. You might see options for loading CMOS defaults (which restore factory settings and can be helpful in troubleshooting) as well as options for exiting with or without saving changes. There might be an option to set user and supervisor passwords as well as a utility to detect IDE hard disk drives automatically.

Now that you're familiar with the way the CMOS setup utility works, you can change the date and time settings. Then you reboot the computer, confirm that the changes are reflected in the operating system, and return the CMOS date and time to the correct settings. Follow these steps:

1. Return to the Standard CMOS setup screen.

2. Highlight the time field(s) and set the time ahead one hour.

3. Move to the date field(s) and set the date ahead one year.

4. Return to the main CMOS setup screen, and click an option named something like **Save Settings and Exit**. If prompted, verify that you want to save the settings.

5. Wait while the system reboots. Allow Windows to load.

6. At the desktop, check the time and date. Are your CMOS setup changes reflected in Windows?

_____

7. Reboot the computer, return to CMOS setup, and set the correct time and date.

8. Verify again that the changes are reflected in Windows.

CRITICAL THINKING (ADDITIONAL 30 MINUTES)

Form workgroups of two to four people, and do the following to practice troubleshooting problems with CMOS:

1. Propose a change you could make to CMOS setup that would prevent a computer from booting successfully. What change did you propose?

_____

2. Have your instructor approve the change because some changes might cause information written to the hard drive to be lost, making it difficult to recover from the problem without reloading the hard drive. Did your instructor approve the change?

_____

3. Now go to another team's computer and make the change to CMOS setup while the other team makes a change to your system.

4. Return to your computer and troubleshoot the problem. Describe the problem as a user would:

_____

_____

5. What steps did you go through to discover the source of the problem and fix it?

_____

_____

6. If you were to encounter this same problem in the future, what might you do differently to troubleshoot it?

_____

_____

REVIEW QUESTIONS

1. Do all systems use the same method to enter CMOS setup? Can you enter CMOS setup after the system has booted?

   _____

2. How are settings usually grouped in the CMOS setup utility?

   _____

3. In what section do you usually find time and date setup in the CMOS setup utility?

   _____

   _____

4. What types of options are shown on the CMOS setup main screen?

   _____

5. What happens automatically after you exit CMOS setup?

   _____

6. What tool in Sandra can you use to find information on your version of BIOS?

   _____

   _____

7. Why does a computer need CMOS?

   _____

   _____

8. When troubleshooting a computer, when might you have to enter CMOS setup? List at least three reasons:

   _____

   _____

   _____

LAB 5.2 USE A HARDWARE INFORMATION UTILITY

OBJECTIVES

The goal of this lab is to help you learn how to use a hardware information utility. After completing this lab, you will be able to:

▲ Download and install the HWiNFO32 utility by Martin Malik

▲ Use the HWiNFO32 utility to examine your system

MATERIALS REQUIRED

This lab requires the following:

- ◢ A computer designated for this lab
- ◢ Windows 2000/XP or Windows 9x operating system
- ◢ Internet access for file downloading only

LAB PREPARATION

Before lab begins, the instructor or lab assistant needs to do the following:

- ◢ Verify that Windows starts with no errors.
- ◢ Verify that Internet access is available.
- ◢ For labs that don't have Internet access, download these files to a file server or other storage media available to students in the lab:
  - ◢ Latest version of HWiNFO32 downloaded from *www.hwinfo.com*. At the time this lab was tested, the latest version is Version 1.59, and the file name is Hw32_159.exe. However, the version number and file name might have changed.
  - ◢ Latest version of HWiNFO downloaded from *www.hwinfo.com*. At the time this lab was tested, the file name was Hwinf497.zip.
  - ◢ For Windows 98 or Windows 2000 systems, download an uncompress utility, such as WinZip from *www.winzip.com*.

ACTIVITY BACKGROUND

A hardware information utility can be useful when you want to identify a hardware component in a system without having to open the computer case. Also, a hardware information utility can help you identify features of a motherboard, video card, or processor installed in a system and establish benchmarks for these components. In this lab, you learn to use HWiNFO32 written by Martin Malik from Slovakia. The utility comes in a Windows version and a DOS version. You can use the Windows version on any Windows 2000/XP or Windows 9x computer, and you can install the DOS version on floppy disks so that the utility is available on any computer you're troubleshooting.

In this lab, you download a shareware Windows version of HWiNFO32 from the Internet and then learn how to use it. Web sites sometimes change, so as you follow the instructions in this lab, you might have to adjust for changes to the *www.hwinfo.com* site. If your lab doesn't have Internet access, ask your instructor for the location of the file downloaded previously for your use. Write the path to that file here:

_____

ESTIMATED COMPLETION TIME: 30 minutes

 Activity

1. Go to the HWiNFO32 Web site at **www.hwinfo.com**. Click **Download**. In the submenu under Download, click **HWiNFO32**. Click one of the download locations, and the File Download dialog box opens. Click **Save**. Select a folder on your computer to save the file, and click **Save**. What is the path and name of the downloaded file?

2. Close your browser, open Windows Explorer, and then double-click the file name to install HWiNFO32 for Windows. If the Security Warning dialog box opens, click **Run** to start setup. Follow the directions on the screen to install the software.

3. After the software is installed, the HWiNFO32 Help window opens. Research this help program to answer the following questions about the utility:

   ◢ Why does the utility's installation program install a driver running in kernel mode?

   _____

   _____

   ◢ The utility was written for Windows 2000/XP but should also work in Windows 9x. What warning is given about running the utility in Windows 9x?

   _____

   ◢ Why is it necessary for the utility to be updated often?

   _____

4. Close the HWiNFO32 Help window.

5. To run the utility, click **Start**, point to **All Programs** (**Programs** for Windows 9x), point to **HWiNFO32**, and click **HWiNFO32 Program**. When a dialog box opens, click **Continue** to close it. The utility examines your system, and then the HWiNFO32 window shown in Figure 5-1 opens.

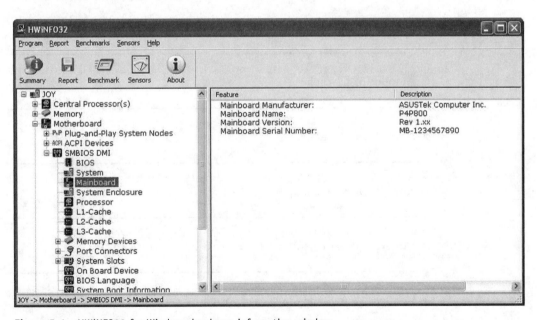

Figure 5-1 HWiNFO32 for Windows hardware information window

Many times you aren't given step-by-step directions when using utility software but must learn how to use it by exploring menus and using the software's help functions. The following steps give you practice in doing that:

1. Use the HWiNFO32 utility to find the following information about your system:

   ◢ Mainboard manufacturer:

   _____

◢ Mainboard name:

_____

◢ Mainboard serial number:

_____

◢ BIOS vendor:

_____

◢ BIOS version:

_____

◢ BIOS release date:

_____

◢ Processor manufacturer:

_____

◢ Processor version:

_____

◢ Current and maximum clock speed of the processor:

_____

◢ Processor socket:

_____

◢ Amount of L1 cache:

_____

◢ Amount of L2 cache:

_____

◢ Amount of L3 cache:

_____

◢ Slot type of the video bus, as reported by the video card:

_____

◢ Slot type of the video bus, as reported by the motherboard:

_____

◢ Amount of video RAM:

_____

2. To identify your motherboard's chipset, look for information under Memory Controller Hub and I/O Controller Hub. Based on this information, what chipset is your motherboard using?

_____

3. Exit the program.

CHALLENGE ACTIVITY (ADDITIONAL 30 MINUTES)

Martin Malik also offers a DOS-based utility for finding information about hardware. If you download and install this DOS version of HWiNFO on a Windows bootable disk, you can boot a system with this disk and run the utility without using Windows. This option can be useful when Windows isn't working or you don't want to take the time to install the utility's 32-bit version in Windows. Also, if you're servicing a customer's computer, you can use the DOS-based utility on a Windows startup disk to get information about the system quickly without installing software on a customer's computer.

Create a bootable floppy disk. Download the DOS version of HWiNFO from the *www.hwinfo.com* Web site and copy it to the disk. Boot from the disk and start the utility on any Windows 2000/XP or Windows 9x computer. Answer the following questions:

1. What is the name of the downloaded compressed file for HWiNFO for DOS?

2. List the steps you took to download the utility and install it on a bootable floppy disk:

3. Describe how the software works using this method:

REVIEW QUESTIONS

1. Why does a Windows driver need to run in kernel mode?

2. In your system, did the type of video slot reported by the video card differ from the type of video slot reported by the motherboard? If so, how can you explain this difference?

3. Using Windows XP, list the steps to create a bootable floppy disk:

4. Can you use a bootable floppy disk created in Windows XP to boot a Windows 2000 computer? A Windows 98 computer?

5. What is an advantage of using the DOS version instead of the Windows version of the HWiNFO utility?

_____

6. List three reasons you might use HWiNFO or HWiNFO32 when troubleshooting or upgrading a PC:

_____

_____

_____

LAB 5.3 IDENTIFY A MOTHERBOARD AND FIND DOCUMENTATION ON THE INTERNET

OBJECTIVES

The goal of this lab is to learn to identify a motherboard and find online documentation for it. After completing this lab, you will be able to:

▲ Identify a motherboard by examining it physically

▲ Determine a motherboard's manufacturer and model

▲ Search the Internet for motherboard documentation

MATERIALS REQUIRED

This lab requires the following:

▲ A computer designated for disassembly

▲ SiSoftware Sandra (installed in Lab 1.3)

▲ Internet access

▲ Adobe Acrobat Reader

▲ A PC toolkit with antistatic ground strap

LAB PREPARATION

Before the lab begins, the instructor or lab assistant needs to do the following:

▲ Verify that Windows starts with no errors.

▲ Verify that Internet access is available.

▲ Verify that SiSoftware Sandra and Adobe Acrobat Reader are installed.

ACTIVITY BACKGROUND

Often a PC technician is asked to repair a PC, but the documentation is lost or not available. Fortunately, you can usually find documentation for a device online, as long as you have the device's manufacturer name and model number. In this lab, you learn how to find the manufacturer's name and model number on a motherboard, and then locate documentation for that device on the Internet.

ESTIMATED COMPLETION TIME: 30 minutes

Activity

1. Boot your PC and use SiSoftware Sandra (installed in Lab 1.3) to find out which type of CPU is installed on your computer. Record that information:

_____

2. Following safety precautions, including using an antistatic ground strap, remove the PC's case cover, and then remove any components obscuring your view of the motherboard. In some cases, you might have to remove the motherboard itself, but usually this step isn't necessary.

3. Look for a stenciled or silkscreened label printed on the circuit board that indicates the manufacturer and model. Note that other components sometimes have labels printed on a sticker affixed to the component. On a motherboard, the label is usually printed directly on the circuit board. Common motherboard manufacturers include Abit, Asus, and Intel.

Also, note that the manufacturer name is usually printed in much larger type than the model number. Model numbers often include both letters and numbers, and many indicate a version number as well. Figure 5-2 shows an example of a motherboard label.

Motherboard manufacturer (ASUS)

Model number (P5A)

Figure 5-2 Label printed directly on motherboard

4. Record the information on the motherboard label:

_____

5. Take your information to a PC with Internet access and open a browser.

6. If you know the manufacturer's URL, go directly to the Web site. (Table 5-2 lists the URLs for some motherboard manufacturers.) If you don't know the manufacturer's URL, search for the manufacturer or model

Notes

For a listing of Web sites about motherboards, including motherboard manufacturers, diagnostics, and product comparisons and reviews, see _www.motherboards.org_.

with your favorite search engine, as shown in Figure 5-3. In the search results, click a link associated with the manufacturer. If this link doesn't take you directly to the documentation, it usually gets you within two or three links. Continue until you find the manufacturer's Web site.

Manufacturer	URL
American Megatrends, Inc.	www.megatrends.com
ASUS	www.asus.com
Dell	www.dell.com
Diamond Multimedia	www.diamondmm.com
First International Computer, Inc.	www.fica.com
Gateway	www.gateway.com
Giga-Byte Technology Co., Ltd.	www.giga-byte.com
IBM	www.ibm.com
Intel Corporation	www.intel.com
Supermicro Computer, Inc.	www.supermicro.com
Tyan Computer Corporation	www.tyan.com

Table 5-2 URLs for major motherboard manufacturers

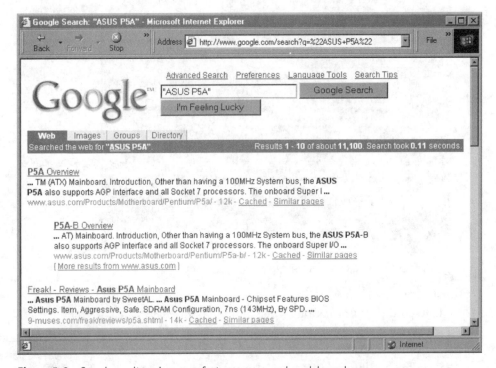

Figure 5-3 Search results using manufacturer name and model number

7. When you have found the site of your motherboard's manufacturer, look for a link to service or support. Click this link, and, if necessary, select a product category and model number. Sometimes knowing the type of CPU the board supports can be useful in finding the right board.

8. Continue working your way through the site until you find the motherboard documentation. The documentation might include a variety of documents covering technical specifications and installation instructions. Often the documentation includes a basic manual, which is usually a combination of technical and installation specifications.

9. When you find the documentation, you might also find a link to updated drivers. If you see such a link, click it and note the release date of these drivers. If they are newer than the current drivers, it's often advisable to update the drivers as well. If possible, record the release dates for updated drivers:

   _____

10. Return to the main documentation page, and, if it's available, select the manual. If it's not available, select the installation instructions.

11. The manual is probably in PDF format, so you need to have Adobe Acrobat Reader installed. If you have the browser plug-in, you can open the document from the source location, or you can download the manual to your computer and then open it. Using your preferred method, open the document and print the motherboard documentation. Save this documentation for use in Lab 5.5.

REVIEW QUESTIONS

1. How is the label usually applied to a motherboard? How is it most often applied to other components?

   _____

2. On the label of a motherboard or other component, how can the manufacturer often be differentiated from the model number?

   _____

3. What type of link on a manufacturer's Web site usually leads you to manuals and other documentation?

   _____

4. What other information about your motherboard might you want to examine on the manufacturer's Web site?

   _____

5. In what format is documentation most often available for download?

   _____

6. What information besides motherboard documentation, such as BIOS updates and drivers, can be found at the manufacturer's Web site?

   _____

LAB 5.4 IDENTIFY MOTHERBOARD COMPONENTS AND FORM FACTORS

OBJECTIVES

The goal of this lab is to help you learn to identify motherboard form factors and components. After completing this lab, you will be able to:

◢ Identify a motherboard's CPU type

◢ Identify connectors

◢ Identify the form factor based on component type and placement

MATERIALS REQUIRED

Instructors are encouraged to supply a variety of motherboards, some common and others not so common. At the very least, this lab requires the following:

◢ Three different motherboards

> **Notes**
>
> If three motherboards aren't available, look on the Web sites of the motherboard manufacturers listed in Lab 5.3 for three boards.

LAB PREPARATION

Before the lab begins, the instructor or lab assistant needs to do the following:

◢ Gather an assortment of motherboards, with at least one AT, ATX, and BTX board, if possible.

ACTIVITY BACKGROUND

As a PC technician, you should be able to look at a motherboard and determine what type of CPU, RAM, and form factor you're working with. You should also be able to recognize any unusual components the board might have. In this lab, you examine different motherboards and note some important information about them.

ESTIMATED COMPLETION TIME: 30 minutes

 Activity

Fill in the following chart for your assigned motherboards. If you have more than three motherboards, use additional paper. When the entry in the Item column is a question such as "AGP slot?", write a yes or no answer.

Item	Motherboard 1	Motherboard 2	Motherboard 3
Manufacturer/model			
BIOS manufacturer			
CPU type			
Chipset			
RAM type/pins			
How many PCI slots?			
How many ISA slots?			
AGP slot?			

Item	Motherboard 1	Motherboard 2	Motherboard 3
How many PCI Express slots?			
Parallel ATA connectors?			
Serial ATA (SATA) connectors?			
SCSI controller?			
Embedded audio, video, and so on			
Jumperless?			
Form factor			
Describe any unusual components			

REVIEW QUESTIONS

1. How can you determine whether a motherboard is an AT or ATX board based on the CPU's location in relation to the expansion slots?

2. How can you determine whether a motherboard is an ATX or a BTX board?

3. Of the motherboards you examined, which do you think is the oldest? Why?

4. Which motherboard best supports old and new technology? Why?

5. Which motherboard seems to provide the best possibility for expansion? Why?

6. Which motherboard is most likely the easiest to configure? Why?

7. Which motherboard do you think is the most expensive? Why?

8. What are some considerations a motherboard manufacturer has to contend with when designing a motherboard? (For example, consider room for large CPUs and cooling fans, where the power supply is located in relationship to the power connector, new technologies, and so forth.)

LAB 5.5 REMOVE AND REPLACE A MOTHERBOARD

OBJECTIVES

The goal of this lab is to familiarize you with the process of replacing an old or faulty motherboard. After completing this lab, you will be able to:

▲ Use SiSoftware Sandra to determine your CPU's specifications

▲ Remove a motherboard

▲ Configure a new motherboard according to its documentation

▲ Install a replacement motherboard

MATERIALS REQUIRED

This lab requires the following:

▲ A computer designated for this lab

▲ SiSoftware Sandra (installed in Lab 1.3)

▲ A workgroup of 2 to 4 students

▲ A PC toolkit with antistatic ground strap

LAB PREPARATION

Before the lab begins, the instructor or lab assistant needs to do the following:

▲ Verify that Windows starts with no errors.

▲ Verify that SiSoftware Sandra has been installed.

ACTIVITY BACKGROUND

In this lab, you exchange a motherboard with another team to simulate the process of replacing a faulty motherboard. When you install the new motherboard, you must configure it for your system by adjusting jumper and CMOS settings according to the documentation you printed in Lab 5.3. Then you install the replacement motherboard.

ESTIMATED COMPLETION TIME: 45 minutes

Activity

In this lab, follow safety precautions while you remove the motherboard. Be sure to use an antistatic ground strap.

1. Launch Sandra (installed in Lab 1.3) and use the **CPU & BIOS Information** utility to examine the CPU in your system. Record the information listed in the Processor section:

   _____

   _____

   _____

2. Power the system down, unplug everything, and remove the case cover. Then remove the cabling and expansion cards from the motherboard. Take all necessary precautions (including using an antistatic ground strap), and make a sketch of cabling and component placement.

3. Six screws usually attach the motherboard to the case via spacers or stand-offs. The spacers prevent the printed circuitry from shorting out on the metal case and provide space for air circulation. Also, it's important that the motherboard be securely attached to the case with enough spacers and screws so that the board won't crack when expansion cards are being inserted. Remove the screws attaching the motherboard, and set them aside in a cup, bag, or bowl so that you don't lose them.

 Tip

In this lab, it's not necessary to remove the spacers from holes in the computer case. However, sometimes you might have to move a spacer from one hole to another, such as when you're replacing a motherboard and the new board lines up over different holes in the computer case. To remove a plastic spacer held in place with barbs, use needlenose pliers to pinch the spacer and slide it out of the hole. To install it in a new hole, push the spacer into the hole until it pops in place. For metal spacers, carefully squeeze the spacer with pliers and remove it from the bracket holding it to the computer case.

4. Carefully lift the motherboard out of the case. You might have to tilt the board to clear the drive bays and power supply. In some cases, you might have to remove the drives to get the motherboard out.

5. Exchange the motherboard and motherboard documentation with that of another team. You might also exchange the CPU and memory, depending on whether your current CPU and memory modules are compatible with the new motherboard. Follow directions from your instructor on what to exchange. Be sure you have the new motherboard's documentation, which you should have found on the Internet in Lab 6.3.

Your instructor might ask you to remove jumpers and reset DIP switches on your motherboard before passing it to the other team. These modifications will make the other team's configuration more challenging. As an alternative, your instructor might have a display motherboard somewhere in the lab that uses jumpers and DIP switches for part of its configuration.

1. With the new motherboard in front of you, consult its documentation and find any jumpers that must be configured to match the system. Older boards use jumpers to adjust clock multipliers and memory speeds and to clear CMOS settings. Unless otherwise instructed, *do not* remove the jumper to clear CMOS settings. Note that newer boards are often "jumperless," with all configuration settings made in CMOS setup. The only jumper these boards have is the one to clear CMOS settings. Remove and replace the jumpers in the configuration specified to match your processor information.

2. Install the motherboard, cabling, expansion cards, and any other components you removed.

3. Have your instructor check your work before you turn on the power.

4. Boot the system and enter the CMOS setup utility. For jumperless motherboards, make any adjustments specified in the motherboard's documentation.

5. Save your settings and exit CMOS setup.

6. Reboot the system and verify that the system is functioning correctly. Describe any error messages:

_____

7. What steps do you plan to take to troubleshoot this error?

_____

CRITICAL THINKING (ADDITIONAL 30 MINUTES)

To learn more about motherboards, do the following:

1. After the PC is working, ask your instructor to configure a power-on password on your computer.

2. Without knowing the password, boot the computer.

3. List the steps required to boot the computer without the power-on password:

_____

_____

_____

REVIEW QUESTIONS

1. How many screws usually attach the motherboard to the computer case?

_____

2. What is the purpose of spacers?

_____

3. A jumperless motherboard is likely to have one jumper. Which jumper is it?

_____

4. Where can you access configuration settings for a jumperless motherboard?

_____

LAB 5.6 FLASH BIOS

OBJECTIVES

The goal of this lab is to help you examine the process of flashing BIOS. After completing this lab, you will be able to:

- ◢ Gather motherboard information
- ◢ Gather BIOS string information
- ◢ Research correct BIOS update information
- ◢ Record current BIOS settings
- ◢ Flash your BIOS, if permitted by your instructor

MATERIALS REQUIRED

This lab requires the following:

- ◢ Windows 2000/XP or Windows 9x operating system
- ◢ Motherboard documentation or SiSoftware Sandra, installed in Lab 1.3
- ◢ Internet access
- ◢ A blank floppy disk

LAB PREPARATION

Before the lab begins, the instructor or lab assistant needs to do the following:

- ◢ Verify that Windows starts with no errors.
- ◢ Verify that Internet access is available.

ACTIVITY BACKGROUND

The BIOS on a motherboard controls many of the system's basic input/output (I/O) functions. You can update the BIOS programming by downloading the latest update from the BIOS or motherboard manufacturer's Web site and then following specific procedures to update (or "flash") the BIOS. Flashing a computer's BIOS is necessary when troubleshooting an unstable motherboard. You might also need to flash a computer's BIOS to provide support for new hardware (such as a processor, hard drive, or CD-ROM drive) or an operating system you're about to install. For example, before upgrading your operating system to Windows 2000/XP Professional, you could update your BIOS to add support for ACPI power management. In this lab, you gather information about your system, including what BIOS you're using and how to flash it. If your instructor permits, you also flash your BIOS.

ESTIMATED COMPLETION TIME: 30 minutes

 Activity

Before making hardware, software, or BIOS changes to a system, it's important to know your starting point so that if problems occur, you know whether the problems already existed or you created them by what you did to the system. Do the following:

1. Verify that your computer can boot successfully to a Windows desktop with no errors.

2. Does the PC boot without errors?

When flashing the BIOS, using the correct BIOS update is critical. Using the wrong BIOS update can render your system inoperable. Follow these steps to gather information on the motherboard chipset and BIOS:

1. Use motherboard documentation or Sandra to find and record the following:

   ◢ Motherboard manufacturer:

   _____

   ◢ Motherboard model number and version/revision:

   _____

   ◢ Chipset manufacturer:

   _____

   ◢ Chipset model number and version/revision:

   _____

2. Next, you need to record the BIOS string and manufacturer information displayed during the boot process. To make it possible to record this information, for an older PC, turn off the PC, unplug your keyboard, and then turn on the PC. In most cases, the first screen contains video BIOS information from the video card and is identified by "VGA BIOS" or "Video BIOS." Ignore this screen and wait for the next screen, which indicates the start of POST. At this point, because you unplugged the keyboard, POST stops and reports the error about a missing keyboard. This freezes the screen so that you can read the BIOS information. For a newer PC, turn off the PC and then turn it on again while pressing the Pause/Break key, which causes POST to halt.

3. Usually, you can find the BIOS manufacturer and version at the top left of the POST screen. You might also see a release date, which is useful in determining whether newer versions of the BIOS are available. The motherboard identification string is usually located at the bottom left and often contains dozens of characters. Make sure you verify that this string is correct so that you get the correct BIOS update. Record your information on the following lines:

   ◢ BIOS manufacturer and version:

   _____

   ◢ BIOS release date, if provided:

   _____

   ◢ Motherboard identification string:

   _____

If you have a name-brand PC that doesn't identify BIOS information during the boot process, you should be able to locate BIOS information on the manufacturer's Web site by computer model number and serial number. Also, some newer computers don't halt the boot process if the keyboard is missing. Alternatively, you can go to CMOS setup and look for the BIOS identifying information on the CMOS main menu screen.

Using the information you gathered, you can search the Web to determine what files you need to update your BIOS:

1. First, search the motherboard manufacturer's Web site and then the BIOS manufacturer's Web site in the Support section for information on updating your BIOS.

Alternatively, search by motherboard model number or BIOS version number. Download the files to update your BIOS or, if your computer is running the latest version of the BIOS, download the files to refresh your existing BIOS. Answer the following questions:

◢ Did you download files to update or refresh your BIOS?

_____

◢ Which manufacturer provided the BIOS: the BIOS manufacturer or motherboard manufacturer?

_____

◢ What is the name of the file you downloaded?

_____

◢ What is the release date of the latest version?

_____

2. Search the manufacturer's Web site for the steps to flash your BIOS. Print this procedure so that you can use it during the upgrade. Does the procedure call for an additional BIOS utility or flash utility? If so, download this utility as well. Research flash utilities on *www.wimsbios.com*. Wim's BIOS is an excellent Web site for researching BIOS information in general. Print information on what BIOS utilities are available.

3. The next step is to record any changes you have made previously to CMOS settings. Generally, when BIOS is updated, settings are returned to their default state, so you probably need to return the settings to their present state after you have flashed BIOS. In addition, you might need to manually input settings for all hard drives (or allow these settings to be detected automatically). Record any settings you know you changed, any hard drive settings that might have to be reconfigured after you update the BIOS, and any additional settings specified by your instructor:

◢ Hard drive information:

_____

_____

◢ Settings you have changed:

_____

_____

◢ Settings specified by your instructor:

_____

_____

4. At this point, if your update procedure requires using a bootable floppy disk, verify that the boot order allows you to boot from drive A before drive C.

5. Prepare to update your BIOS. Uncompress any files, double-check procedures, read any Readme.txt files included in the upgrade files (which often contain last-minute adjustments to the procedure), and create the upgrade boot disk, if necessary.

6. If your instructor permits, follow the BIOS update procedure to flash your BIOS. During the procedure, if you're given the opportunity to save your old BIOS, do so. This information makes it possible to return to the previous BIOS version if you encounter problems with the new BIOS.

7. Reboot, verify CMOS settings, and verify that the computer boots to a Windows desktop successfully.

REVIEW QUESTIONS

1. At what point in the boot process is BIOS information displayed?

   _____

2. How can you freeze the screen during POST so that you can read the BIOS information?

   _____

   _____

3. Why is it so important to record BIOS and motherboard information correctly?

   _____

   _____

4. What files might contain last-minute adjustments to the upgrade procedures?

   _____

5. In what state are CMOS settings usually placed after a BIOS update?

   _____

6. If given the opportunity during the update, what should you always do and why?

   _____

   _____

Upgrading Memory

Labs included in this chapter:

- **Lab 6.1:** Research RAM on the Internet

- **Lab 6.2:** Explore the Kingston Web Site

- **Lab 6.3:** Upgrade RAM

- **Lab 6.4:** Troubleshoot Memory Problems

- **Lab 6.5:** Use Himem.sys in Windows 98

LAB 6.1 RESEARCH RAM ON THE INTERNET

OBJECTIVES

The goal of this lab is to help you learn how to find important information about RAM that you need when upgrading memory. After completing this lab, you will be able to:

◢ Find documentation on your system's motherboard

◢ Read documentation for your system's RAM specifications

◢ Search the Internet for RAM prices and availability

MATERIALS REQUIRED

This lab requires the following:

◢ Windows 2000/XP or Windows 98 operating system

◢ Internet access

◢ *Optional*: A workgroup of 2 to 4 students

LAB PREPARATION

Before the lab begins, the instructor or lab assistant needs to do the following:

◢ Verify that Internet access is available.

ACTIVITY BACKGROUND

In the past, RAM was literally worth more than its weight in gold. When building a system, most people made do with the minimum amount of RAM needed for adequate performance. These days, RAM is more inexpensive, which means you can probably buy all the RAM you need to make your system perform at top speed. Graphics-editing software, in particular, benefits from additional RAM. In this lab, you research how to optimize RAM on a graphics workstation with a memory upgrade budget of $150.

ESTIMATED COMPLETION TIME: 30 minutes

 Activity

1. Use My Computer to determine the amount of RAM currently installed. Record the amount of RAM here:

   _____

2. Using skills you learned in Lab 5.3, determine your motherboard's manufacturer and model. (If you don't have the motherboard documentation available, search for it on the Web and print it.)

Use the documentation for your motherboard to answer these questions:

1. What type (or types) of memory does your motherboard support? Be sure to include the speed as well as the category (such as SDRAM or DDR2):

   _____

   _____

2. How many slots for memory modules are included on your motherboard?

_____

3. How many memory slots on your motherboard are used, and how much RAM is installed in each slot?

_____

_____

4. What is the maximum amount of memory your motherboard supports?

_____

5. What size and how many memory modules would be needed to upgrade your system to the maximum amount of supported memory?

_____

Now that you have the necessary information about your system's memory, go to a local computer store that sells memory, or go to *http://pricewatch.com* or a similar Web site, and answer the following questions:

1. What is the price of the memory modules required to configure your system for maximum memory?

_____

2. Does your budget allow you to install the maximum supported amount of RAM?

_____

3. Can you use the existing memory modules to upgrade to the maximum amount of supported memory?

_____

4. What is the most additional memory you could install and still stay within your budget? (Assume you'll use the existing memory modules.)

_____

Explore other types of memory on *http://pricewatch.com* or another similar Web site, and answer the following questions:

1. On average, what is the least expensive type of memory per MB you can find? What is its price?

_____

_____

2. On average, what is the most expensive type of memory per MB you can find? What is its price?

_____

3. Is SO-DIMM memory for a notebook computer more or less expensive than an equivalent amount of DDR2 memory for a desktop PC? Give specific information to support your answer:

_____

_____

REVIEW QUESTIONS

1. Why might you want to upgrade RAM on a system?

_____

_____

2. How many pins are on the different types of DIMMs?

_____

3. Which is more expensive: DDR-DIMM or RIMM?

_____

4. What is a disadvantage of using two 64 MB modules instead of a single 128 MB module in a system with three slots for memory modules?

_____

_____

5. What are two disadvantages of using only one 256 MB module rather than two 128 MB modules?

_____

_____

_____

LAB 6.2 EXPLORE THE KINGSTON WEB SITE

OBJECTIVES

The goal of this lab is to use the Kingston Web site to learn about RAM. After completing this lab, you will be able to:

◢ Identify types of RAM
◢ Determine appropriate memory types for a system

MATERIALS REQUIRED

This lab requires the following:

◢ Internet access

LAB PREPARATION

Before the lab begins, the instructor or lab assistant needs to do the following:

◢ Verify that Internet access is available.

ACTIVITY BACKGROUND

RAM comes in a variety of shapes, sizes, and speeds. Not every type of RAM works with every system. In this lab, you use the Kingston Technology (a major RAM manufacturer) Web site to learn about RAM and see how to make sure you have the right memory module to upgrade your system.

ESTIMATED COMPLETION TIME: 30 minutes

 Activity

Do the following to begin learning about system memory:

1. Open your browser and go to **www.kingston.com**.

2. Notice that you can use the site's Memory Search section to search for memory based on the type of system you have. What other three ways can you search for memory?

_____

_____

_____

When you search the site based on your system, the results include a list of compatible memory types with prices, maximum memory your system supports, processors supported, and number of expansion slots on your system for memory modules. Do the following to find information about a memory upgrade for a motherboard:

1. Select one of the motherboards from the table in Lab 5.4. Which motherboard did you select?

_____

2. Perform a memory search on the Kingston site for information on this motherboard. Answer the following questions:

◢ What types of memory modules can this board can use?

_____

_____

_____

◢ What types of processors does the board support?

_____

_____

_____

▲ How many memory slots are on the board?

_____

▲ What is the maximum amount of memory the board supports?

_____

Now continue exploring the Kingston site by following these steps:

1. Return to the Kingston home page.
2. Click the **Memory Tools** link. A drop-down list displays several tools, one being the Memory Assessor. With this tool, you specify which OS you're researching, and Kingston displays a recommended amount of physical RAM based on usage criteria.
3. Using these tools, and perhaps other areas of the site, answer the following questions:

   ▲ In general, do operating systems for desktops and workstations require more or less memory than operating systems for servers?

   _____

   _____

   ▲ How wide is the data path on a 168-pin DIMM?

   _____

   ▲ DDR is an extension of what older memory technology?

   _____

   _____

   ▲ What does the SO in SO-DIMM represent?

   _____

   ▲ What is an advantage of loading applications entirely into RAM rather than loading part of an application into virtual memory (a page file)?

   _____

   _____

   _____

   ▲ What is another term for a page file, and why are page files used?

   _____

   _____

   _____

   ▲ How many bits of information does a single cell of a memory chip on a 256 MB PC2700 DDR module hold?

   _____

◢ Why would you have problems with a system in which you installed three known good RIMMs?

_____

_____

_____

◢ One memory technology uses only a 16-bit path. What acronym is used for this type of memory?

_____

◢ What type of material is used to make a memory "chip"?

_____

_____

◢ What function(s) does the aluminum plate on a RIMM serve?

_____

_____

◢ Why might you not mind using slower memory (in MHz) if faster memory is available for a marginal price difference?

_____

_____

◢ What is the system's bank schema, and why is it important when installing RAM?

_____

_____

◢ What is a memory performance measurement in which the lower the number, the better the performance?

_____

◢ What memory technology achieves better performance by using both the rising and falling sides of the clock cycle?

_____

_____

◢ List five considerations when upgrading memory:

_____

_____

_____

_____

_____

◢ If a motherboard can support SDRAM or EDO, which would result in better performance?

_____

◢ What memory technology uses a heat spreader?

_____

◢ What types of memory do notebook computers typically use?

_____

◢ Name two characteristics of a system using RAMBUS licensed memory:

_____

_____

REVIEW QUESTIONS

1. Is a DIMM or RIMM more expensive, given that both hold the same amount of memory? Why do you think this is the case?

_____

_____

2. Summarize why adding RAM offers a performance advantage:

_____

_____

3. Which tool on the Kingston Web site could you use to find Kingston modules for your system if you know the model number of your system's motherboard?

_____

4. If you were planning to buy a new system, would you choose a motherboard that uses DIMMs or RIMMs? Why?

_____

_____

LAB 6.3 UPGRADE RAM

OBJECTIVES

The goal of this lab is to learn how to plan a memory upgrade and then perform the upgrade. After completing this lab, you will be able to:

◢ Estimate how much free memory your system has available during typical and stressed use

◢ Determine how much and what kind of memory is needed for an upgrade

◢ Upgrade RAM in your system

MATERIALS REQUIRED

This lab requires the following:

◢ Windows 2000/XP or Windows 9x operating system

◢ SiSoftware Sandra, installed in Lab 1.3

◢ Internet access

◢ A PC designated for disassembly

◢ A PC toolkit and antistatic ground strap

◢ Additional memory module compatible with your system

LAB PREPARATION

Before the lab begins, the instructor or lab assistant needs to do the following:

◢ Verify that a computer designated for disassembly and a compatible memory module are available to each student or workgroup.

◢ Verify that Internet access is available.

ACTIVITY BACKGROUND

In this lab, you examine your system, gather information on its memory subsystem, and establish a memory usage baseline. Using this information, you then determine through further research whether the system can support a RAM upgrade required to run a computer-aided design (CAD) application. Finally, you install an additional memory module, examine your system again, and compare it against the baseline.

ESTIMATED COMPLETION TIME: 45 minutes

 Activity

1. Start SiSoftware Sandra, and use it to answer the following questions about your system:

   ◢ What OS are you running?

   _____

   ◢ What type of processor is your system using?

   _____

   ◢ What is your motherboard's manufacturer and model?

   _____

◢ How many MB of RAM are currently installed?

◢ What type of memory modules are installed? Be as specific as you can:

◢ At what speed does the memory bus operate?

To establish a memory usage baseline, follow these steps:

1. Leaving Sandra open, launch one instance each of Windows Explorer, Paint, and Internet Explorer.
2. Use the Windows Memory Information tool in Sandra and record the amount of free physical memory. This is your memory baseline. How much memory is free?

---

3. Open six more instances of Internet Explorer, browsing to a different site on each instance. Try to view a movie trailer or video, because this activity is memory intensive compared with displaying a static Web page.
4. Refresh the information in the Windows Memory Information tool by clicking the blue arrow. Record the free physical memory. How much memory is free now?

The change is the result of the demands of running and displaying six additional Web pages.

Suppose your employer's Engineering Department is interested in deploying a CAD program that requires 1 GB of RAM more than what's currently in your system. Use your investigating skills to gather information on supporting the additional required RAM:

1. Can you upgrade your system's RAM without removing any of the current memory modules?

---

2. What would be the least expensive upgrade to meet the new requirements?

---

3. How would your answers to Questions 1 and 2 change if the CAD program required an additional 4 GB of RAM?

Next, you simulate making the upgrade by following these steps:

1. Shut down your system and remove all exterior cabling.
2. Be sure you're wearing your antistatic ground strap. Open the system case and locate the slots for memory modules.

3. Remove any data cabling and other devices preventing you from getting at the slots. Answer the following questions:

◢ How many modules are currently installed?

_____

◢ Are there any empty slots in which to install an additional module?

_____

4. Notice that the slots have a retaining mechanism at each end to secure the modules in the slot. Typically, these mechanisms are plastic levers that you spread outward to unseat and remove modules. Modules are inserted and removed straight up and down. Spread the plastic levers apart before inserting or removing the memory modules.

5. Examine an empty slot and note the raised ridges that line up with notches on the memory module's pin edge. Because modules are designed to be inserted in only one orientation, these ridges prevent them from being inserted incorrectly.

6. With the module oriented correctly, insert the module and gently but firmly push it in.

7. Reassemble your system.

Although purchasing a bad memory module is extremely rare, it's a good idea to give the system every opportunity to detect faulty memory. BIOS tests physical memory each time the system is booted. If a module is drastically flawed, usually the system won't boot. Instead, it issues a beep code indicating memory problems. Assuming that the module is in fairly good shape and the video has initialized, the system BIOS's POST routine typically displays a memory count in bytes as it tests memory.

Most POST routines run through the test three times before proceeding. You can skip this redundant testing by enabling a Quick POST in CMOS setup. Quick POST is great for cutting down bootup time during normal use, but when installing new RAM, it's best to give the system every opportunity to detect a problem. Therefore, you should disable Quick POST until you're confident the module has no obvious problem. With this in mind, follow these steps to verify that the system recognizes the upgrade:

1. Boot the system and enter CMOS setup.

Notes

The first time you boot after a memory upgrade, the BIOS might display a memory mismatch error to let you know the memory has been changed.

2. Verify that Quick POST is disabled, and specify that you have installed additional memory, if necessary. (Telling CMOS about new memory isn't necessary unless you have a very old motherboard.)

3. Save your settings and reboot. Record whether the additional memory was recognized and how many times it was tested:

_____

4. Being careful to duplicate the steps, perform the same baseline tests that you did earlier in this lab. Record the results here:

◢ Amount of free memory with Sandra, Windows Explorer, Paint, and Internet Explorer open:

_____

◢ Amount of free memory with the system heavily used:

_____

5. When you have finished, remove the additional memory and return the system to its previous configuration.

REVIEW QUESTIONS

1. What is the minimum and recommended memory requirement for the OS your system is running?

_____

_____

2. What are at least two ways you can determine how much RAM is installed?

_____

_____

3. Which Sandra module(s) can be used to display information about system memory?

_____

_____

4. What feature is used on memory slots and modules to prevent modules from being inserted incorrectly?

_____

_____

5. In what situation might you want to disable Quick POST, and why?

_____

_____

LAB 6.4 TROUBLESHOOT MEMORY PROBLEMS

OBJECTIVES

The goal of this lab is to give you hands-on experience in troubleshooting memory problems. After completing this lab, you will be able to:

◢ Identify some symptoms that indicate memory problems

◢ Identify a faulty module

◢ Use DocMemory to test installed RAM

MATERIALS REQUIRED

This lab requires the following:

◢ Internet access (to download files)

◢ Windows 2000/XP or Windows 9x operating system

◢ SiSoftware Sandra, installed in Lab 1.3

◢ A printer

◢ A blank floppy disk

◢ Adobe Acrobat Reader

◢ A PC designated for disassembly

◢ A PC toolkit and antistatic ground strap

LAB PREPARATION

Before the lab begins, the instructor or lab assistant needs to do the following:

◢ Verify that a computer designated for disassembly and a printer are available to each student or workgroup.

◢ Verify that Internet access is available. For labs that don't have Internet access, download these files from *www.docmemory.com* to a file server or other storage media available to students in the lab: DocMem1_45a.exe, Docguide.pdf, and Docmem2_2b.zip.

◢ Go to the *www.docmemory.com* Web site and register at the site with an e-mail address and password. Students use this information later on the Members Login page.

ACTIVITY BACKGROUND

The symptoms of faulty RAM are many and varied. Faulty memory can cause a complete failure to boot, fatal exception errors while working with an application, or catastrophic data loss. However, sometimes faulty memory is noticeable only as annoying interruptions while you're working. RAM that's outright dead is fairly easy to identify. If the dead module is the only module installed, the system won't boot. If it's one of several modules, you'll notice that the system reports less memory than you expected.

However, it's not common for a module to fail absolutely. More often, a module develops intermittent problems that cause data corruption, applications hanging at unexpected times, or Windows 2000/XP hanging and displaying the Blue Screen of Death. In this lab, you learn how to detect and isolate faulty memory modules to prevent these problems.

ESTIMATED COMPLETION TIME: 60 minutes

Activity

Reliable memory function is essential to system operation. Therefore, when the system is booted, if memory isn't detected or has major problems, the startup BIOS begins emitting a beep code to define a general or particular memory problem. If startup BIOS finds memory to be adequate, during POST startup, BIOS does a thorough test of physical memory, which is usually repeated three times before the system summary is displayed and booting continues. Then while Windows is loading, it tests memory again.

These tests are all well and good at startup, but often partially corrupted modules don't show a problem until they're running at certain temperatures. Because these faults show up only at certain times and temperatures, they are referred to as "thermal intermittents." Although these problems are difficult to nail down and document, they are actually fairly easy to remedy if the fault is on the memory module instead of the motherboard.

DocMemory is a utility that allows you to use a quick test or a burn-in test that runs until an error is encountered or there's human intervention. This burn-in test is particularly useful in discovering a thermal intermittent fault.

In the following steps, you use DocMemory to test installed RAM. The installation process for DocMemory creates a bootable disk. First, you create a boot disk with the DocMemory software on it, and then use the boot disk to boot a PC and test memory on that PC. Follow these steps:

1. Open your browser, and go to **www.docmemory.com**. Click the **Download Docmemory SPD Reader Software** link. On the next page, you must enter an e-mail address and password. Ask your instructor for that information and enter it. Click **Submit**.

   ◢ E-mail: _____

   ◢ Password: _____

2. On the next page, shown in Figure 6-1, click the **DocMemory User Guide** link at the bottom and print the user guide for later use. Click your browser's **Back** button to return to the previous page.

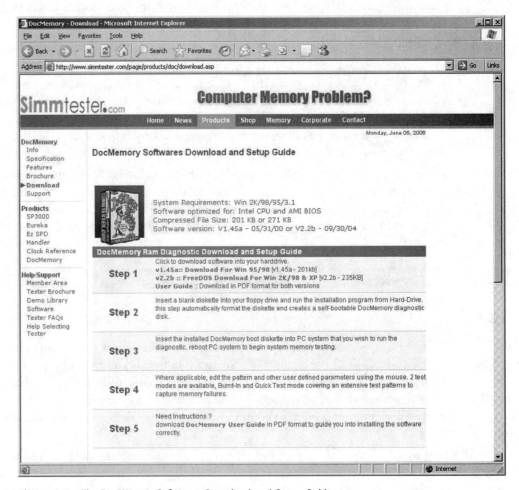

Figure 6-1   The DocMemory Softwares Download and Setup Guide page

3. To download the software, for a Windows 9x system, click **Download For Win 95/98**. For a Windows 2000/XP system, click **FreeDOS Download For Win 2K/98 & XP**. Save the file to a location on your hard drive. What's the location of the downloaded file?

   _____

4. In Windows 2000/XP, double-click the downloaded file to extract the compressed files. Save the uncompressed files to a folder on your hard drive named **C:\Test**. Open a command

prompt window, type the command **CD C:\test**, and press **Enter**. The prompt becomes C:\test> (see Figure 6-2). Type **Install** and press **Enter** to begin the installation process.

Figure 6-2 Prepare a boot disk with the DocMemory software installed

5. In Windows 9x, double-click the downloaded file DocMem1_45a.exe to run it. DocMemory then opens in a command prompt window. Use the arrow keys and Enter key or the mouse to select **Make Boot Disk**.

6. Regardless of the OS you're using, a license agreement appears next. Scroll down and accept the license agreement. Next, a prompt is displayed asking you to insert a blank formatted disk. Insert the disk and press **Enter**.

7. The installation process begins. When the installation is finished, a message is displayed indicating that the process is complete. Close any open windows.

8. The disk is now ready to be used on any computer. For the purpose of this lab, leave the disk in the system and reboot.

9. The system boots into the DocMemory utility. Purchase information is displayed and then the Select Type of Test dialog box opens with options for Burn-in Test, Quick Test, or Cancel. To test for a thermal intermittent, the Burn-in Test option is the best choice. However, in the interest of time, click **Quick Test** for this lab.

10. The test begins and the status is displayed at the upper-left side. Your processor and RAM are identified at the upper-right side, and the bottom of the screen displays pass/fail results. This portion of the lab varies in time because of differences in systems' amount of RAM and processor speeds.

11. While waiting for the test to finish, consult the documentation and answer the following questions:

▲ What two things happen when a fault is detected?

_____

_____

▲ What two areas can DocMemory test?

_____

_____

▲ What type of fault is the Walk Data "0" & "1" test designed to uncover?

_____

_____

12. When the test ends or errors are found, record the results here:

_____

_____

_____

Follow these steps to observe the effects of a faulty memory module and interpret beep codes:

1. Use Sandra to determine the BIOS manufacturer for your system, and record it here:

_____

2. Search documentation or the Internet for a list of beep codes for that manufacturer.

3. Shut down the system and remove all external cabling.

4. Put on your antistatic ground strap, open the case, remove all memory modules, and set them aside in an antistatic bag.

5. Reassemble the system, leaving out the memory.

6. Power up the system and describe the outcome, including any beep codes:

_____

_____

_____

7. If you heard beep codes, using the information you found in Step 2, interpret their meaning:

_____

_____

8. Shut down the system, disassemble it, install the RAM, and reassemble.

9. Boot the system to verify that the system is functional.

Using the documentation for DocMemory, summarize the process of using a known good memory module to provide strong evidence that a memory module is faulty:

_____

_____

_____

_____

REVIEW QUESTIONS

1. What are some common symptoms of a thermal intermittent?

_____

_____

2. How many times does POST usually test memory?

_____

3. Why must the DocMemory software run from a boot disk?

_____

_____

4. Describe the symptoms caused by a dead memory module:

_____

_____

_____

5. Which DocMemory test would be ideal for diagnosing a thermal intermittent?

_____

LAB 6.5 USE HIMEM.SYS IN WINDOWS 98

OBJECTIVES

The goal of this lab is to help you investigate ways memory can be used by observing the effects of Himem.sys. After completing this lab, you will be able to:

▲ Configure Himem.sys
▲ Configure Msdos.sys to stay in text mode throughout the boot
▲ Observe the effects Himem.sys has on the system

MATERIALS REQUIRED

This lab requires the following:

▲ Windows 98 operating system
▲ Two blank floppy disks
▲ Windows 98 setup CD or setup files

LAB PREPARATION

Before the lab begins, the instructor or lab assistant needs to do the following:

▲ Verify that the Windows 98 computer starts with no errors.
▲ Provide each student with access to the Windows 98 setup files, if needed.

ACTIVITY BACKGROUND

If you often need to run programs in MS-DOS mode, setting up Config.sys and Autoexec.bat is important because these files help set environmental variables in MS-DOS mode. Himem.sys is necessary to use many DOS utilities. Another key function of Himem.sys is that it tests RAM independently during booting. By observing the effects of changing how the system uses Himem.sys, you can get an idea of its various functions. In this lab, you configure and observe Himem.sys.

 Activity

To configure your system to remain in text mode throughout bootup, complete the following steps:

1. In Windows Explorer, right-click **Msdos.sys** in the root directory of the system partition. Click **Properties** from the shortcut menu to open the Msdos.sys Properties dialog box.

2. In the Attributes section, click to clear the check box indicating that the file is read-only. Click **OK** to apply your change and close the dialog box.

3. Again, right-click **Msdos.sys**, this time clicking **Open with** from the shortcut menu to open the Open with dialog box.

4. In the Choose the program you want to use drop-down list, click **Notepad**. If necessary, click to clear the **Always use this program to open this type of file** check box, and then click **OK**. Notepad opens and displays the entries in Msdos.sys.

5. Under the [Options] heading, add the line **Logo=0**. (Be sure to type a zero, not an uppercase "O.") Using the File menu, save the changes and close Notepad.

6. Reboot the computer and record any messages you see about Himem.sys. Notice that the Windows logo screen never appears during startup. This allows you to observe the entire text-based boot sequence, which can be useful in observing and diagnosing boot problems.

_____

_____

_____

In DOS and Windows 3.x, Himem.sys was always loaded by using a Device= command line in Config.sys. Windows 9x loads Himem.sys automatically, even if a Config.sys file isn't present. However, you can use Config.sys in Windows 9x to load Himem.sys and configure how Himem.sys loads. To do this, you create a Config.sys file and add the Himem.sys command line with the appropriate switches. To configure Himem.sys and watch it load, follow these steps:

1. In the root of the system partition, right-click **Config.sys**. Click **Open with** from the shortcut menu to open the Open with dialog box.

2. In the Choose the program you want to use drop-down list, click **NOTEPAD**. If necessary, click to clear the **Always use this program to open this type of file** check box, and click **OK**. Notepad opens, displaying the entries in Config.sys.

3. In Config.sys, add the line **Device=C:\Windows\himem.sys**. Using the File menu, save your changes and close Notepad.

4. Reboot the computer, recording any messages you see concerning Himem.sys.

_____

_____

_____

5. Following Steps 1 through 4, add the **/V** switch (be sure to type an uppercase "V") to the Device= line. The resulting line should be Device=C:\Windows\Himem.sys /V, with a space before the switch. "V" stands for verbose or descriptive, meaning text is displayed to keep you informed of the command's progress. Reboot the system (if necessary, more than once), and answer the following questions:

◢ How much high memory did Himem.sys report available?

_____

◢ What version of Himem.sys is loaded?

_____

6. Following the previous process to edit Config.sys, add the **/TestMem:ON** switch. Reboot and record any changes:

_____

_____

_____

Next, you create a Windows 98 startup disk by using the Add/Remove Programs applet in Control Panel. Then you use Scandisk on the startup disk to scan your hard drive for errors, which is a first step in demonstrating why loading Himem.sys from Config.sys is important. Follow these steps:

1. From Control Panel, open the Add/Remove Programs applet.

2. When the applet opens, click the **Startup disk** tab.

3. Click the **Create Disk** button and, if prompted, enter the location of the Windows setup files.

4. Insert the floppy disk when prompted, and click **OK** to continue and create a startup disk.

5. When the startup disk has been created, examine its contents in Windows Explorer. Does the startup disk contain both Config.sys and Himem.sys? Open the Config.sys file and write the command line that loads Himem.sys:

_____

6. With the startup disk in the floppy drive, reboot the computer.

7. When prompted, select the option to start the computer without CD-ROM support.

8. When you arrive at the command prompt, type **Scandisk C:** and press **Enter** to scan the hard drive for errors.

9. Observe while Scandisk performs a data scan on drive C. When prompted, don't perform a surface scan. Press **X** to return to the command prompt.

10. Remove the startup disk and reboot the system.

Next, follow these steps to create a bootable disk, copy the Scandisk utility to it, and then attempt to use Scandisk without having Himem.sys loaded:

1. In Windows Explorer, insert the second blank floppy disk, and right-click the 3½ **Floppy (A:)** drive.

2. Click **Format** in the shortcut menu to open the Format dialog box.

3. Click both **Quick (erase)** and **Copy system files**, and then click the **Start** button.

4. When the summary appears, click **Close** and then click **Close** again to exit. You have created a bootable disk. Using Windows Explorer, examine the disk and list the files on the disk:

_____

_____

_____

5. Now copy **Scandisk.exe** from the C:\Windows\Command folder to the bootable disk.

6. Reboot the system with the bootable disk in the drive. At the command prompt, type **Scandisk C:** and press **Enter** to attempt to scan the hard drive again for errors. Describe what happens:

_____

_____

_____

7. What two files must be put on the bootable disk for Scandisk to work?

_____

REVIEW QUESTIONS

1. Other than providing access to memory, what valuable function does Himem.sys include?

_____

2. What system file is modified to make text messages during startup easier to view?

_____

3. In a command line, when more than one switch is used, what should come before each switch?

_____

4. Based on the knowledge you have gained in this lab, name three configuration files that can be used to alter the way an OS loads:

_____

5. Name one MS-DOS utility that requires Himem.sys to be loaded for the utility to run. What does Himem.sys do for this utility?

_____

_____

Hard Drives

Labs included in this chapter:

- **Lab 7.1:** Format a Floppy Disk

- **Lab 7.2:** Test Hard Drive Performance Using Sandra

- **Lab 7.3:** Use Disk Management

- **Lab 7.4:** Use Hard Drive Utilities

- **Lab 7.5:** Troubleshoot Hard Drives

- **Lab 7.6:** Critical Thinking: Use Debug to Examine Disk Information

- **Lab 7.7:** Critical Thinking: Sabotage and Repair a Hard Drive Subsystem

LAB 7.1 FORMAT A FLOPPY DISK

OBJECTIVES

The goal of this lab is to help you use formatting options available from the command prompt and in Windows Explorer. After completing this lab, you will be able to:

⊿ Use command-line switches for different formatting options

⊿ Format a floppy disk using Windows Explorer

MATERIALS REQUIRED

This lab requires the following:

⊿ Windows 2000/XP or Windows 9x operating system

⊿ A blank unformatted floppy disk

LAB PREPARATION

Before the lab begins, the instructor or lab assistant needs to do the following:

⊿ Verify that Windows starts with no errors.

ACTIVITY BACKGROUND

Floppy disks must be formatted before you can use them. These days, floppy disks usually come preformatted from the factory, but you might need to reformat a used disk. The formatting process defines track and sector spacing so that data can be written to a known location. Formatting also creates the file allocation table (FAT), which lists the locations of files on the disk. You can format a disk in Windows Explorer or from the command line. When formatting disks from the command line, you can use switches to decide exactly how to format the disk. These switches enable you to cut some corners to speed the formatting process or to streamline the process of making a bootable disk. In this lab, you format a floppy disk in several different ways.

ESTIMATED COMPLETION TIME: 45 minutes

 Activity

To practice formatting a floppy disk in Windows Explorer, follow these steps:

1. Open Windows Explorer.

2. With the floppy disk inserted in drive A, right-click **3½ Floppy (A:)**, and then click **Format** in the shortcut menu. The Format dialog box opens.

3. Observe the layout of the Format dialog box, and describe the available options:

It's also a good idea to know how to format disks from the command line in case the GUI isn't available or you want to use switches to speed the formatting process. Follow the procedure for the operating system you're using to practice formatting a floppy disk from the command prompt.

In Windows XP, follow these steps:

1. Insert a blank unformatted floppy disk into drive A, if necessary.

2. Open a command prompt window. Use the **Dir** command to examine drive A. Describe what you see on the screen:

   _____

   _____

3. The system can't provide information about the disk's contents because the disk hasn't been formatted yet. Type **format /?** and press **Enter**. This command displays a list of nine switches you can use to modify the Format command. What is the correct syntax for a Format command to format a 1.44 MB floppy disk?

   _____

4. To format the disk, type **format A:** and press **Enter**. Time how long it takes for the formatting to reach 100%.

5. When prompted, press **Enter**. The formatting process begins. Throughout the process, you see a message indicating the percent completed.

6. When the formatting reaches 100%, the system gives you the opportunity to name the volume. Name the volume **FTEST**, and then press **Enter**.

7. Next, the system displays the formatting summary and prompts you to format another. Type **n** and press **Enter**.

8. Use the **Dir** command to examine drive A. Now the system can give you information about the floppy disk because it has been formatted.

9. A quick format doesn't write track and sector markings on the disk and is a fast way to reformat a previously formatted disk. To do a quick format, type **format A: /q** and press **Enter**. Continue through the formatting procedure. Compare the time it took to do a quick format to the time required for a full format:

   _____

10. Again, use the **Dir** command to examine drive A. Is there a difference between the outcome of the quick format and the full format?

    _____

In Windows 2000, follow these steps:

1. Insert a blank unformatted floppy disk into drive A, if nceessary.

2. Open a command prompt window. Use the **Dir** command to examine drive A. Describe what you see on the screen:

   _____

   _____

3. The system can't provide information about the disk's contents because the disk hasn't been formatted yet. Type **format /?** and press **Enter**. This command displays a list of 12 switches you can use to modify the Format command. What is the correct syntax for a Format command to format only one side of a disk?

   _____

4. To format the disk, type **format A:** and press **Enter**. Time how long it takes for the formatting to reach 100%.

5. When prompted, press **Enter**. The formatting process begins. Throughout the process, you see a message indicating the percent completed.

6. When the formatting reaches 100%, the system gives you the opportunity to name the volume. Name the volume **FTEST**, and then press **Enter**.

7. Next, the system displays the formatting summary and prompts you to format another. Type **n** and press **Enter**.

8. Use the **Dir** command to examine drive A. Now the system can give you information about the floppy disk because it has been formatted.

9. A quick format doesn't write track and sector markings on the disk and is a fast way to reformat a previously formatted disk. To do a quick format, type **format A: /q** and press **Enter**. Continue through the formatting procedure. Compare the time it took to do a quick format to the time required for a full format:

_____

10. Again, use the **Dir** command to examine drive A. Is there a difference between the outcome of the quick format and the full format?

_____

In Windows 98, follow these steps:

1. Insert a blank unformatted floppy disk into drive A, if necessary.

2. Open a command prompt window. Use the **Dir** command to examine drive A. Describe what you see on the screen:

_____

_____

3. The system can't provide information about the disk's contents because the disk hasn't been formatted yet. Type **format /?** and press **Enter**. This command displays a list of 11 switches you can use to modify the Format command. What is the correct syntax for a Format command to test clusters on the disk in drive A that are currently marked as bad?

_____

4. To format the disk, type **format A:** and press **Enter**. Time how long it takes for the formatting to reach 100%.

5. When prompted, press **Enter**. The formatting process begins. Throughout the process, you see a message indicating the percent completed.

6. When the formatting reaches 100%, the system gives you the opportunity to name the volume. Name the volume **FTEST**, and then press **Enter**.

7. Next, the system displays the formatting summary and prompts you to format another. Type **n** and press **Enter**.

8. Use the **Dir** command to examine drive A. Now the system can give you information about the floppy disk because it has been formatted.

9. A quick format doesn't write track and sector markings on the disk and is a fast way to reformat a previously formatted disk. To do a quick format, type **format A: /q** and

press **Enter**. Compare the time it took to do a quick format to the time required for a full format:

10. Again, use the **Dir** command to examine drive A. Is there a difference between the outcome of the quick format and the full format?

Suppose you want to make a bootable floppy disk so that you could add utilities and use the disk for troubleshooting. You can use more than one switch at a time with most commands. To demonstrate this fact with the Format command, complete the steps for the operating system you're using.

In Windows XP, follow these steps:

1. Type **format A: /q /s** and press **Enter**. This command instructs the system to do a quick format and then copy the system files required to make the disk bootable.

2. What error message did you receive about creating a Windows XP bootable floppy disk?

3. Describe the formatting process:

4. How many bytes of free space are now included on the disk? What command did you use to get your answer?

5. Close the command prompt window.

In Windows 2000, follow these steps:

1. Type **format A: /q /s** and press **Enter**. This command instructs the system to do a quick format and then copy the system files required to make the disk bootable.

2. What error message did you receive? Suppose you have a copy of a bootable floppy disk. What command could you use to create another bootable floppy disk using the one you already have?

3. Describe the format process:

4. What command did you use to find out how many bytes of free space are included on a disk?

5. Close the command prompt window.

In Windows 98, follow these steps:

1. Type **format A: /q /s** and press **Enter**. This command instructs the system to do a quick format and then copy the system files required to make the disk bootable.

2. Describe the format process:

   _____

   _____

   _____

   _____

3. How many bytes of free space are now included on the disk? What command did you use to get your answer?

   _____

4. Close the command prompt window.

REVIEW QUESTIONS

1. Suppose you formatted a floppy disk on a Windows 98 system. Would you then be able to reformat the same disk by using the /q switch on another Windows 98 system? Why or why not?

   _____

2. Suppose you want to format a disk in drive B, making it a bootable disk. What command do you use in Windows 98?

   _____

3. In general, what difference did you see in a disk's directory listing after formatting the disk with the /s switch?

   _____

4. Why might it be less important for Windows 2000/XP to provide a switch for creating a bootable floppy disk?

   _____

   _____

5. What's the difference between a Windows 98 startup disk and a boot disk created with the Format A: /s command?

   _____

   _____

LAB 7.2 TEST HARD DRIVE PERFORMANCE USING SANDRA

OBJECTIVES

The goal of this lab is to help you use Sandra to compare the performance of your system's drives against similar drives. After completing this lab, you will be able to:

◢ Use Sandra to test your drives' performance

◢ Use Sandra to compare your system's drives with similar drives

MATERIALS REQUIRED

This lab requires the following:

◢ Windows 2000/XP or Windows 9x operating system

◢ SiSoftware Sandra, installed in Lab 1.3

LAB PREPARATION

Before the lab begins, the instructor or lab assistant needs to do the following:

◢ Verify that Windows starts with no errors.

ACTIVITY BACKGROUND

You can use Sandra to run a routine of several tests on your drive, report the results, and compare your drive to a selection of comparable drives. This lab gives you an indication of how your drive is performing and whether another product is available that better meets your performance needs. Some tasks, such as video editing, are demanding on the drive where files are stored; a faster drive can increase productivity. When making an upgrade decision, it's helpful to compare results reported by Sandra to information on other hard drives. In this lab, you use Sandra to test your drive.

ESTIMATED COMPLETION TIME: 30 minutes

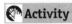 **Activity**

Follow these steps to test your drive:

1. Start Sandra.

2. Double-click the **Drives Benchmark** icon to open the Drives Benchmark window. (If you don't see the Drives Benchmark icon, you installed the wrong version of Sandra. You should be using the Standard version.)

3. Click the **Select Drive** list arrow, and then click the letter of the drive you're testing. What message is displayed after you select drive C?

_____

_____

4. Wait until Sandra has finished testing your drive before moving your mouse or doing anything else with the system. After the test is finished, a summary is displayed. Use the summary to answer the following questions:

◢ In the Current Drive field, what drive index is reported?

_____

◢ What drives were compared to the current drive?

_____

_____

5. Click the drop-down menu of one of the compared drives to view it. Note that you can compare your drive against several drives.

6. One by one, select each drive, and note its performance ratings. List drives with a lower performance rating than the current drive:

_____

_____

7. List the size and rpm of the two drives with the lowest performance:

_____

_____

8. Use the bottom field of the Drives Benchmark window to fill in the following chart. (Scroll down as necessary to display the information you need.)

Category	Value
Drive class	
Total space	
Sequential read	
Random read	
Buffered write	
Sequential write	
Random write	
Average access time	

REVIEW QUESTIONS

1. Why might you want to test your drive with Sandra?

_____

_____

2. Based on the drive ratings information you got from Sandra, does a drive perform better if it spins faster or slower?

_____

3. Based on the drive ratings information you got from Sandra, does a drive perform better if it reads data randomly or sequentially?

_____

4. Why shouldn't you use the system when Sandra is testing a drive?

_____

_____

LAB 7.3 USE DISK MANAGEMENT

OBJECTIVES

The goal of this lab is to help you use Disk Management to work with local hard drives. After completing this lab, you will be able to:

- Create a partition from unused disk space
- Specify a file system
- Format a partition
- Delete a partition

MATERIALS REQUIRED

This lab requires the following:

- Windows 2000/XP Professional operating system
- A printer
- Windows 2000/XP Professional installation CD or installation files
- Unallocated disk space

LAB PREPARATION

Before the lab begins, the instructor or lab assistant needs to do the following:

- Verify that Windows starts with no errors.
- Provide each student with access to the Windows 2000/XP Professional installation files, if needed.
- Verify that there's unallocated space on the hard drive.

ACTIVITY BACKGROUND

Disk Management is a Microsoft Management Console (MMC) snap-in and an administrative tool installed in the Computer Management console by default. To start Disk Management, you need to start Computer Management first. Unlike Fdisk, Disk Management allows you to partition and format disk space from within Windows. In this lab, you create and delete two different partitions using unallocated disk space.

ESTIMATED COMPLETION TIME: 30 minutes

 Activity

To work with your local hard drive using Disk Management, follow these steps:

1. Log on with an administrator account. In Windows XP, open Control Panel, click **Performance and Maintenance**, and then click **Administrative Tools**. In Windows 2000,

open Control Panel and double-click the **Administrative Tools** icon. The Administrative Tools window opens.

2. Double-click **Computer Management**. The Computer Management snap-in opens in an MMC. In the left pane, click **Disk Management**. The Disk Management interface opens in the right pane (see Figure 7-1).

Figure 7-1 Use Disk Management to manage hard drives

3. Use the information at the top of the right pane to complete the following chart:

Volume	Layout	Type	File System	Status	Capacity

4. Information about each physical drive is displayed in the bottom section of the right pane. In addition, a graphic shows each drive's space distribution. Note that drives are labeled with numbers (0, 1, and so forth) and logical drives or volumes are labeled with letters (C, D, E, and so forth). If a hard drive has just been installed and not yet partitioned, the graphic shows all unallocated (unpartitioned) space, as in Figure 7-1. What drive letters are used on your system?

5. Right-click a blank area of the C drive space in the Disk Management interface. A shortcut menu opens with the following options:

   ◢ *Open*—Displays the drive's contents in a window similar to My Computer.

   ◢ *Explore*—Displays the drive's contents in a window similar to Windows Explorer.

◢ *Mark Active Partition*—Marks the current partition as the partition from which Windows is loaded.

◢ *Change Drive Letter and Path*—Allows you to select a new letter for the drive. For instance, you can change the drive letter from C to F.

◢ *Format*—Allows you to format a partition and make partition-related choices, including specifying the file system and sector size. *Note*: Windows XP protects itself by disabling Format on the (System) partition.

◢ *Delete Partition*—Allows you to delete an entire partition and all its contents.

◢ *Properties*—Displays information about the partition, such as how it's formatted.

◢ *Help*—Provides information about Disk Management.

6. Right-click the unpartitioned area of the disk drive, which is labeled Unallocated. List the differences between the options in this shortcut menu and the menu you examined in Step 5:

_____

_____

In the next set of steps, you create a new partition from unpartitioned space. Note that the partition you're creating should use only *currently unpartitioned* space. Follow these steps:

1. Using *only unpartitioned space*, create and format a new partition using the FAT32 file system and drive letter S. List the steps to perform this task:

_____

_____

_____

_____

2. Print a screen shot of the Disk Management window showing the FAT32 drive S.

3. Delete the partition you just created. List the steps to perform this task:

_____

_____

4. Using *only unpartitioned space*, create and format a new NTFS partition using the drive letter H. List the steps to perform this task:

_____

_____

_____

5. Print a screen shot of the Disk Management window showing the NTFS drive H.

6. Close the Computer Management window.

CRITICAL THINKING: MANAGING PARTITIONS FROM THE RECOVERY CONSOLE (ADDITIONAL 60 MINUTES)

Do the following to practice managing partitions from the Recovery Console:

1. Open the Windows 2000/XP Recovery Console. List the steps to perform this task:

_____

_____

_____

2. Open Help and display information about the Diskpart command, including possible command-line options. List the steps to perform this task:

_____

_____

_____

3. Delete the NTFS partition you created earlier using Disk Management. List the steps to perform this task:

_____

_____

_____

4. Create and format a new NTFS partition, using the drive letter R. List the steps to perform this task:

_____

_____

_____

5. Delete the newly created partition. List the steps to perform this task:

_____

_____

_____

REVIEW QUESTIONS

1. Name an advantage that Disk Management has over Fdisk:

_____

2. What happens to all the information in a partition if you delete the partition?

_____

_____

3. What feature opens if you choose Explore from a shortcut menu in Disk Management?

_____

4. Is it possible to create two partitions, using different file systems, from one area of unallocated disk space? Explain:

_____

_____

_____

5. List the steps for removing two empty partitions and creating one single NTFS partition assigned the drive letter T:

_____

_____

_____

_____

_____

_____

_____

_____

LAB 7.4 USE HARD DRIVE UTILITIES

OBJECTIVES

The goal of this lab is to give you an opportunity to work with utilities from hard drive manufacturers that examine and diagnose hard drive problems. After completing this lab, you will be able to:

◢ Identify your hard drive manufacturer

◢ Evaluate utilities that hard drive manufacturers provide for their drives

◢ Test for hard drive problems

MATERIALS REQUIRED

This lab requires the following:

◢ Windows 2000/XP or Windows 9x operating system

◢ Internet access

◢ A printer

◢ A blank floppy disk or burnable CD

LAB PREPARATION

Before the lab begins, the instructor or lab assistant needs to do the following:

▲ Verify that Windows starts with no errors.

▲ Verify that Internet access is available.

ACTIVITY BACKGROUND

Hard drive problems can manifest themselves in different ways. The drive might exhibit immediate and total failure so that it doesn't operate at all. If the failure is caused by a problem with the platters, you might not be able to boot at all if the area where system files are stored is affected. If system files aren't affected, you might be able to boot and work normally but could have file loss or file corruption. Then again, you might never realize you have a hard drive problem if your hard drive has bad sectors because data might not be saved to that particular physical area of the disk. More often, however, when a disk begins to fail, you notice errors. One tool you can use to diagnose hard drive problems is diagnostic software that your hard drive manufacturer supplies. In this lab, you identify your drive manufacturer and use its software to examine your drive.

ESTIMATED COMPLETION TIME: 60 minutes

 Activity

When you need to use a hard drive diagnostic utility, first you must identify your hard drive's manufacturer. To do that, you use a utility for that purpose from Seagate. Follow these steps to identify your drive:

1. Open your browser, and go to **www.seagate.com/support/seatools/index.html**.

2. Look for the section under SeaTools Online, and follow the links to learn more about and run the SeaTools Online Data Safe Drive Self Test. Click the **English** link to run the software in English. A new window opens, displaying the SeaTools Online testing options.

3. In the new window, click the **Drive Self Test** link to do a quick test of your drive. You might receive a warning about trusting content from Seagate or Ontrack. If you see this prompt, click **Yes** to receive the content. If your browser displays a message in the address bar asking permission to install an ActiveX control, click the address bar to continue. By doing this, you're allowing a small program to be downloaded to your PC and run to identify your drive. Follow instructions to download and run the program.

4. A window now lists your drive information. Record the drive information on the following lines as it's displayed. If you have more than one hard drive, all the drives in your system are listed. Included in the list is the hard drive manufacturer. You use the drive manufacturer information later in this lab. (Note that if the drive name begins with ST, the drive is made by Seagate.)

_____

_____

5. To select the drive to test, click the check box to the left of your drive information, and then click **Next**. A list of tests is displayed in the next window.

6. Click the **Run Short Drive Self Test,** and then click **Next.** The test begins in the same window. The test might take a few minutes. When it's done, record the results:

_____

_____

_____

_____

_____

7. When you have recorded your results, close the window. A message box informs you that you might not want to navigate away from the site. Click **OK** to close it and continue the lab.

Next, you find out about hard drive utilities supplied by several hard drive manufacturers.

Maxtor offers PowerMax to support its hard drives. Do the following to find out about this software:

1. In your Web browser, go to **www.maxtor.com.** Click the **Software Downloads** link and then the **Top Downloads** link. Answer the following questions:

   ◢ What is the purpose of the MaxBlast software?

   _____

   ◢ When might you want to use the MaxBlast software?

   _____

2. Now click the **PowerMax** link. Examine the information on the page and answer these questions:

   ◢ What types of problems does the software identify?

   _____

   _____

   _____

   ◢ How do you run the PowerMax utility?

   _____

   _____

   ◢ List the three main steps to prepare to run the utility:

   _____

   _____

   _____

3. If you have a Maxtor drive, click the link to download PowerMax and follow the directions onscreen to save it in its own folder. What is the file name and path to the file?

   _____

The IBM line of hard drives was purchased by Hitachi, which provides Drive Fitness Test for its hard drives. Do the following to find out about this software:

1. In your Web browser, go to **www.hitachigst.com**. Click **Support**, and then click **Downloads**. The software can be run from a bootable floppy disk or CD.

2. Search the information about the product, and answer the following questions:

   ▲ What types of drives are supported and what three types are expressly not supported?

   _____

   _____

   ▲ What types of analysis does the software perform?

   _____

   _____

   ▲ If you have Linux installed on your system, how can you still create a bootable floppy disk to use the utility?

   _____

   _____

3. If you have an IBM or Hitachi drive, click the link to download the Drive Fitness Test utility and save it in its own folder. What is the file name and path to the file?

   _____

Western Digital provides Data Lifeguard. Do the following to find out about this software:

1. In your Web browser, go to **http://support.wdc.com/download**, and click the link in the Data Lifeguard Tools section to download Data Lifeguard Diagnostic for Windows.

2. Examine the information and answer these questions:

   ▲ What versions of Windows can use this software?

   _____

   ▲ What is the purpose of the Write-Zeroes-To-Drive feature of the software? When would you want to use this feature?

   _____

   _____

3. If you have a Western Digital drive, click the link to download the utility and save it to its own folder. What is the file name and path to the file?

   _____

Seagate offers Data Lifeguard. Do the following to find out about this software:

1. In your Web browser, go to **www.seagate.com/support/seatools/index.html**, and click the **Learn More** link for SeaTools Desktop.

2. Examine the information and answer these questions:

   ▲ What percentage of drives returned to Seagate are found to be healthy?

   _____

◢ The utility you download runs in Windows only one time. What is the purpose of this one-time run?

_____

3. If you have a Seagate drive, click the link to download this utility and save the file to its own folder. What is the file name and path to the file?

_____

Next, follow these steps to use a manufacturer's utility to test your drive:

1. If your drive is from one of the previous manufacturers, follow the instructions on your drive manufacturer's Web site to create a bootable floppy disk and use it to perform the test for your hard drive.

2. Summarize the process and results:

_____

_____

_____

_____

If your hard drive isn't made by one of the previous manufacturers, go to your manufacturer's Web site and search for diagnostic software. What software did you find?

_____

REVIEW QUESTIONS

1. What are some symptoms of hard drive problems listed on the hard drive manufacturers' Web sites? List three in order of seriousness:

_____

_____

_____

2. Which hard drive manufacturer's Web site was the most informative and easiest to use? Why?

_____

_____

_____

3. Which utility from a hard drive manufacturer seemed to be the most powerful? Why?

_____

_____

_____

4. What was the most common method used to run the utilities?

_____

5. Why is it useful to run the utility from a bootable floppy disk or CD rather than from Windows?

_____

6. What operating system is used on the bootable floppy disk or CD?

_____

7. How do you determine that your system is set to boot from a floppy disk or CD?

_____

LAB 7.5 TROUBLESHOOT HARD DRIVES

OBJECTIVES

The goal of this lab is to help you troubleshoot common hard drive problems. After completing this lab, you will be able to:

▲ Simulate common hard drive problems

▲ Diagnose and repair common hard drive problems

▲ Document the process

MATERIALS REQUIRED

This lab requires the following:

▲ A computer with a hard drive subsystem that you can sabotage

▲ A bootable disk

▲ A PC toolkit with antistatic ground strap

▲ A workgroup of 2 to 4 students

LAB PREPARATION

Before the lab begins, the instructor or lab assistant needs to do the following:

▲ Verify that Windows starts with no errors.

▲ Verify that a computer with a hard drive that can be sabotaged is available for each student or workgroup.

ACTIVITY BACKGROUND

This lab gives you practice diagnosing and remedying common hard drive problems.

ESTIMATED COMPLETION TIME: 45 minutes

 Activity

1. Verify that your hard drive is working by using a command prompt window or Windows Explorer to display files on the drive.

2. Switch computers with another team.

3. Sabotage the other team's computer by doing one of the following:

   ◢ Remove or incorrectly configure the drive jumpers.

   ◢ Remove the power connector from the drive.

   ◢ Switch data cables to place devices on incorrect IDE channels.

   ◢ Disable IDE controllers in CMOS setup.

   ◢ If allowed by your instructor, delete partitions on the hard drive.

4. Return to your computer and examine it for any symptoms of a problem.

5. On a separate piece of paper, answer the following questions about the problem's symptoms:

   ◢ What symptoms would a user notice? (Describe the symptoms as a user might describe them.)

   ◢ Does the system boot from the hard drive?

   ◢ Does POST display the hard drive?

   ◢ Can you boot from a floppy disk and change to the drive in question?

   ◢ Does the CMOS HDD Autodetect option detect the hard drive?

6. On a separate piece of paper, before you actually begin your investigation, state your initial diagnosis.

7. Diagnose and repair the problem.

8. On a separate piece of paper, list the steps to confirm your diagnosis and solve the problem.

9. Answer the following questions about your final conclusions:

   ◢ What was the problem?

   _____

   ◢ What did you do to correct the problem?

   _____

   _____

   _____

   ◢ Was your preliminary diagnosis correct?

   _____

10. Repeat Steps 1 through 9, choosing actions at random from the list in Step 3, until your team has performed all the actions. Be sure to write down the relevant information (as instructed in the steps) for each problem.

REVIEW QUESTIONS

1. What was the first indication that the power was disconnected from your drive?

   _____

   _____

2. In what incorrect drive configuration would you be able to access files on the hard drive by booting from the floppy drive?

   _____

   _____

3. What incorrect configurations have similar symptoms?

_____

_____

4. What problem resulted in no drives being detected except for the floppy drive?

_____

_____

5. List the steps to use a drive whose partitions have been deleted:

_____

_____

_____

_____

_____

_____

LAB 7.6 CRITICAL THINKING: USE DEBUG TO EXAMINE DISK INFORMATION

OBJECTIVES

The goal of this lab is to help you use the Debug utility to examine the beginning of a floppy drive. After completing this lab, you will be able to:

◢ Use Debug commands

◢ Explain how Debug displays information

◢ Examine the boot record on a floppy disk

MATERIALS REQUIRED

This lab requires the following:

◢ Windows XP operating system

◢ A blank floppy disk

LAB PREPARATION

Before the lab begins, the instructor or lab assistant needs to do the following:

◢ Verify that Windows starts with no errors.

ACTIVITY BACKGROUND

In this lab, you use the Debug tool to examine the boot record of a startup floppy disk. The file system on a floppy disk is similar to that of a hard drive, so the concepts you learn here about floppy disks can be applied to hard drives.

Using Debug, you can view the contents of a disk or memory location. This information helps you gain the strong technical insight you need to take advantage of more user-friendly data recovery software and to be confident that you understand how these products work. The better you understand how data is constructed on the disk and exactly what problems can happen, the better your chances of recovering lost or damaged data.

ESTIMATED COMPLETION TIME: 45 minutes

Activity

Follow these steps to examine the boot record of a startup disk:

1. Boot your PC into Windows and then insert a blank floppy disk.

2. Click **Start, My Computer**. In the My Computer window, right-click the 3½ **Floppy (A:)** icon, and click **Format** in the shortcut menu. Click **Create an MS-DOS startup disk**, and then click **Start**. In the warning message box that opens, click **OK**. After the formatting is completed, you'll have a bootable startup disk. Click **OK** to close the completion message box, and then close the Format dialog box.

3. Click **Start, Run**. Type **cmd** and click **OK** to open a command prompt window. At the command prompt, type **debug** and press **Enter**. The Debug utility starts, and the prompt changes to a dash (–).

The Debug utility can be used to examine and change the contents of a location in memory. Although Debug can't edit storage devices directly, it can also be used to view data on a storage device, such as a floppy disk or hard drive, by copying the data into memory first. To examine the startup disk you just created, first you have to copy some of its contents into memory. Follow these steps:

Notes

You can see a full list of Debug commands by typing ? at the prompt.

1. To view information, you're going to use the D command (which stands for "dump"). Type D and press **Enter**.

2. Observe the output of the D command, which shows the contents of memory beginning with a memory address (see Figure 7-2). Note that this command displays memory 128 bytes at a time. The information is in lines of 16 bytes each, with the start address at the left side, the hex value of each byte in the middle, and the ASCII interpretation (if any) of each byte at the right side.

Figure 7-2 Results of the Debug D command showing the contents of 128 bytes of memory

3. Each time you dump memory, the pointer in memory moves to the next group of 128 bytes. By using successive dump commands, you can move through memory consecutively, dumping 128 bytes of memory to the screen with each command. To view the next 128 bytes, simply type **D** and press **Enter** again.

4. If the contents of memory aren't ASCII text, the attempt to display the ASCII interpretation looks like gibberish in that section. Continue to scan each 128-byte section until you find a section of data that's readable in ASCII. This shouldn't take more than a few minutes. What does the code at these memory addresses refer to?

_____

_____

5. The next step is to copy, or load, the boot record from the floppy disk into memory. Type **L0 0 0 1** and press **Enter**. You should hear the floppy drive run. Answer these questions to decipher the command:

◢ What does "L" stand for?

_____

◢ What does the first 0 indicate?

_____

◢ What does the second 0 indicate?

_____

◢ What does the third 0 indicate?

_____

◢ What does the 1 indicate?

_____

6. The information from this sector of the floppy disk is now loaded in system memory. To view this information, type **D0** and press **Enter**. Can you see any indication of which file system is used to format the floppy disk? Explain:

_____

_____

7. Figure 7-3 shows the result of this dump command for a startup disk formatted with DOS. Compare it to your dump. What differences do you see? Table 7-1 lists the items in a boot record to help you with your comparisons.

_____

_____

_____

_____

8. To exit Debug, type **Q** and press **Enter**. You return to the command prompt.

Figure 7-3 The first 128 bytes of the boot record of a floppy disk formatted with DOS

Description	Number of bytes
Machine code	11
Bytes per sector	2
Sectors per cluster	1
Reserved	2
Number of FATs	1
Number of root directory entries	2
Number of logical sectors	2
Medium descriptor byte	1
Sectors per FAT	2
Sectors per track	2
Heads	2
Number of hidden sectors	2
Total sectors in logical volume	4
Physical drive number	1
Reserved	1
Extended boot signature record	1
32-bit binary volume ID	4
Volume label	11
Type of file system (FAT12, FAT16, or FAT32)	8
Program to load operating system (bootstrap loader)	Remainder of the sector

Table 7-1 Layout of the boot record of a floppy disk or hard drive

REVIEW QUESTIONS

1. Why do storage devices have to be copied into memory before their contents can be viewed in Debug?

   _____

   _____

2. What Debug command dumps data at the beginning of the memory address space?

   _____

3. What command loads two sectors from the C drive, starting at the sixth sector?

   _____

   _____

4. Debug displays data _____ bytes at a time.

5. Why do you think it's important to be careful when tinkering with the Debug utility?

   _____

   _____

LAB 7.7 CRITICAL THINKING: SABOTAGE AND REPAIR A HARD DRIVE SUBSYSTEM

OBJECTIVES

The goal of this lab is to learn to troubleshoot a hard drive by repairing a sabotaged system.

MATERIALS REQUIRED

This lab requires the following:

▲ A PC designated for sabotage (containing no important data)

▲ A workgroup of 2 to 4 students

LAB PREPARATION

Before the lab begins, the instructor or lab assistant needs to do the following:

◢ Verify that Windows starts with no errors.

◢ Verify that a PC that can be sabotaged is available for each student or workgroup.

ACTIVITY BACKGROUND

You have learned about several tools and methods for troubleshooting and recovering from a hard drive failure. This lab gives you the opportunity to use these skills in a troubleshooting situation. Your group will work with another group to sabotage a system, and then you recover your own sabotaged system.

ESTIMATED COMPLETION TIME: 45 minutes

 Activity

1. If your system's hard drive contains important data, back it up to another medium. Is there anything else you would like to back up before another group sabotages the system?

   _____

2. Trade systems with another group and sabotage the other group's system while that group sabotages your system. Do one thing that will cause the hard drive to fail to work or return errors after the boot. Use any of the problems suggested in Lab 7.5, or you can introduce a new problem. (Do *not* alter the operating system files.) What did you do to sabotage the other group's system?

   _____

   _____

3. Return to your system and troubleshoot it.

4. Describe the problem as a user would describe it to you if you were working at a help desk:

   _____

   _____

5. What is your first guess as to the source of the problem?

   _____

6. List the steps you took in the troubleshooting process:

   _____

   _____

   _____

   _____

   _____

7. What did you do that finally solved the problem and returned the system to good working order?

   _____

   _____

REVIEW QUESTIONS

1. Now that you have been through this troubleshooting experience, what would you do differently the next time the same symptoms are exhibited?

   _____

2. What operating system utilities did you use or could you have used to solve the problem?

   _____

3. Is there any third-party software that might have been useful in solving this problem?

   _____

4. In a real-life situation, what might happen that would cause this problem to occur? List three things:

   _____

   _____

   _____

Installing and Supporting I/O Devices

Labs included in this chapter:

Critical Thinking

LAB 8.1 GATHER INFORMATION ON YOUR SYSTEM

OBJECTIVES

The goal of this lab is to teach you how to use Sandra, Control Panel, and other sources to compile information on your system specifications. After completing this lab, you will be able to:

- ▲ Use various Sandra modules to get information about your system
- ▲ Use Control Panel applets to get information about your system
- ▲ Compile a documentation notebook

MATERIALS REQUIRED

This lab requires the following:

- ▲ Windows 2000/XP or Windows 9x operating system
- ▲ Documentation you collected about your computer in Lab 3.4
- ▲ SiSoftware Sandra, installed in Lab 1.3

LAB PREPARATION

Before the lab begins, the instructor or lab assistant needs to do the following:

- ▲ Verify that Windows starts with no errors.
- ▲ Verify that Sandra is installed or available.

ACTIVITY BACKGROUND

As you continue to work with different kinds of computers, you'll find it extremely useful to maintain a report listing the components installed on each computer. This report is especially important if you're responsible for many computers. In this lab, you create such a report. (Note that you need to refer to this document in future labs.) You can also use Sandra in this lab, which you installed in Lab 1.3.

ESTIMATED COMPLETION TIME: 45 minutes

 Activity

Fill in Tables 8-1 through 8-3, which will become part of the total documentation you keep about your PC. When necessary, refer to the documentation about your computer that you collected in Lab 3.4 or use the Sandra software. After you have finished the tables, make copies of them and place them in your computer's documentation notebook. If you aren't sure which menus and applets to use in Sandra, experiment to find the information you need. Some information can be found in more than one place.

Location of computer	
Owner	
Date purchased	
Date warranty expires	
Size and speed of CPU	
Type of motherboard	
Amount of RAM	
Type of monitor	
Type of video card	
Hard drive type and size	
Size of disk drive A	
Size of disk drive B (if present)	

Table 8-1 Computer fact sheet

Software install name	Version	Installed by	Date

Table 8-2 Software installed

Name of device	IRQ	I/O address	DMA channel device	Driver file name
Serial port 1				
Serial port 2				
Parallel port				
Mouse				
Modem				
CD-ROM drive				
Display adapter				
Network card				

Table 8-3 Other devices

Create a documentation notebook or binder for your computer that includes copies of these tables as well as any other documentation you have collected about your computer. Save space for troubleshooting steps you learn in future labs. You'll need this notebook in future labs.

REVIEW QUESTIONS

1. How did you determine the CPU type?

2. How did you determine the driver your display adapter uses?

_____

_____

3. List two ways to determine the amount of RAM installed on a system:

_____

_____

4. Why is it important for PC technicians to keep documentation on computers they are responsible for?

_____

_____

LAB 8.2 IDENTIFY HARDWARE CONFLICTS USING DEVICE MANAGER

OBJECTIVES

The goal of this lab is to help you learn to use Device Manager to identify hardware conflicts. After completing this lab, you will be able to:

- Use Device Manager to investigate your system specifications
- Detect hardware conflicts using Device Manager
- Use Device Manager properties to determine which resources are causing a conflict

MATERIALS REQUIRED

This lab requires the following:

- Windows 2000/XP or Windows 9x operating system
- A PC with no hardware resource conflicts
- A hardware device, such as a sound card, you can install to create a hardware resource conflict
- Windows installation CD or installation files

LAB PREPARATION

Before the lab begins, the instructor or lab assistant needs to do the following:

- Verify that Windows starts with no errors.
- Verify that the system is free of resource conflicts.
- Provide a device that can be used to create a resource conflict.
- Provide each student with access to the the Windows installation files, if needed.

ACTIVITY BACKGROUND

Device Manager is an excellent tool for finding information about hardware specifications. You can also use it to diagnose problems with hardware devices, including those caused by two or more devices attempting to use the same system resources (a situation called a hardware resource conflict). Among other things, Device Manager can identify faulty or disabled devices, conflicting devices, and resources currently in use. This lab teaches you how to use Device Manager to find this information. You start by examining your system and verifying that no hardware resource conflicts currently exist on your system. Then you install a device that creates a resource conflict and observe the effects.

ESTIMATED COMPLETION TIME: 30 minutes

 Activity

You can use Device Manager to print a report about your system. Printing one when your system is working correctly is a good idea because you can use that report later as a baseline comparison when troubleshooting conflicts or other problems.

1. Open Device Manager, and click **Action, Print** from the menu. In the Report type section, click the **All devices and system summary** option button. If you're using a lab PC that doesn't have access to a printer, you can save the report to a floppy disk and go to another computer to print it.

2. Answer the following:

   ◢ How many pages are in the report?

   _____

   ◢ In one or two sentences, describe the type of information included on the report:

   _____

   _____

   ◢ List two items in the report that aren't displayed in Device Manager windows:

   _____

   _____

3. Put the Device Manager report in your documentation notebook (which you created in Lab 8.1).

Next, you use Device Manager to verify that there are no hardware conflicts:

1. Using Device Manager, check for conflicts among devices. Conflicts are indicated by a yellow triangle with an exclamation point. (Note that if a device has been disabled and isn't working at all, a red circle with a slash appears over the yellow triangle and exclamation point.)

2. Shut down the system, and install the component and its drivers that your instructor supplied. This component should conflict with another component already installed on the system. If you don't have a device that causes a conflict, remove a nonessential device, such as a modem card or sound card, which at least causes Device Manager to report an error.

3. Reboot and install drivers if prompted. You might be asked to provide access to Windows setup files. Did you see a message indicating a conflict or other error? If so, record it here:

   _____

   _____

4. Open Device Manager. Does Device Manager report any conflicting devices? Describe the problem as Device Manager reports it, listing all devices causing conflicts:

_____

_____

5. For each device reporting a conflict, open the device's Properties dialog box by right-clicking the device and clicking **Properties** in the shortcut menu. What messages do you see in the Device status section?

_____

_____

6. Next, click the **Resource** tab in the Properties dialog box. What message do you see in the Conflicting device list section?

_____

7. Examine the information in the Resource type and Settings columns. What resources is the device using?

_____

_____

8. Does it seem that you might be able to change settings for this device?

_____

9. Close the device's Properties dialog box, but leave Device Manager open if you're doing the Critical Thinking Activity.

CRITICAL THINKING (ADDITIONAL 15 MINUTES)

While the two devices are in conflict, use Device Manager to print a report on your system. Remember that if your PC isn't connected to a printer, you can save the report to a floppy disk and print it from another computer. Compare the report created when the system was working correctly to the report created when conflicts existed, and note the differences.

Now that you have observed two devices in conflict, you remove one of the conflicting devices. When you remove a device, you should uninstall it in Device Manager before removing it from your system. If you don't, when you want to install a similar or the same device later, you end up with two devices installed under Device Manager, which can cause the new device not to work.

Follow these steps to uninstall the device in Device Manager and then remove it:

1. In Windows 2000/XP, right-click the device, and then click **Uninstall** in the shortcut menu. In the Confirm Device Removal dialog box that opens, click **OK**. In Windows 9x, click to select the problem device in Device Manager and click **Remove**. If prompted to restart the computer, click **No**.

2. Close Device Manager and shut down the system.

3. Remove the device you installed earlier.

4. Restart the computer, open Device Manager, and verify that no conflicts exist.

REVIEW QUESTIONS

1. What symbol in Device Manager indicates that a component isn't working correctly?

_____

2. What two devices in your system were in conflict?

_____

3. What resources were causing a conflict?

_____

_____

4. Before physically removing a device from a system, what should you do?

_____

5. What would happen if you didn't uninstall the device before removing it from your system?

_____

LAB 8.3 SIMULATE SERIAL PORT COMMUNICATION

OBJECTIVES

The goal of this lab is to show how serial communication works by using a game. After completing this lab, you will be able to:

▲ Identify pin arrangements

▲ Explain which pins are used for handshake and data transfer

MATERIALS REQUIRED

This lab requires the following:

▲ Seven pieces of string, each approximately 4 feet long

▲ A workgroup of 8 students

LAB PREPARATION

Before the lab begins, the instructor or lab assistant needs to do the following:

▲ Divide the class into groups of 8 students.

▲ Give each group of students seven 4-foot pieces of string.

ACTIVITY BACKGROUND

RS-232 standards specify cabling and communication methods for PCs. Among other things, they specify the sequence of signals that must travel across a serial cable to complete a handshake and transmit data between devices. In this lab, to keep things simple, you simulate a handshake and data transfer on a null modem cable. You and your fellow students play the part of the serial ports, using pieces of string for the cable.

ESTIMATED COMPLETION TIME: 30 minutes

Activity

Follow these steps to simulate a cable connection between two devices:

1. Position eight students in two rows facing each other, with four on each side. Designate the students on one side as Students A through D and the students on the other side as Students E through H. Students E and A should be facing each other, as should Students B and F, and so on down the line. The two groups of students make up Computer ABCD and Computer EFGH.

2. Stretch seven strings between the eight students, as shown in Figure 8-1. Student A's left hand and Student E's right hand are Pin 1 on their respective serial ports. The numbers should proceed down the line until Pin 8 is Student D's right hand and Student H's left hand. Table 8-4 describes the null modem cable communication your workgroup is simulating. Notice that Pins 1 and 9 aren't used in null modem cable communication and are, therefore, omitted from this simulation.

Figure 8-1   Simulating null modem cable communication

Pin number on one connector	Pin number on the other connector	How the wire connecting the two pins is used
1	1	Not used
2 (RXD)	3 (TXD)	Data sent by one computer is received by the other
3 (TXD)	2 (RXD)	Data received by one computer is sent by the other
4 (DTR)	6 (DSR)	One end says to the other end "I'm able to talk"
5 (Ground)	5 (Ground)	Both ends are grounded
6 (DSR)	4 (DTR)	One end hears the other end say "I'm able to talk"
7 (RTS)	8 (CTS)	One end says to the other "I'm ready to talk"
8 (CTS)	7 (RTS)	One end hears the other say "I'm ready to talk"
9	9	Not used

Table 8-4   Pin connections for a 9-pin null modem cable

Here are the meanings of the abbreviations in the table and figure:

- *RXD*—Receive data
- *TXD*—Transmit data
- *DTR*—Data terminal ready
- *DSR*—Data set ready
- *CTS*—Clear to send
- *RTS*—Request to send

Follow these steps to perform the handshake and then send and receive data. Suppose that Computer EFGH has initiated communication to Computer ABCD, and Computer ABCD is ready to receive data from Computer EFGH.

1. Student G raises his left hand indicating that he's able to talk (DSR high).
2. Student B raises her hand on the other end of the same string to indicate that she has received Student G's communication.
3. Student C raises his right hand, indicating he understands that Computer EFGH is able to talk (DTR high).
4. Student F raises her left hand, indicating she has received the communication.
5. Student H raises his right hand, indicating he's ready to talk (RTS high).
6. Student D raises her right hand, indicating she has received the communication.
7. Student D raises her left hand, indicating she's ready to receive data from Computer EFGH.
8. Student H raises his left hand, indicating he has received the communication.

   Computer ABCD has just indicated that it's able and ready to have a conversation. (DTR indicates that Computer ABCD is open to having a conversation, and RTS tells Computer EFGH to go ahead and start talking.) Computer EFGH is now ready to start talking to Computer ABCD.

9. Student F repeatedly raises and lowers her hand—which represents the TXD pin—to indicate that data is being sent. (Each raise of the hand represents one bit transmitted.)
10. Student A sees this signal and repeatedly raises and lowers his right hand—which represents the RXD pin—to indicate the reception of each bit.

    Now suppose that computer EFGH has been transmitting for a while and Computer ABCD has noticed that its buffer is getting full. (That is, it has to process what Computer EFGH has said.) This capability of the receiving computer to stop a transmission so that it can catch up is called flow control.

11. Student D lowers her left hand (RTS) to indicate that Computer ABCD is processing and doesn't want to hear any more right now.
12. Student H quits receiving CTS high and lowers his hand to indicate he has received the communication.
13. Other students keep their hands raised, indicating that the conversation still isn't over.
14. Student F quits sending data and keeps her hand down.

    At this point, Computer EFGH has quit talking but hasn't yet finished sending all the data. After a pause, Computer ABCD finishes processing and the buffer is empty. Computer ABCD is now ready to listen again.

15. Student D raises her left hand, indicating RTS high.
16. Student H raises his hand, indicating CTS high. In response, Student F starts sending data again until all data is sent.
17. Students H and G lower their hands, indicating that Computer EFGH has nothing more to say and wants to end the conversation.

18. All students then lower their hands in response to Students H and G. The conversation is ended.

Now that you have seen how Computer EFGH sends data to Computer ABCD, answer the following questions about communication from Computer ABCD to Computer EFGH:

▲ Which hands should be raised to indicate that Computer EFGH is able to communicate with Computer ABCD?

_____

▲ Which hands should be raised to indicate that Computer EFGH is ready to receive data?

_____

▲ Which hands should be raised to indicate data flowing from Computer ABCD to Computer EFGH?

_____

▲ Which hands should be lowered when Computer EFGH's buffers are full?

_____

▲ Which hands should be lowered when the communication is finished?

_____

19. Now raise and lower your hands to simulate communication from Computer ABCD to Computer EFGH.

REVIEW QUESTIONS

1. What does a signal raised on Pin 8 indicate?

_____

2. Pin 4 on one end of the cable is connected to Pin _____ on the other end of the cable.

3. Data passes from Pin _____ on one end of the cable to Pin _____ on the other end of the cable.

4. What is the sole purpose of Pin 5's participation in network communication?

_____

LAB 8.4 DIAGNOSE SIMPLE HARDWARE PROBLEMS

OBJECTIVES

The goal of this lab is to give you practice diagnosing and repairing simple hardware problems. After completing this lab, you will be able to:

▲ Start with a functioning PC, introduce a problem, and remedy the problem

▲ Diagnose a problem caused by someone else

▲ Record the troubleshooting process

MATERIALS REQUIRED

This lab requires the following:

▲ Windows 2000/XP or Windows 9x operating system

▲ A PC toolkit including screwdrivers and an antistatic ground strap

▲ Pen and paper

▲ The documentation notebook you began creating in Lab 8.1

▲ A workgroup of 2 to 4 students

LAB PREPARATION

Before the lab begins, the instructor or lab assistant needs to do the following:

▲ Verify that Windows starts with no errors.

ACTIVITY BACKGROUND

If you have worked in a computer repair shop dealing with the general public, you know that about half the problems you see are the result of an inexperienced person making a slight mistake when configuring a system and lacking the knowledge to diagnose and remedy the problem. Unless you're very skilled and lucky, you'll make many of the same mistakes from time to time. Your advantage is that you'll have the experience to narrow down and identify the problem and then fix it. This lab gives you experience troubleshooting and repairing simple problems. Before you begin, team up with another workgroup in your class. Your team works with this other group throughout the lab.

ESTIMATED COMPLETION TIME: 60 minutes

Activity

1. Verify that your team's system is working correctly. Also, verify that you have the completed charts for your system from Lab 8.1.

2. Make one of the following changes to your team's system:

   ▲ Remove the power cable from the hard drive on the primary interface or highest SCSI ID.

   ▲ Reverse the data cable for the floppy drive.

   ▲ Remove the RAM and place it safely inside the case so that the other team can't see it.

   ▲ Disable IDE, SCSI, or serial ATA controllers in CMOS.

   ▲ Remove the power-on wire from the motherboard connection.

   ▲ Partially remove the data cable from the hard drive.

   ▲ For IDE drives, swap master/slave jumper assignments or set both drives to the same setting.

3. Switch places with the other team, and then diagnose and remedy the problem on your team's PC. Record the troubleshooting process on a separate sheet of paper, making sure you answer the following questions:

   ▲ Describe the problem as a user would describe it to you if you were working at a Help desk.

   ▲ What is your first guess as to the source of the problem?

   ▲ What did you do that solved the problem and returned the system to good working order?

4. Repeat Steps 1 through 3, choosing items at random from the list in Step 2. Continue until your team has made all the changes listed in Step 2.

CRITICAL THINKING (ADDITIONAL 30 MINUTES)

If time permits, try introducing two changes at a time. This procedure can prove much more difficult.

REVIEW QUESTIONS

1. What problems resulted in a "non-system disk" error?

   _____

2. Typically, what's the first indication that RAM has been removed?

   _____

3. What was the first indication of a problem with drive assignments?

   _____

   _____

4. Name three problems resulting in symptoms similar to those for a problem with the primary slave drive:

   _____

   _____

   _____

5. What was the first indication of a floppy drive problem?

   _____

LAB 8.5 USE A MULTIMETER TO INSPECT CABLES

OBJECTIVES

The goal of this lab is to teach you how to use a multimeter to test cables. After completing this lab, you will be able to:

▲ Set up a multimeter to measure resistance

▲ Test cables for resistance to determine pin arrangements

▲ Test cables for broken connections

▲ Measure resistance in a resistor

MATERIALS REQUIRED

This lab requires the following:

▲ A multimeter

▲ Three assorted cables

▲ Assorted resistors

▲ *Optional*: Internet access

▲ A workgroup of 2 to 4 students

LAB PREPARATION

Before the lab begins, the instructor or lab assistant needs to do the following:

▲ Provide students with the required multimeter, cables, and resistors.

▲ *Optional*: Verify that Internet access is available.

ACTIVITY BACKGROUND

One of a multimeter's many uses is to determine whether a cable is good or bad. You can also use a multimeter to determine a cable's pin arrangement. Both are done by measuring resistance in the cable. Resistance is measured in ohms. Infinite ohms (resistance) indicate that no electricity can flow; a measure of zero ohms means that electricity can flow (a state referred to as continuity). A resistor is a device that resists or controls the flow of electricity in a circuit, and a multimeter can be used to measure a resistor. You begin the lab by setting up and testing your multimeter. Then you measure resistance in cables and resistors.

ESTIMATED COMPLETION TIME: 45 minutes

 Activity

Follow these steps to set up and test your multimeter:

1. Set the multimeter to measure resistance (sometimes represented by the symbol Ω).

2. With the probes not in contact with anything, observe the reading on the meter. The reading should be infinity, open, 99999.99999, or similar.

3. With the probes touching each other, observe the reading on the meter. The reading should be 0 or similar.

Now that you have verified that your multimeter is working correctly, you can use it to measure the resistance or continuity in a cable. Examine the cables your instructor supplied. In the following steps, you use your multimeter to discover the pin-outs for each cable:

1. On a separate piece of paper, create a table for each cable indicating the cable's pin-outs. Can you identify the cable from your table and your knowledge of cables?

2. For Cable 1, complete the following:

   ▲ Description of cable connectors:

   _____

   ▲ Number of pins on each end of the cable:

   _____

   ▲ Number of pins on each end of the cable that are used:

   _____

   ▲ Type of cable:

   _____

3. For Cable 2, complete the following:

   ◢ Description of cable connectors:

   _____

   ◢ Number of pins on each end of the cable:

   _____

   ◢ Number of pins on each end of the cable that are used:

   _____

   ◢ Type of cable:

   _____

4. For Cable 3, complete the following:

   ◢ Description of cable connectors:

   _____

   ◢ Number of pins on each end of the cable:

   _____

   ◢ Number of pins on each end of the cable that are used:

   _____

   ◢ Type of cable:

   _____

Suppose a user comes to you with a problem. He has a cable that connects his computer's serial port to a serial printer. He needs to order more of the same cable but doesn't know whether it's a regular serial cable or a specialized cable made specifically for this printer. One connector on the cable is 9-pin, and the other connector is 25-pin. Using this information, answer the following:

1. Describe how to determine what kind of cable he needs to order:

   _____

   _____

   _____

   _____

2. Suppose the cable is not a regular serial cable but a specialized cable. How might you give the user the pin-outs necessary to order new custom-made cables?

   _____

   _____

   _____

   _____

So far you have used a multimeter to discover cable specifications. Next, you use the multimeter to measure the resistances of several resistors.

1. Measure each resistor and record the results in the following chart. Note that resistors have colored bands indicating their intended resistance. If you're testing more than four resistors, use a separate piece of paper to record your results.

Resistor	Resistance reading

CRITICAL THINKING (ADDITIONAL 45 MINUTES)

On an Ethernet network, a patch cable is used to connect a PC to a hub or other network device, but a crossover cable is used for PC-to-PC or hub-to-hub connections. Answer the following questions:

1. How many pins does an RJ-45 patch cable or crossover cable have?

_____

2. Research the Internet for the pin-outs of a crossover cable and a patch cable. Draw a diagram of each cable's pin-outs.

3. Have your instructor give you one patch cable and one crossover cable. Can you tell which cable is which by examining them physically?

_____

4. Use your multimeter to confirm which cable is the patch cable and which is the crossover cable. Which pins did you examine?

_____

REVIEW QUESTIONS

1. When a multimeter is set to measure resistance, what reading would you expect when the probes are touching?

_____

2. When a multimeter is set to measure resistance, what reading would you expect when the probes aren't touching anything?

_____

3. Suppose all pins match pin-outs except one at each end, and these nonmatching pins have no continuity with any other pin. What is the likely condition of the cable?

_____

_____

4. What do the colors on resistors indicate?

5. When you're measuring resistance, is there enough electricity in the wire to cause you harm?

LAB 8.6 CRITICAL THINKING: SABOTAGE AND REPAIR A SYSTEM

OBJECTIVES

The goal of this lab is to learn to troubleshoot a system by recovering from a sabotaged system.

MATERIALS REQUIRED

This lab requires the following:

◢ A PC (containing no important data) that has been designated for sabotage

◢ A workgroup of 2 to 4 students

LAB PREPARATION

Before the lab begins, the instructor or lab assistant needs to do the following:

◢ Verify that Windows starts with no errors.

◢ Verify that students' PCs contain no important data and can be sabotaged.

ACTIVITY BACKGROUND

You have learned about several tools and methods you can use to troubleshoot and repair a failed system or failed hardware devices. This lab gives you the opportunity to use these skills in a simulated troubleshooting situation. Your group will work with another group to sabotage a system and then repair another failed system.

ESTIMATED COMPLETION TIME: 45 minutes

 Activity

1. If the hard drive contains important data, back it up to another medium. Back up anything else you would like to save before another group sabotages the system and note it here:

2. Trade systems with another group and sabotage the other group's system while that group sabotages your system. Do one thing that will cause the system to fail to work or give errors after booting. Use any of the problems listed in Lab 8.4 or introduce a new problem. (Do *not* alter the operating system files.) What did you do to sabotage the other team's system?

3. Return to your system and troubleshoot it.

4. Describe the problem as a user would describe it to you if you were working at a help desk:

_____

_____

5. What is your first guess as to the source of the problem?

_____

6. List the steps you took in the troubleshooting process:

_____

_____

_____

_____

_____

7. What did you do that finally solved the problem and returned the system to good working order?

_____

_____

REVIEW QUESTIONS

1. Thinking back on this troubleshooting experience, what would you do differently the next time you encounter the same symptoms?

_____

_____

2. What software utilities did you use or could you have used to solve the problem?

_____

3. What third-party software utility or hardware device might have been useful in solving this problem?

_____

4. In a real-life situation, what might cause this problem to occur? List three possible causes:

_____

_____

_____

CHAPTER 9

Multimedia Devices and Mass Storage

Labs included in this chapter:

LAB 9.1 INSTALL A SOUND CARD

OBJECTIVES

The goal of this lab is to help you learn how to install a sound card. After completing this lab, you will be able to:

- Physically install a sound card
- Install device drivers
- Test the card and adjust the volume

MATERIALS REQUIRED

This lab requires the following:

- Windows 2000/XP operating system
- Windows 2000/XP installation CD or installation files
- An empty expansion slot
- A compatible sound card with speakers or headphones
- Sound card device drivers
- Motherboard documentation, if your system uses embedded audio
- A PC toolkit with antistatic ground strap
- *Optional*: Internet access

LAB PREPARATION

Before the lab begins, the instructor or lab assistant needs to do the following:

- Verify that Windows starts with no errors.
- Verify access to motherboard and sound card documentation.
- *Optional:* Verify that Internet access is available.
- Provide each student with access to the Windows installation files, if needed.

ACTIVITY BACKGROUND

Two of the most popular multimedia devices are the sound card and the embedded audio device. A sound card enables a computer to receive sound input and to output sound, as when playing a music CD. Many newer systems have audio embedded on the motherboard. As an A+ computer technician, you need to know how to install a sound card, whether you're putting together a computer from scratch, repairing a failed device, or upgrading components on an existing system. In this lab, you install, configure, and test a sound card.

ESTIMATED COMPLETION TIME: 45 minutes

 Activity

First, you need to find out whether your system has a sound card, an embedded audio device, or perhaps both or neither. Use the skills you have learned to discover and describe what audio configuration your system currently has. Describe the configuration, and then work through the steps to complete the lab in the following general order:

- Disable any existing audio devices in Windows.
- Remove or disable the hardware device(s).

◢ Verify that the audio is disabled.

◢ Physically install the sound card.

◢ Install the drivers in Windows.

◢ Verify the function of audio features.

◢ Return the system to its original state (optional, per instructor's directions).

Follow these steps to uninstall a sound card or embedded audio device in Windows:

1. After you have logged on as an administrator, open Control Panel.

2. Click **Add/Remove Hardware** to start the Add/Remove Hardware Wizard.

3. Click the **Uninstall/Unplug a device** option button, and then click **Next** to continue.

4. In the Choose a Removal Task window, click the **Uninstall a device** option button, as shown in Figure 9-1, and then click **Next** to continue.

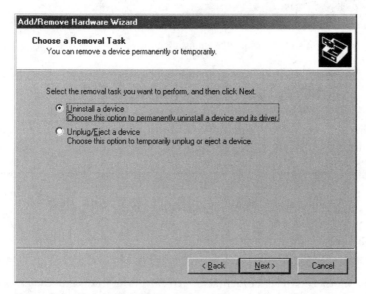

Figure 9-1   Use the Uninstall a device option to uninstall the sound card or embedded audio device

5. In the Devices list box, scroll down until you locate your audio device. Click your device to select it, and then click **Next** to continue.

6. Click the **Yes, I want to uninstall this device** option button, as shown in Figure 9-2, and then click **Next** to continue.

7. When the Add/Remove Hardware Wizard reports that you have uninstalled your audio device successfully, click **Finish** to close the window.

8. Close any open windows, log off, and shut down your computer.

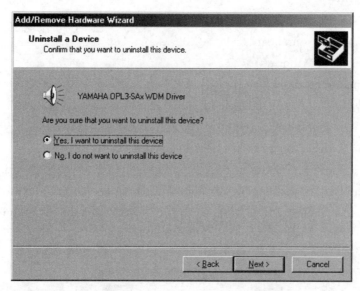

Figure 9-2 Confirm that this device should be uninstalled

Follow these steps to remove the sound card:

1. Disconnect all external cables from the case.

2. Remove the case cover and locate the sound card. List any cables connected to the sound card:

   _____

3. Disconnect any cables from the sound card and secure them. Remove the sound card and place it in a safe place.

4. Reassemble the system and boot to Windows to verify that the audio doesn't function.

Follow these steps to disable the embedded audio device:

1. Consult the motherboard documentation to learn how to disable the embedded audio device. Also, take note of any internal audio cables. The way to disable the device is often a jumper setting, but sometimes you might have to disable the device in the CMOS setup utility. If you must disable the device in CMOS, describe the steps you took on the following lines, and then complete Steps 2 and 3:

   _____

   _____

   _____

2. Disconnect all external cables. Remove the case cover and locate the way to disable the embedded audio (if applicable). List the steps, and then remove and secure any internal audio cables:

   _____

   _____

3. Reassemble the system and boot to Windows to verify that the audio doesn't function.

Follow these steps to physically install a sound card:

1. Shut down the computer and disconnect all external cables from the case.

2. Remove the case cover.

3. Locate an empty expansion slot that you can use for the sound card. On some systems, expansion cards are attached to a riser card, which you might have to remove at this time. If necessary, remove the expansion slot faceplate on the case so that the sound card fits into the expansion slot.

4. Insert the sound card into the expansion slot on the motherboard (or insert the sound card into the riser card and the riser card into the motherboard). Line up the sound card on the slot and press it straight down, making sure the tab on the backplate (the metal plate on the rear of the card where sound ports are located) fits into the slot on the case. Normally, seating the card requires a little effort, but don't force it. If you can't insert the card with just a little effort, something is preventing it from seating. Check for obstructions and try again, removing components that are in the way, if needed.

5. After the card is installed, secure it with a screw. The screw goes through a hole in the card's backplate, securing the backplate to the case.

6. Attach any cable required to carry an audio signal from other multimedia devices, such as a CD-ROM drive.

7. Replace any components you removed while installing the sound card, and replace and secure the cover on the case.

8. Reattach all cables from external devices to the correct ports. Attach speakers or headphones. (Some speakers receive power from the computer, and others have to be plugged into an external power source, such as a wall outlet.)

Next, you configure the drivers and other software for your sound card. If you have the documentation for your sound card, follow those instructions. Otherwise, follow these general steps to install software for most sound cards, keeping in mind that your sound card might require a slightly different procedure:

1. Start the computer, and log on as an administrator. The Found New Hardware dialog box opens, attempts to determine what type of new hardware is present, and displays the result.

2. The New Hardware Wizard launches, informing you that it will help you install a driver. Click **Next** to continue.

3. The New Hardware Wizard displays a message asking how you want to install the software. Click the **Search for a suitable driver for my device (Recommended)** option button, and then click **Next** to continue.

4. The New Hardware Wizard displays a message asking where the drivers for the new device are located (see Figure 9-3). Insert the floppy disk or CD containing the drivers, and click the check box to indicate the location of the drivers. (If the CD Autorun program launches when you insert the CD, close it.) Click **Next** to continue. If your files aren't located on removable media, click the **Specify a location** check box. A dialog box opens, prompting you to type the path or browse to the file location. Use either method you prefer, and when you finish, click **OK** to continue.

5. If the New Hardware Wizard can locate the correct driver, it displays a message identifying the sound card model name, driver location, and driver file name. Click **Next** to continue and then skip to Step 7. If the wizard reports that it is unable to find the drivers, proceed to Step 6.

6. If the New Hardware Wizard reports that it was unable to locate the drivers, click **Back** and repeat Step 4, but this time click the **Specify Location** option, and then click **Browse** to open the Browse for a Folder dialog box.

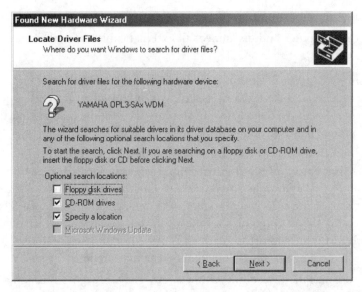

Figure 9-3 Direct the New Hardware Wizard to the correct location of the drivers

Browse to the location of the setup files, expanding folders as needed, and look for a folder named Win2000, Win2k, or similar. (If you aren't sure which .inf file to choose, consult the Readme.txt file, which should include instructions and last-minute information. Don't be surprised if you're instructed to use Windows NT 4 drivers for some devices!) After you select the correct folder, click **OK** to close the Browse for a Folder dialog box, and then click **Next** in the New Hardware Wizard. If the wizard finds the driver, continue to Step 7; otherwise, consult the documentation again for the correct installation procedure.

7. After locating and installing the drivers, the New Hardware Wizard displays a message notifying you that the device installation is completed. Click **Finish** to close the wizard. At some point, you might be required to supply the location of the i386 directory holding Windows installation files.

8. After the sound card is completely installed, Windows might detect additional devices. Sound cards sometimes include embedded features, such as MIDI Wave Audio, SB16 Emulation, Game Port, and so on. The New Hardware Wizard launches as needed to install these devices separately. Follow the preceding steps to install each device.

9. When Windows finishes installing software, you might be prompted to reboot. If so, go ahead and reboot. You should hear the Microsoft sound (the default sound played on startup) after you log on.

Follow these steps to adjust the volume in Windows and then test the sound card:

1. Open Control Panel. In Windows XP, click **Sounds, Speech, and Audio Devices**, and then click **Sounds and Audio Devices**. The Sounds and Audio Devices Properties dialog box opens. In Windows 2000, double-click **Sounds and Multimedia**. The Sounds and Multimedia Properties dialog box opens.

2. In Windows XP, click the **Volume** tab. In the Device volume section, make sure the **Place volume icon in taskbar** check box is selected, and drag the volume slider all the way to High. In Windows 2000, click the **Sounds** tab, if necessary. Make sure the **Show volume control on the taskbar** check box at the bottom of the tab is selected, and then move the volume slider all the way to High (see Figure 9-4). Click **OK** to close the dialog box, close Control Panel, and reboot the system.

Figure 9-4   Check the settings in the Sounds tab

3. On the right side of the taskbar, you should see the speaker volume setting represented by a speaker icon. Click the speaker icon. A pop-up window opens with a slider for adjusting speaker volume.

4. Drag the volume slider all the way to the top, and then click on the desktop to close the pop-up window.

5. Double-click the speaker icon. The Volume Control dialog box opens. Note that this dialog box gives you more control than the pop-up window you used in Step 4. Among other things, you can adjust the volume of various inputs, including the overall volume control, which controls the actual volume of the signal fed to the speakers. On the following lines, list the volume controls from left to right, and identify two settings (other than volume) that can be changed:

6. Set the volume slider on the far left to half volume, and then close the Volume Control dialog box.

7. Next, if you have Internet access, you can do a further test of your sound card. Use a search engine, locate a Lion.wav file, and play it to hear a lion's roar. What was the Web site where you found the file?

REVIEW QUESTIONS

1. What Windows feature walks you through the process of installing drivers for a new device?

2. Other than driver files included with the sound card, what other information might Windows request when configuring a new sound card?

3. What other devices embedded on the sound card might Windows detect after the sound card installation is finished?

_____

_____

4. How does Windows handle the installation of these additional devices?

_____

_____

5. What Control Panel applet, and which tab in its Properties dialog box, do you use to adjust the volume in Windows?

_____

6. Besides output to the speakers on the sound card or embedded audio device interface, what other outputs and inputs are available on the sound card? What are their uses?

_____

_____

_____

LAB 9.2 INSTALL A PC VIDEO CAMERA

OBJECTIVES

The goal of this lab is to help you complete the process of installing and testing a PC camera. After completing this lab, you will be able to:

◢ Install a PC video camera

◢ Use Windows XP Movie Maker to test your PC camera

◢ Use Windows 98 NetMeeting to test your PC camera

MATERIALS REQUIRED

This lab requires the following:

◢ Windows XP and Windows 98 operating systems

◢ Windows installation CD or installation files

◢ A USB-connected PC camera compatible with your system

◢ A spare USB port on the system

◢ Device drivers for the camera

◢ Sound card, speakers, and optional microphone

◢ _Optional_: Internet access

LAB PREPARATION

Before the lab begins, the instructor or lab assistant needs to do the following:

◢ Verify that Windows starts with no errors.

◢ Provide each student with access to the necessary installation files or drivers.

◢ *Optional:* Verify that Internet access is available.

ACTIVITY BACKGROUND

PC cameras are becoming increasingly popular. Using these cameras, you can set up a video conference, record or send video images to your family and friends, and monitor your house over the Internet. You can even detach some PC cameras and use them to take still pictures while away from your system, uploading them to the computer when you return. Most PC cameras install via the USB port, making physical installation fairly simple. In this lab, you install, configure, and test a basic PC camera.

ESTIMATED COMPLETION TIME: 45 minutes

 Activity

In Windows XP, follow these steps to install a PC camera:

1. Start the computer and, if necessary, log on as an administrator.

2. Locate an unused USB port. Insert the PC camera's cable into the USB port. (Don't force the cable. If you can't insert it easily, flip the connector over, and try again; it should insert easily.)

3. Windows detects the new USB device and the Found New Hardware icon appears in the taskbar's notification area. A balloon tip above the icon informs you that new hardware has been found. Next, the balloon tip identifies the hardware as a camera, and then notifies you that it has identified the particular camera model. Finally, the balloon tip notifies you that the camera has been installed successfully. Windows XP probably won't give you the opportunity to use the camera manufacturer's device drivers. However, if requested, insert the camera installation CD or floppy disk. (If the Autorun program launches, close it.)

Next, you use My Computer to collect information about your camera by following these steps:

1. Open My Computer. Note the section title under which the camera is listed in the right pane of My Computer:

_____

2. Right-click the icon for your camera and click **Properties** in the shortcut menu. The *Cameraname* Properties dialog box opens. List the five types of information available in the Camera Status section of the General tab:

_____

_____

_____

3. Click the **Test Camera** button in the Diagnostics section. On the following lines, describe the results reported in the message box that opens, and then click **OK** to

close the message box. Click **OK** again to close the *Cameraname* Properties dialog box.

---

4. Now double-click the camera icon in My Computer. Record what happens and what tasks are available in the Camera Tasks section:

---

5. Use what you know about Windows and list two ways, other than My Computer or Windows Explorer but in Windows XP, where you can find information about the camera. Briefly describe any differences from My Computer on the amount of information available or the way it's presented:

Next, you use Windows Movie Maker, a feature new to Windows XP, to put your camera to use. Complete the following steps:

1. Click **Start**, point to **All Programs**, point to **Accessories**, point to **Entertainment**, and then click **Windows Movie Maker**. Windows Movie Maker opens, as shown in Figure 9-5.

Figure 9-5 The Windows Movie Maker main window

2. On the Windows Movie Maker toolbar, click **Record**. The Record dialog box opens.

3. Click the **Record** list arrow, and list the choices you have for recording:

_____

_____

4. Click the **Change Device** button. The Change Device dialog box opens. What devices are currently selected?

_____

5. Click the **Line** list arrow, and click the microphone on the camera. If your camera doesn't have a microphone, leave the default setting. Click **OK** to close the dialog box.

6. To record a video clip, click the **Record** button in the Record dialog box (see Figure 9-6). The Record button changes to Stop, and the Elapsed time counter starts ticking. Take several seconds of footage, and then click **Stop**. What's the name of the dialog box that opens? What is the default path in the new dialog box?

_____

_____

 Notes

If the Video Capture Wizard starts, go through the steps to select a device and so forth. Also, note that steps and screens might differ slightly for you, depending on the version of Windows XP you're using.

Figure 9-6 The Record dialog box for Windows Movie Maker

7. Save your file as a test with the default extension. The Record dialog box closes, and the Creating Clips dialog box opens to show the save progress. When the clip is saved, the Creating Clips dialog box closes automatically. Where does your clip appear in the Windows Movie Maker window?

_____

_____

8. When you click a clip to select it, you can play that clip in the interface on the right side of the window. In addition, you can drag a clip to the Timeline/Storyboard interface at the bottom of Windows Movie Maker to edit it. Take a few minutes to explore Windows Movie Maker, and then record and save a clip describing what features you find interesting about the capability to record and edit video on your system.

In Windows 98, follow these steps to install a PC camera:

1. Start the computer and log on, if necessary.

2. Insert the PC camera's installation CD or floppy disk. (If the CD Autorun program launches, close it.)

3. Locate an unused USB port. Insert the PC camera's cable into the USB port. (Don't force the cable. If you can't insert it easily, flip the connector over and try again; it should insert easily.)

4. Windows detects the new USB device and the Found New Hardware dialog box opens, informing you that a USB device has been detected. A second dialog box opens, informing you that Windows is forming a New Driver Database; when the new database is finished, the second dialog box closes as well as the Found New Hardware dialog box. (If Windows doesn't detect the camera, check Device Manager or BIOS settings to discover whether the USB controller has problems or has been disabled. If necessary, enable the USB controller in Device Manager and CMOS setup, and begin again with Step 1.)

5. The New Hardware Wizard opens and indicates that it will begin searching for drivers for a USB device. Click **Next** to continue.

6. The wizard prompts you to specify a driver or search for the best driver. Click the **Search for the best driver for your device (Recommended)** option button, and then click **Next** to continue.

7. Locate the installation files, as you learned how to do in Lab 9.1, and click **Next**.

8. The wizard indicates that it has found the driver for the PC camera and displays the driver's location and file name. Click **Next** to continue.

9. The wizard copies all necessary files and displays a message indicating that the installation is complete. Click **Finish** to close the wizard. Many PC cameras have built-in microphones as well as other devices. If this is the case, the wizard might start again for each device. In addition, during any installation, the wizard might prompt you to provide the location of Windows 98 installation files.

Now you use Windows 98 NetMeeting to test your camera. NetMeeting is video conferencing software included with Windows 98. To conduct a full video conference with two or more people, you can use a directory server, an online database that NetMeeting uses to locate participants in a NetMeeting conference. One directory server is Microsoft Internet Directory. When you install NetMeeting, you're prompted to enter information about yourself and are then given the opportunity to be added to Microsoft Internet Directory. The following steps tell you to use the Microsoft Internet Directory, although your instructor might ask you to use a different directory server. Follow these steps to install NetMeeting if it's not already installed:

1. Open Control Panel, open the Add or Remove Programs applet, and then click the **Windows Setup** tab. Windows searches for Windows components.

2. Double-click the **Communications** group in the Components list box. The Communications dialog box opens.

3. Scroll down the Components list box, click the **Microsoft NetMeeting** check box, and then click **OK**. The Communications dialog box closes.

4. Click **OK** to close the Add or Remove Properties dialog box. The Copying Files dialog box opens, indicating that the copying process has begun. If prompted, supply the

location of Windows 98 installation files. When the files are copied, the Copying Files dialog box closes. Restart your PC if prompted to do so.

Follow these steps to start and configure Windows 98 NetMeeting:

1. Click **Start**, point to **Programs**, and then look for Microsoft NetMeeting on one of the submenus. You might find it under Internet Explorer or Accessories, Communications.

2. Click **Microsoft NetMeeting**.

3. Microsoft NetMeeting begins configuring your connection. Click **Next** to continue.

4. In the NetMeeting dialog box shown in Figure 9-7, accept Microsoft Internet Directory as the server name (unless your instructor gives you different directions), and then click **Next**.

Figure 9-7 By default, installing NetMeeting adds you to Microsoft Internet Directory

5. Supply the requested identification information, including your name and e-mail address, and then click **Next** to continue. (Keep in mind that your identification information will be available to other NetMeeting users on the directory server.)

6. What you see on the next screen depends on the version of NetMeeting that's installed. You might see a screen asking you what category to use for your personal info (personal use for all ages, business use for all ages, or adults-only use). Select a category, and then click **Next**. For some versions of NetMeeting, the screen gives you the option of selecting a directory server. In this case, the default is Microsoft Internet Directory. Leave the default selected, and then click **Next**.

7. On the next screen, you're asked to specify your connection speed. Click **Local Area Network** (or other speed specified by your instructor), and then click **Next** to continue.

8. Next, you're asked to specify your video capturing device. Click your camera in the drop-down list, if it's not already selected, and then click **Next** to continue.

9. NetMeeting informs you that it will help tune your audio settings. Click **Next** to continue.

10. Set and test your audio settings. When they are satisfactory, click **Next** to continue.

11. When the installation is completed, click **Finish**. NetMeeting launches.

12. Click **Current Call**, and then click the **Play** button in the My Video frame. You should be able to see video supplied by your PC camera in the My Video frame, which indicates that your video camera was installed correctly.

CRITICAL THINKING (ADDITIONAL 20 MINUTES)

If others in the lab are connected to NetMeeting and you have access to a sound card, speakers, and microphone, join someone else in a video conference. To make the connection, you can use an IP address of another computer on the LAN, instead of using a directory server. To use Windows 98 to determine a workstation IP address, type winipcfg in the Run dialog box, and then click the network adapter in the drop-down list. Figure 9-8 shows a full NetMeeting video conference complete with a shared whiteboard, chat window, and video window.

Figure 9-8   NetMeeting provides three windows during a session

REVIEW QUESTIONS

1. Typically, via what type of port do PC cameras attach to a system?

2. What type of audio device might be embedded in a PC camera?

3. Do you have to power down the system before connecting a USB camera? Why or why not?

4. What feature of Windows XP is designed to create video content?

5. What application can you use to test the video supplied by your PC camera?

6. When would using a PC camera be beneficial to you?

_____

_____

LAB 9.3 COMPARE CD AND DVD TECHNOLOGIES

OBJECTIVES

The goal of this lab is to help you use the Internet to research CD and DVD standards. After completing this lab, you will be able to:

◢ Recognize CD and DVD specifications

MATERIALS REQUIRED

This lab requires the following:

◢ Internet access

LAB PREPARATION

Before the lab begins, the instructor or lab assistant needs to do the following:

◢ Verify that Internet access is available.

ACTIVITY BACKGROUND

Many multimedia PCs include CD or DVD drives (and sometimes both). These drives can be of three types: read-only (ROM), write/record (R), or write/record and rewrite (RW or RAM). (The last two types can write and record only to specialized disks.) You research the features and limitations of CD and DVD standards in this lab.

> **ESTIMATED COMPLETION TIME: 60 minutes**

Activity

Use the Internet and your favorite search sites, such as Google (*www.google.com*) or Yahoo! (*www.yahoo.com*), to answer the following questions on CD standards. Print the source page or pages supporting your answers.

1. What is the maximum storage capacity of a CD?

_____

2. Briefly, how is information recorded on a CD-ROM disk?

_____

_____

3. Are CDs capable of storing data on both sides of the disk?

_____

4. What type or color of laser is used in a CD drive?

_____

5. What is a limitation of a CD-R drive that isn't an issue with a CD-RW drive?

_____

6. What kind of problems might occur if you tried to use an older CD-ROM drive or a CD player to play a CD-R or CD-RW disk?

_____

_____

7. Define "constant angular velocity" and explain how it applies to CD standards:

_____

_____

8. Define "constant linear velocity" and explain how it applies to CD standards:

_____

_____

9. What term is used for the process of writing data to a disk?

_____

10. Can any CD hold video data? Explain:

_____

11. On a CD, is data written in concentric circles or a continuous spiral track?

_____

12. What are three common standards CD drives use to interface with a system?

_____

_____

13. What does the X factor of a drive indicate? What is the specification of one X?

_____

_____

14. Briefly describe how a CD-RW writes data to a disk and how it's able to rewrite data:

_____

_____

_____

_____

15. How much would you pay for a package of CD-Rs? How much for a package of CD-RWs? How many discs are in a package of each type?

_____

_____

Use the Internet and your favorite search sites to answer the following questions on DVD standards. Print the source page or pages supporting your answers.

1. What is the maximum storage capacity of a DVD?

_____

2. What two characteristics give a DVD more storage capacity than a CD?

_____

_____

3. Describe the difference between DVD-R and DVD-RAM:

_____

_____

_____

4. Besides DVD-R, what other standards are available for burning DVDs?

_____

_____

5. Explain how DVD audio and CD audio differ:

_____

_____

_____

6. How many CDs worth of data can a single DVD hold?

_____

7. How many layers of data can be stored on one side of a DVD?

_____

8. How many data areas are on a single side of a DVD-R?

_____

9. List the versions and maximum capacities of DVD-RAM:

_____

_____

10. Can DVDs be used in CD devices? Explain:

_____

11. Explain the use of the UDF file system and how it applies to a DVD:

_____

_____

_____

_____

_____

REVIEW QUESTIONS

1. What factors, other than storage capacity, would you consider when choosing between a DVD drive and a CD drive?

_____

_____

_____

2. What characteristics do DVD and CD drives share?

_____

_____

3. If you wanted to create a disc that would never need to be altered and could be used on the maximum number of systems, what type of disc would you use and why?

_____

_____

_____

4. Why do you think motion pictures are released on DVDs instead of CDs?

_____

_____

LAB 9.4 INSTALL DUAL MONITORS IN WINDOWS XP

OBJECTIVES

The goal of this lab is to help you set up a second monitor on a system. After completing this lab, you will be able to:

◢ Install a display adapter and its drivers

◢ Attach a second monitor

◢ Configure the system to use both monitors at the same time

MATERIALS REQUIRED

This lab requires the following:

◢ Windows XP operating system

◢ A PC toolkit with antistatic ground strap

◢ A second display adapter with drivers

◢ A second monitor

LAB PREPARATION

Before the lab begins, the instructor or lab assistant needs to do the following:

◢ Verify that Windows starts with no errors.

ACTIVITY BACKGROUND

Having two monitors on a system is often quite handy. For instance, you can have a Web browser displayed on one and a video-editing application on the other. Using two monitors has the effect of making your desktop larger and making it easier to work with multiple applications simultaneously, which is often useful when developing multimedia presentations. In this lab, you install and configure a second monitor on a computer.

ESTIMATED COMPLETION TIME: 45 minutes

 Activity

It's important to verify that the original hardware is working correctly before you try to add a second display adapter and monitor. That way, if a problem comes up after you install new hardware, you can be fairly sure something is amiss with the newly added components rather than the original equipment. Also, you should make sure the hardware is on the Windows XP HCL (recommended) or, at the very least, the device manufacturer offers drivers and specific instructions for use with Windows XP.

Follow these steps to physically install the second display adapter:

1. Check to make sure the original display adapter uses the PCI or AGP standard, and decide whether it will be the primary or secondary monitor.

2. Install the second adapter card in the PCI slot nearest to the AGP slot (if the original is an AGP adapter) or the PCI slot immediately next to the original PCI adapter (if the original is a PCI adapter). If you need additional guidance on installing a card, refer to Lab 9.1.

3. Attach the second monitor to the port on the back of the display adapter.

4. Boot your PC and enter CMOS setup. If your setup has display settings for dual monitors, adjust them so that the primary display adapter is initialized first. If you don't see this setting, your BIOS doesn't support it, so you can exit CMOS setup and wait for your system to reboot.

5. Enter CMOS setup again. If you see settings for dual monitors, for a system with an AGP slot, make sure the AGP adapter is selected as the primary adapter and the PCI adapter as the secondary adapter. For a system that uses two PCI adapters, it doesn't matter which adapter is the primary one; you can leave the setting as is. For additional guidance on adjusting BIOS settings, refer to Lab 5.1. Exit CMOS setup and wait for your system to reboot.

Follow these steps to install device drivers and adjust Windows display settings:

1. When the system reboots, log on as an administrator. Windows XP recognizes the new adapter and displays a Found New Hardware icon in the taskbar's notification area. Above the Found New Hardware icon, a balloon tip appears with the notification.

2. At this point, Windows might install the drivers automatically for you (if the drivers were available when XP was published) or launch the New Hardware Wizard if the adapter is new enough that XP isn't aware of the correct drivers. Complete the steps in the wizard to install the adapter. When the installation is completed, reboot. Refer to Lab 9.1 if you need additional information on using the wizard.

Before you use a second monitor, you must activate it. To do so, follow these steps:

1. Log on as an administrator, open Control Panel, and click **Appearance and Themes.** Then click the **Display** link to open the Display Properties dialog box.

2. Click the **Settings** tab in the Display Properties dialog box, as shown in Figure 9-9. The area at the top of the Settings tab now displays two monitors. Click the image of the monitor with the number 2, or in the Display list box, click the video adapter you just installed.

Figure 9-9 You must activate a second monitor before Windows can use it

3. Adjust the resolution and color settings to your preference, and then click the **Extend my Windows desktop onto this monitor** check box.

4. Click **Apply** to apply the settings. The second monitor displays the desktop.

Follow these steps to test your dual-monitor configuration:

1. Open Paint, and then drag it to the second monitor. Does your desktop extend to the second monitor as expected?

2. Open Windows Explorer, and maximize it on the original monitor. Can you see your mouse move as expected from one monitor to the next? Does the mouse interact with applications on each monitor?

3. Close Paint and Windows Explorer, and open Device Manager.

Follow these steps to remove the second adapter and return to a single-monitor configuration:

1. Open Device Manager, find the second display adapter, and click to select it. (Make sure you're looking at the second adapter, not the first.)

2. Click **Uninstall**. If prompted, verify that you do want to remove the device, and when asked if you want to restart the computer, click **No**.

3. Shut down the computer. Don't restart the computer at this time.

4. Remove the second monitor and adapter card. If necessary, reverse any BIOS changes you made that affect the display initialization sequence, and reboot the system to verify that the system no longer recognizes the adapter card.

REVIEW QUESTIONS

1. Before installing a second monitor, why is it important to know whether your existing configuration is working correctly?

2. Why might it be necessary to change the sequence in which the system initializes display adapters?

3. In Display Properties, what is one way to select the monitor you want to adjust?

4. What would probably happen if the new adapter was on the Windows XP HCL and was in production before the release of Windows XP?

5. Does adjusting the settings of one monitor affect the settings of the other?

6. Why might you want to install multiple monitors on a system?

7. Which would be less expensive: adding a second 17-inch monitor to an existing system or buying a 21-inch monitor in single-monitor mode?

8. How did you arrive at your answer to Question 7?

LAB 9.5 RESEARCH DIGITAL CAMERAS

OBJECTIVES

The goal of this lab is to help you research digital cameras and learn how you can integrate them with a multimedia PC. In this lab, you will research:

◢ Camera picture quality and compatibility

◢ Camera storage technology

◢ Methods of transferring images to a PC

MATERIALS REQUIRED

This lab requires the following:

◢ Internet access

LAB PREPARATION

Before the lab begins, the instructor or lab assistant needs to do the following:

◢ Verify that Internet access is available.

ACTIVITY BACKGROUND

As digital cameras have become more common and popular, they have also become more sophisticated. Their special features, image quality, methods of file storage, and methods of transferring image data to the PC have improved over earlier models. Also, the prices of digital cameras have decreased dramatically. In this lab, you research digital cameras and learn how they are used with multimedia PCs.

ESTIMATED COMPLETION TIME: 60 minutes

 Activity

Research digital photography on the Internet. Try searching for "digital camera" or "digital photography" on your favorite search engine. Web sites that might be useful include the following:

◢ CNET Networks, Inc., *www.cnet.com*

◢ Digital Photography Review, *www.dpreview.com*

◢ Shutterline, *www.shutterline.com*

◢ KeyWorlds.com, *www.keyworlds.com/d/digital_photography.htm*

Answer these questions about general camera topics. Print the Web page or pages supporting your answer.

1. How is image quality measured? Do all digital cameras produce the same image quality?

2. What are three storage technologies that digital cameras might use to store images in a camera?

_____

_____

_____

3. Name four technologies a camera might use to transfer images to a PC. What requirements must a PC meet for each?

_____

_____

_____

_____

4. Find and print information about at least two digital cameras that offer features such as changeable lenses, manual focus, aperture settings (f-stops), and shutter-speed settings (exposure). List the two digital cameras you selected on the following lines:

_____

_____

Answer these questions on basic image characteristics:

1. What three file types might a digital camera use to store images?

_____

2. Name three factors that affect the number of images that a camera can store on a single storage device:

_____

_____

_____

3. Do most digital cameras offer the capability to control image quality? Explain:

_____

4. Can you remove an image you don't like from a camera without transferring the image to a PC? Explain:

_____

_____

5. What are three means of printing a photo taken by a digital camera?

_____

_____

_____

6. Can digital cameras record images other than still shots?

_____

Answer these questions about how cameras transfer images to a PC:

1. Which transfer method offers the highest transfer speed? What is that speed?

_____

2. Which transfer method requires the least specialized hardware on a PC?

_____

3. Which storage technologies allow direct image transfer by removing the storage device from the camera and inserting it into the PC?

_____

_____

4. What devices can be added to a PC to allow it to read flash memory cards directly?

_____

_____

_____

5. What image transfer method doesn't require removing a device from the camera or using cabling to the PC?

_____

6. Does image resolution have any effect on transfer speed? Explain:

_____

_____

_____

Answer these questions about photo-quality printers:

1. What resolution would you recommend for a printer capable of reproducing digital pictures?

_____

2. Do you need special paper to get the best quality in photo printing? Explain:

_____

3. Describe one way you could get pictures from your digital camera to the printer:

_____

_____

REVIEW QUESTIONS

1. What are three advantages of a digital camera over a 35mm camera?

_____

_____

_____

2. What are some disadvantages of a digital camera compared with a 35mm camera?

_____

_____

_____

3. What are some features you would like on a digital camera? Explain your choices:

_____

_____

_____

4. What can you do to maximize the number of images stored on a camera without modifying the storage device capacity?

_____

_____

_____

5. Would all 3.1 megapixel cameras have the same picture quality? Why or why not?

_____

_____

6. What factors should you consider when purchasing a photo printer?

_____

_____

LAB 9.6 EXPLORE WINDOWS XP AUDIO FEATURES

OBJECTIVES

The goal of this lab is to give you the opportunity to experiment with different audio features and capabilities of Windows XP. After completing this lab, you will be able to:

▲ Identify audio media types

▲ Download and install Nullsoft Winamp, a third-party sound application

⊿ Control audio CD playback with Windows Media Player and Nullsoft Winamp

⊿ Customize sounds that Windows plays for events

MATERIALS REQUIRED

This lab requires the following:

⊿ Windows XP operating system

⊿ Windows XP installation CD or installation files

⊿ Internet access

⊿ CD-ROM drive and an audio CD

LAB PREPARATION

Before the lab begins, the instructor or lab assistant needs to do the following:

⊿ Verify that Windows starts with no errors.

⊿ Provide each student with access to the Windows XP installation files, if needed.

⊿ Verify that Internet access is available.

ACTIVITY BACKGROUND

Windows XP offers features that let you use audio files in different ways. For example, Windows events can be configured to play a certain sound when the event occurs. These features can be used simply to make using Windows more enjoyable for average users, but to a sight-impaired user, they can be vital tools.

Windows XP provides Windows Media Player to play audio CDs as well as other multimedia types. Some people also install third-party media players with additional features, such as built-in codecs. In this lab, you experiment with Windows audio capabilities and use Nullsoft Winamp, a third-party sound application.

ESTIMATED COMPLETION TIME: 40 minutes

 Activity

Follow these steps to control which sounds play for certain Windows events:

Notes

Refer to Lab 9.1 for a reminder on how to adjust the volume level in Windows.

1. Open Control Panel, click **Sounds, Speech, and Audio Devices,** and then click **Sounds and Audio Devices.** The Sounds and Audio Devices Properties dialog box opens. Click the **Sounds** tab, and scroll down the Program events list box; note that each event with a speaker icon has a sound assigned that plays when the event occurs, as shown in Figure 9-10.

Figure 9-10 A speaker icon indicates which events have sounds associated with them

2. Fill in the following chart by clicking each event in the table and writing down the sound associated with it. (The sound file associated with the selected event is displayed in the Sounds text box.) Also, note that not all Windows events are assigned a sound.

Event	Sound name
Critical Stop	
Exit Windows	
Empty Recycle Bin	

3. Click **Start Windows** in the Program events list box, and then click the **Play sound** button (to the left of the Browse button). The Windows XP Startup sound plays. If you don't hear the sound, check your volume levels and make sure the volume is not muted.

4. In the Sounds drop-down list, select and play several different sounds for Start Windows until you find one you like better than the Windows default. Click the **Save As** button at the top, type **Custom** in the dialog box that opens, and click **OK** to save the new settings. (You could also apply the Windows Default scheme by selecting it in the Sound scheme drop-down list.)

5. Click **OK** to apply and save the sound properties. To test the new sound, restart Windows and log on to the same account.

6. After you have verified that the new sound plays, repeat the process and return the sound to the original settings.

Follow these steps to play an audio CD with Windows Media Player:

1. Insert the audio disc in the CD-ROM drive. In the Audio CD dialog box that opens, click **Play Audio CD using Windows Media Player**, and then click **OK** to close the dialog box.

2. Windows Media Player should start and begin playing the CD automatically. Adjust the volume so that it's not distracting to others.

3. The right pane of Windows Media Player lists the tracks on the CD. The center section displays different images to accompany the audio output. Experiment with customizing this image by right-clicking this section and selecting another choice in the shortcut menu. List three of your favorite selections:

---

4. Windows Media Player has the standard set of control features you would expect with a CD player. At the left are a number of other features. Experiment with Windows Media Player and answer the following questions:

◢ Which feature changes the appearance of the entire Windows Media Player interface?

◢ What are some featured stations in Radio Tuner?

◢ What types of information are available via Media Guide?

Follow these steps to install Winamp and use it to play the audio CD. Bear in mind that new versions of software are released often, so these directions might differ slightly, depending on the latest release:

1. Open your Web browser, and go to **www.winamp.com**. Click the **Download Now!** icon, and download the default version of Winamp. What is the name of the file you found to download?

---

2. Open Windows Explorer, find your download location, and double-click the file you downloaded to launch Winamp Setup and begin the installation process. Winamp Setup is similar to other installation wizards you have used. Step through the installation, using default settings for everything. If you don't want to receive e-mail from Nullsoft, click the **Stop Bugging Me** check box if it appears on the information screen for Winamp Setup. When prompted, click **Run Winamp** to launch Winamp, which then downloads additional information in the Winamp browser.

3. Close Winamp and the Winamp browser. Remove the audio CD, and then insert it again. This time, when the Audio CD dialog box opens, click **Play Audio CD using Winamp**. Winamp starts again and begins playing your audio CD.

4. Experiment with Winamp to answer these questions:

◢ Does Winamp have the same basic features as Windows Media Player?

◢ What feature does Winamp have for customizing the sound tone?

▲ Name three popular music file types that Winamp supports:

_____

▲ Could you set up a playlist for playing files on your CD in an order you choose, instead of first to last? Explain your answer:

_____

_____

_____

REVIEW QUESTIONS

1. What Control Panel applet, and which tab in its Properties dialog box, do you use to change the sound that plays for an event?

_____

2. What feature of Windows Media Player enables you to listen to streaming audio content?

_____

3. What is the default sound played during Windows XP startup?

_____

4. Which audio player provided more features, and which was easier to use? Explain your answers:

_____

_____

_____

PCs on a Network

Labs included in this chapter:

- Lab 10.1: Install and Test an Ethernet NIC
- Lab 10.2: Inspect Cables
- Lab 10.3: Compare Options for a Home LAN
- Lab 10.4: Troubleshoot with TCP/IP Utilities
- Lab 10.5: Practice Solving Network Connectivity Problems
- Lab 10.6: Use AT Commands to Control a Modem
- Lab 10.7: Simulate Modem Problems

LAB 10.1 INSTALL AND TEST AN ETHERNET NIC

OBJECTIVES

The goal of this lab is to install and configure an Ethernet network interface card (NIC). After completing this lab, you will be able to:

◢ Remove a NIC (and network protocols, if necessary)

◢ Install a NIC (and network protocols, if necessary)

◢ Perform a loopback test

MATERIALS REQUIRED

This lab requires the following:

◢ Windows 2000/XP operating system or Windows 98 with no modem or dial-up networking installed

◢ A NIC and drivers

◢ Windows installation CD or installation files

◢ A PC toolkit with antistatic ground strap

◢ A crossover cable

◢ A workgroup partner

LAB PREPARATION

Before the lab begins, the instructor or lab assistant needs to do the following:

◢ Verify that Windows starts with no errors.

◢ Provide each student with access to the Windows installation files, if needed.

ACTIVITY BACKGROUND

A computer connects to a wired network through a network interface card (NIC). In this lab, you install a NIC, configure necessary network settings, and verify that the NIC is functioning correctly. Working with a partner, you create a simple network of two PCs. By default, Windows 98 doesn't install network protocols needed to support a network, but Windows 2000/XP has these components installed, which makes installing a NIC much simpler in these operating systems.

ESTIMATED COMPLETION TIME: 30 minutes

 Activity

In Windows 2000/XP, follow these steps to install and configure your NIC:

1. Physically install your NIC as you would other expansion cards. If you need a refresher on the process, review Lab 9.1.

2. Boot the system. The Found New Hardware Wizard detects the NIC and begins the driver installation process. In some cases, Windows XP doesn't allow using non-Microsoft drivers. If this option is available, however, click **Have Disk** and provide the manufacturer's drivers for the NIC. Reboot if prompted to do so.

Next, you give the computer an IP address, a computer name, and a workgroup name as shown in the following chart. Write your name and your partner's name in the chart, and then follow these steps to assign an IP address to the computer:

 Notes

If you want to force Windows XP to use manufacturers' drivers, run the setup program on the CD or floppy disk that comes bundled with the NIC *before* you physically install the NIC. After you boot with the new card installed, Windows then finds the already installed manufacturers' drivers and uses them.

Your names:		
IP address:	192.168.1.1	192.168.1.2
Computer name:	Lab 1	Lab 2
Workgroup name:	NIC Lab	NIC Lab

1. Right-click **My Network Places** and click **Properties** in the shortcut menu. The Network Connections window appears.

2. Right-click **Local Area Connection** and click **Properties** in the shortcut menu. The Local Area Connection Properties dialog box opens.

3. In the list of connection items, click **Internet Protocol (TCP/IP)**, and then click the **Properties** button. The Internet Protocol (TCP/IP) Properties dialog box opens. Click **Use the following IP address** and enter your IP address (192.168.1.1 or 192.168.1.2) and subnet mask (255.255.255.0). Click **OK** twice to close all open windows.

Next, you assign a computer name and workgroup name to your computer:

1. Right-click **My Computer** and click **Properties** in the shortcut menu. The System Properties dialog box opens.

2. In Windows XP, click the **Computer Name** tab, and then click the **Change** button. The Computer Name Changes dialog box opens (see Figure 10-1). In Windows 2000, click the **Network Identification** tab, and then click the **Properties** button. The Identification Changes dialog box opens.

Figure 10-1   Assigning a host name to a computer on a network

3. Enter the computer name (**Lab 1** in the example shown in Figure 10-1). Each computer name must be unique within a workgroup or domain.

4. Click **Workgroup** and enter the name of the workgroup (**NIC Lab** in this example).

5. Click **OK** twice to close all open windows. Restart your computer when prompted for changes to take effect.

For Windows 98, if your computer doesn't already have a NIC installed, skip to the next set of steps. Otherwise, follow these steps on your Windows 98 computer to remove the computer's networking components:

1. Right-click the **Network Neighborhood** icon and click **Properties** in the shortcut menu. The Network Properties dialog box opens.

2. If necessary, click the **Configuration** tab, click **Client for Microsoft Networks**, and then click **Properties**. The Client for Microsoft Networks Properties dialog box opens.

3. In the General section, make sure the **Log on to Windows NT domain** check box is not selected, and then click **OK** to close the Client for Microsoft Networks Properties dialog box. Close the Network Properties dialog box and reboot when prompted.

4. After the computer has rebooted, open the Network Properties dialog box again. If necessary, click the **Configuration** tab, click your NIC (indicated by an adapter symbol), and then click **Remove**. The NIC and any protocol associated with it are uninstalled; Client for Microsoft Networks is also uninstalled.

5. Click **OK** to close the Network Properties dialog box. You might see a message stating that the network is incomplete.

6. Click **Yes** to continue. When you're prompted to restart your computer, click **No**.

7. Shut down your computer, but do not reboot.

8. Remove your computer's NIC, or if your instructor directs you to do so, remove the network cable but leave the NIC in place.

In Windows 98, follow these steps to install and configure your NIC:

1. If your NIC isn't installed, physically install it as you would other expansion cards. If you need a refresher on the process, review Lab 9.1.

2. Boot the system. The Add New Hardware Wizard detects the NIC and begins the driver installation process. Step through the Add New Hardware Wizard as in previous labs. Reboot when prompted.

3. The Network Neighborhood icon is displayed on the desktop again. Right-click the **Network Neighborhood** icon and then click **Properties**. The Network Properties dialog box opens.

4. Click the **Configuration** tab, examine the installed network components that are listed, and record them here:

_____

_____

_____

_____

_____

5. Verify that your NIC is in the list and that TCP/IP is installed and bound to the NIC, as indicated by an item that includes TCP/IP with an arrow that points to the name of your NIC. Click this item and then click **Properties**. The TCP/IP dialog box opens.

6. Click the **IP Address** tab, if necessary, and then click the **Specify an IP Address** option button.

7. Next, you configure the network connection. You and your partner need an IP address, a computer name, and a workgroup name, which are listed in the following chart. Write your name and your partner's name in the chart.

Your names:		
IP address:	192.168.1.1	192.168.1.2
Computer name:	Lab 1	Lab 2
Workgroup name:	NIC Lab	NIC Lab

8. In the IP Address text box of the TCP/IP Properties dialog box, type **192.168.1.1** or **192.168.1.2**. (Your lab partner should use one and you the other.) In the Subnet Mask text box, type **255.255.255.0**. (Both you and your partner should enter this information.) Note that it's possible for a server (called a DHCP server) to assign these two values that enable TCP/IP communications, but in this lab, you don't assume this server is available.

9. Click **OK** to close the TCP/IP dialog box.

10. To identify each computer on the network, click the **Identification** tab in the Network Properties dialog box. Replace the computer name in the Computer Name text box with **Lab 1** or **Lab 2**. (Again, your partner should use one of these names while you use the other.) In the Workgroup text box, type **NIC Lab**. Although it's not necessary, you can type a description for your computer if you want. When you're browsing the network, this description is displayed in the computer's Properties dialog box (under the Comment heading). This description can help users determine what resources might be available on the computer. What description, if any, did you enter?

_____

11. Click **OK** to close the Network Properties dialog box and save your settings. Supply the Windows 98 CD or the location of the installation files, if prompted. If you see a message stating that a file being copied is older than the current file, click **Yes** to keep the current file. (This is usually the best practice, unless you suspect the newer file has been the source of an existing problem.)

12. Click **Yes** when prompted to restart the computer.

In Windows 2000/XP or Windows 98, follow these steps to test your NIC:

1. Open a command prompt window.

2. Type **ping 127.0.0.1** and press **Enter**. Ping is a TCP/IP utility used to test whether an address can be reached and is able to respond. Any 127.x.x.x address is a loopback address, which is essentially a stand-in for your computer's own address. When you use a loopback address in a ping test, the Ping utility sends packets to your local computer's NIC, thereby allowing you to verify that your computer's NIC has a functioning TCP/IP connection. If your computer is connected to a printer, take a screen shot of the results of the loopback Ping command and print it.

3. Examine the results of the loopback test and answer these questions:

◢ How many bytes were sent in each packet?

_____

◢ How many packets were sent with one Ping command?

_____

◢ How many responses were received from one Ping command?

_____

◢ Were any packets lost?

_____

In Windows 2000/XP, use the Ipconfig utility to verify your IP configuration. Do the following to check your NIC's configuration:

1. At the command prompt, type **ipconfig /all |more** and press **Enter**. An IP configuration report is displayed one screen at a time. If necessary, press **Enter** to see each new line. Answer the following:

◢ Is the configuration the same information you configured originally?

_____

◢ What is the physical address (MAC address) of your NIC?

_____

In Windows 98, use the Winipcfg utility to verify your IP configuration. Do the following to check your NIC's configuration:

1. At the command prompt, type **winipcfg** and press **Enter**.
2. Click your NIC in the drop-down list and examine your IP configuration. Answer the following:

◢ Is the configuration the same information you configured originally?

_____

◢ What is the MAC address of your NIC?

_____

In Windows 2000/XP or Windows 98, another way to test an NIC is to use its assigned IP address in a ping test:

1. Use the Ping command with the IP address you assigned to your computer. The results should be similar or identical to the loopback test results, except for the address listed in the Ping results.
2. Now ping your partner's IP address. Describe what happened to the request:

_____

_____

_____

Next, you connect the two PCs with the crossover cable, and then test your network:

1. Close the command prompt window, and shut down both computers.

2. Connect one end of the crossover cable to the NIC on your partner's computer and the other end to the NIC on your computer.

3. Reboot the computers, and open a command prompt window.

4. Ping your partner's IP address. If your computer is connected to a printer, take and print a screen shot of the results. How do these results differ from your earlier attempt to ping your partner's IP address?

_____

_____

REVIEW QUESTIONS

1. Where do you configure network adapters and protocols?

_____

2. What two text boxes are used to identify a computer on a workgroup?

_____

_____

3. Other than the IP address, what information is required for TCP/IP communication?

_____

4. What are two ways to use the Ping utility to test a local computer's NIC?

_____

_____

5. What conclusion should you draw from a loopback test that reports dropped packets or an unreachable host?

_____

_____

LAB 10.2 INSPECT CABLES

OBJECTIVES

The goal of this lab is to help you visually inspect a set of cables and use a multimeter to test them. After completing this lab, you will be able to:

◢ Identify two Cat 5 wiring systems

◢ Test cables with a multimeter

◢ Draw pin-outs for cable connectors

◢ Determine whether a cable is a patch cable (also known as a straight-through cable) or a crossover cable

◢ Visually inspect cables and connectors

MATERIALS REQUIRED

This lab requires the following:

◢ A variety of cables, including a patch cable and a crossover cable

◢ A multimeter

◢ Internet access

LAB PREPARATION

Before the lab begins, the instructor or lab assistant needs to do the following:

◢ Verify that Internet access is available.

ACTIVITY BACKGROUND

After you narrow down a problem to physical connectivity, you must inspect the connections to verify that they aren't loose. If you eliminate that possibility, you can assume the cable is the problem. In this lab, you physically inspect cables and the connector, and then test the cable for continuity and pin-outs using a multimeter.

ESTIMATED COMPLETION TIME: 45 minutes

 Activity

1. Open your browser, and go to **www.atcomservices.com/highlights/cat5notes.htm**. You can also search the Internet for information about a patch cable diagram, a crossover cable diagram, and a Cat 5 wiring diagram. List the two standards for Cat 5 wiring schemes. What Web site did you use?

2. For both wiring schemes, print a wiring diagram for a patch cable and a crossover cable.

Follow these steps to visually inspect cables:

1. Examine the length of the cable for obvious damage, such as a cut or abrasion in the outer sleeve with further damage to the twisted pairs inside. A completely cut strand is an obvious problem, but the conductor inside the cable might be broken even if the insulator is intact. Any visible copper is an indication you need a new cable.

2. Inspect the RJ-45 connectors. In particular, look for exposed twisted pairs between the clear plastic connector and the cable sleeve. This indicates that the cable was assembled improperly or excessive force was used when pulling on the cable. The cable sleeve should be crimped inside the RJ-45 connector. Sometimes you can identify a nonconforming wiring scheme by noting the color of the insulation through the clear connector, but you should check the cable with a multimeter to verify its condition.

3. Next, verify that the retaining clip on the connector is present. When an assembled cable is pulled, this clip often snags on carpet or other cables and breaks off. This results in a connector that's likely to become loose or fall out of the jack. Worse still, this connection might be intermittent. Some cables have hooded guards to prevent the clip from snagging when pulled, but these guards can cause problems when seating the connector in the jack if the guard has slid too far toward the end of the cable.

4. Test your cables with a multimeter, and fill in Table 10-1.

	Pin #	End A		End B		Questions About the Cable
		Insulator color	Pin tied to pin at End B	Insulator color	Pin tied to pin at End A	Is the cable good or bad?
Cable 1	1					
	2					Wired with what scheme?
	3					
	4					
	5					Is the cable a
	6					crossover or
	7					patch cable?
	8					
	Pin #	Insulator color	Pin tied to pin at End B	Insulator color	Pin tied to pin at End A	Is the cable good or bad?
Cable 2	1					
	2					Wired with what scheme?
	3					
	4					
	5					Is the cable a
	6					crossover or
	7					patch cable?
	8					
	Pin #	Insulator color	Pin tied to pin at End B	Insulator color	Pin tied to pin at End A	Is the cable good or bad?
Cable 3	1					
	2					Wired with what scheme?
	3					
	4					
	5					Is the cable a
	6					crossover or
	7					patch cable?
	8					

Table 10-1   Pin connections for selected cables

REVIEW QUESTIONS

1. If you can see a copper conductor in a cable, what should you do with the cable?

_____

2. What type of connector is used with Cat 5 cable?

_____

3. Based on your research, what cabling scheme is more common?

_____

4. On a patch cable, pin 3 on one end connects to pin _____ on the opposite end of the cable.

5. On a crossover cable, pin 2 on one end connects to pin _____ on the other end of the cable.

LAB 10.3 COMPARE OPTIONS FOR A HOME LAN

OBJECTIVES

The goal of this lab is to help you research the costs and capabilities of wired and wireless home LANs. After completing this lab, you will be able to:

◢ Research wired and wireless Ethernet

◢ Research 802.11 standards

◢ Identify the strengths and weaknesses of each option

MATERIALS REQUIRED

This lab requires the following:

◢ Internet access

LAB PREPARATION

Before the lab begins, the instructor or lab assistant needs to do the following:

◢ Verify that Internet access is available.

ACTIVITY BACKGROUND

As the price of equipment and computers fall, installing a home LAN has become increasingly popular. In this lab, you research wired and wireless Ethernet and determine which option is best in certain situations.

ESTIMATED COMPLETION TIME: 30 minutes

 Activity

Use your favorite search site to investigate and answer the following questions about wireless LAN standards:

1. List the 802.x standards for specifying wireless networks:

_____

2. What industry name is associated with 802.11b?

_____

3. What is the simplest form of a wireless network? What devices are needed to create this type of network, and what mode does this type of network use?

_____

_____

_____

4. What device connects wireless users to a wired network?

_____

5. What standard speeds are supported by 802.11x?

_____

_____

_____

6. What kind of encryption is used with 802.11b?

_____

7. Give four examples of devices (besides PCs) that will probably eventually run on wireless LANs:

_____

_____

_____

_____

8. What does the acronym Wi-Fi stand for?

_____

9. What is the approximate maximum range for 802.11b technology?

_____

10. What inherent feature of 802.11b, seen as a major problem by businesses, might affect your decision to use Wi-Fi at home?

_____

_____

11. In the context of how they physically interface with a computer, what are the three basic types of wireless adapters?

_____

_____

_____

12. What mode requires a wireless access point?

_____

13. How many 802.11b devices can be used at one time with a single access point?

_____

14. What radio band and speed does 802.11a use?

_____

15. Which standard offers a faster transfer rate: 802.11a or 802.11b? List their transfer rates:

_____

_____

16. List the components required to connect four PCs in ad hoc mode and include their prices. List the device and extra expense needed to connect the same four PCs to a cable modem:

_____

_____

_____

_____

Use the Internet to research and answer these questions on an Ethernet home LAN:

1. What is the maximum cable length for a 100BaseT Ethernet LAN?

_____

2. Must you use a hub to connect three PCs? Two PCs? Explain:

_____

_____

_____

3. What type of cabling is typically used for 100BaseT?

_____

4. Are special tools required when working with Cat 5 cabling to create patch or crossover cables?

_____

5. What feature of Windows 2000/XP or Windows 98 allows more than one computer to share a connection to the Internet?

_____

6. What type of cable connector is used for fast Ethernet?

_____

7. What standard supports a speed of 100 Mbps using two sets of Cat 3 cable?

_____

8. What is the name for a cable that connects a computer to a hub?

_____

9. Suppose you have a LAN consisting of a 100BaseT hub, two computers with 10BaseT NICs, and a computer with a 10/100BaseT NIC. At what speed would this LAN operate? Why?

_____

_____

10. Given a budget of $200 to connect five computers, would you choose 100BaseT or 10BaseT? Explain your choice:

_____

_____

_____

11. What is the name for a cable that connects a hub to a hub?

_____

12. In theory, if a file is transferred in 4.5 seconds on a fast Ethernet LAN, how long would the same file transfer take on a 10BaseT LAN?

_____

13. Give three examples of ways to physically interface a NIC to a computer:

_____

_____

_____

14. What device can you use to connect two or more PCs to a single cable modem?

_____

15. List the components, including cables, required to connect four PCs. Include the price of each component. List the changes and additional devices required to connect all four PCs to a cable modem and provide a hardware firewall:

_____

_____

_____

_____

_____

REVIEW QUESTIONS

1. Based on your research, does wireless or 100BaseT offer the best performance for the money?

_____

_____

2. Is wireless or 100BaseT easier to configure in a home? Why?

_____

_____

3. What factors dictate the transmission range of 802.11x?

_____

_____

_____

4. What determines the speed of a LAN that consists of both 10 Mbps and 100 Mbps devices?

_____

_____

5. Does a wired or wireless LAN offer better security?

_____

6. Could you combine a wireless and wired LAN in the same home? Why would you?

_____

_____

_____

LAB 10.4 TROUBLESHOOT WITH TCP/IP UTILITIES

OBJECTIVES

The goal of this lab is to help you use Windows 2000/XP TCP/IP utilities to troubleshoot connectivity problems. After completing this lab, you will be able to:

- ⊿ Use the Ipconfig utility
- ⊿ Use the Ping utility
- ⊿ Use the Tracert utility
- ⊿ Identify the point at which your packets will no longer travel

MATERIALS REQUIRED

This lab requires the following:

- ⊿ Windows 2000/XP operating system
- ⊿ A DHCP server
- ⊿ Internet access

LAB PREPARATION

Before the lab begins, the instructor or lab assistant needs to do the following:

- ⊿ Verify that Windows starts with no errors.
- ⊿ Verify that Internet access is available.

ACTIVITY BACKGROUND

Perhaps nothing frustrates users more than a suddenly unavailable network connection. As a PC technician, you might be asked to restore these connections, and sometimes you even have to deal with several failed connections at one time. When troubleshooting network connections, it helps to know whether many users in one area of a network are having the same connection problem. That information can help you narrow down the source of the problem. After you have an idea of what machine is causing the problem, you can use a few TCP/IP utilities to test your theory without physically checking the system. In this lab, you learn to use TCP/IP utilities to isolate connection problems.

ESTIMATED COMPLETION TIME: 30 minutes

 Activity

Follow these steps to display IP settings in Windows 2000/XP:

1. Right-click **My Network Places** and click **Properties** in the shortcut menu. In, Windows XP, the Network Connections window opens; in Windows 2000, the Network and Dial-up Connections window opens.

2. Right-click **Local Area Connection** and click **Properties** in the shortcut menu. The Local Area Connection Properties dialog box opens.

3. Click **Internet Protocol (TCP/IP)**, and then click the **Properties** button. When the Internet Protocol (TCP/IP) dialog box opens, notice the different options. What two ways can you set up the IP configuration?

_____

_____

4. Verify that **Obtain an IP address automatically** is selected.

5. Click **OK** to close the Internet Protocol (TCP/IP) dialog box, and then close the Local Area Connection Properties dialog box. Close the Network and Dialup Connections window (Windows 2000) or the Network Connections window (Windows XP).

Follow these steps to adjust the command prompt so that you can view more information at a time:

1. Open a command prompt window.

2. Right-click the title bar of the command prompt window and click **Properties** in the shortcut menu. The Command Prompt Properties dialog box opens.

3. Click the **Layout** tab, if necessary. In the Screen Buffer Size section, type **150** for width and **300** for height. These settings enable you to scroll in the command prompt window and view the last 300 lines of 150 characters. If you want, you can adjust settings in the Window Size section, but generally, it's best to adjust a command prompt window after it opens so that you don't make the window too large for your monitor's display settings. Click **OK** to save the settings.

4. The Apply Properties to Shortcut dialog box opens. To specify that you want to apply the properties every time you open a command prompt window, click **Modify the shortcut that started this window**, and then click **OK**.

Follow these steps to learn how to display IP information from the command line:

1. Open a command prompt window.

2. Type **ipconfig** and press **Enter**. List the three types of information that are displayed:

_____

_____

_____

3. To get more information about your IP settings, type **ipconfig /all** and press **Enter**. Take a screen shot of these results, print the screen shot, and answer these questions:

◢ What is the purpose of DHCP?

_____

_____

◢ What is the address of the DHCP server?

_____

4. Because your system is using DHCP to obtain an IP address, type **ipconfig /renew** and press **Enter**. The command prompt window again displays IP information.

5. Again, type **ipconfig /all** and press **Enter**. Compare the current IP address lease information to the information in the screen shot. What information changed?

_____

_____

6. Next, type **ipconfig /release** and press **Enter**. What message is displayed? What implications do you predict this command will have on connectivity?

_____

_____

7. Using your screen shot as a reference, attempt to ping the DHCP server and the DNS server. What are the results?

_____

_____

8. Type **ipconfig** and press **Enter**. Note that your adapter has no IP address and no subnet mask. These two parameters are necessary to communicate with TCP/IP.

9. To get an IP address lease again, type **ipconfig /renew** and press **Enter**. New IP information, which might be the same address as before, is assigned.

10. Find your new IP address lease information. List the command you used to find this information and the lease information:

_____

_____

_____

11. In Windows XP, you can use the Network Connections window to release and renew the IP address. Right-click **My Network Places** and click **Properties** in the shortcut menu. The Network Connections window opens. Click the network connection you want to repair, and then click **Repair this connection**. You can also right-click the network connection you want to repair and click Repair in the shortcut menu.

If you're connected to the Internet, follow these steps to determine what route your packets take to reach an Internet address:

1. Open a command prompt window.

2. Type **tracert** followed by a single space and then a domain name on the Internet (for example, **tracert www.yahoo.com**). Press **Enter**.

3. The DNS server resolves the domain name to an IP address, and that address is listed, indicating you can reach at least one DNS server. This information tells you that your packets are traveling at least that far. Next, each hop (or router your packet passed through) is listed with the time in milliseconds the packet took to reach its destination. How many hops did the packet take to reach the domain you specified?

_____

4. Now use the Tracert command with an illegal name, such as **www.mydomain.c**. What are the results of this command?

_____

When troubleshooting connectivity problems, always consider the number of users experiencing the problem. If many users have similar difficulties, it's unlikely the problem lies with any one user's computer. Therefore, you can probably eliminate the need to run extensive local tests on each computer. Instead, you can examine a device that all computers commonly use.

As a general rule, when troubleshooting, you should start by examining devices close to the computer exhibiting problems and then move farther away. The following steps show you how to apply this principle by examining the local computer first, and then moving outward to other devices on the network.

1. Verify that the computer is physically connected (that both ends of the cable are connected).

2. Verify that the NIC is installed and TCP/IP is bound to the NIC.

3. Perform a loopback test to verify that the NIC is functioning correctly.

4. Check the IP settings with the **ipconfig /all** command. Verify that an IP address is assigned.

5. Ping other computers on the local network. If you get no response, begin by examining a hub or punchdown panel (a panel where cables convene before connecting to a hub).

6. If you can ping other computers on the local network, ping the default gateway, which is the first stop for transmissions being sent to addresses that aren't on the local network.

7. Continue troubleshooting connections, beginning with nearby devices and working outward until you discover an IP address that returns no response. That device will be the source of the trouble.

8. If the device is under your supervision, take the necessary steps to repair it. If the device is out of your control, contact the appropriate administrator.

REVIEW QUESTIONS

1. Name four additional pieces of information that the Ipconfig command with the /all switch provides that the Ipconfig command alone does not:

_____

_____

_____

_____

2. What type of server resolves a domain name to an IP address?

_____

3. In Windows 2000/XP, what command discards the IP address?

_____

4. What command do you use to determine whether you can reach another computer on the local network? Would this command work if the default gateway were down?

_____

_____

5. If many users suddenly encountered connection problems, would you suspect problems with their local computers or problems with other devices on the network? Explain:

_____

_____

_____

LAB 10.5 PRACTICE SOLVING NETWORK CONNECTIVITY PROBLEMS

OBJECTIVES

The goal of this lab is to troubleshoot and remedy common network connectivity problems. After completing this lab, you will be able to:

◢ Diagnose and solve connectivity problems

◢ Document the process

MATERIALS REQUIRED

This lab requires the following:

◢ Windows 2000/XP or Windows 98 operating system

◢ A PC connected to a network and to the Internet

◢ Windows installation CD or installation files

◢ A PC toolkit with antistatic ground strap

◢ A workgroup partner

LAB PREPARATION

Before the lab begins, the instructor or lab assistant needs to do the following:

◢ Verify that Windows starts with no errors.

◢ Provide each student with access to the Windows installation files, if needed.

ACTIVITY BACKGROUND

To a casual user, Internet and network connections can be confusing. When users have a connectivity problem, they usually have no idea how to remedy the situation. In this lab, you introduce and solve common connectivity problems.

ESTIMATED COMPLETION TIME: 30 minutes

Activity

1. Verify that your network is working correctly by browsing the network and connecting to a Web site.

2. Do one of the following:

    ◢ Change your PC's IP address.

    ◢ Change your PC's subnet mask.

    ◢ Remove your PC's network cable.

▲ Remove TCP/IP from your PC.

▲ Remove your PC's adapter in the Network Properties dialog box.

▲ Unseat or remove your PC's NIC, but leave it installed in the Network Properties dialog box.

▲ Disable your PC's NIC in Device Manager.

▲ Release your PC's IP address (if DHCP is enabled).

3. Swap PCs with your partner and troubleshoot your partner's PC.

4. On a separate sheet of paper, answer these questions about the problem you solved:

   ▲ What is the initial symptom of the problem as user might describe it?

   _____

   _____

   ▲ What steps did you take to discover the source of the problem?

   _____

   _____

   _____

   _____

   ▲ What steps did you take to solve the problem?

   _____

   _____

   _____

   _____

5. Repeat Steps 1 through 4 until you and your partner have used all the options listed in Step 2. Be sure to answer the questions in Step 4 for each troubleshooting situation.

REVIEW QUESTIONS

1. What problem could you solve by issuing only one command? What was the command you used?

   _____

   _____

2. Which problem (or problems) forced you to reboot the computer after repairing it?

   _____

   _____

   _____

   _____

3. What two pieces of information are necessary for TCP/IP communication on the local network?

_____

4. When using Windows 98, what problem (or problems) caused the Network Neighborhood icon to disappear?

_____

5. What TCP/IP utility was the most useful, in your opinion, for troubleshooting these problems? Why?

_____

_____

6. What situation doesn't necessarily cause a communication problem if a network protocol other than TCP/IP (such as NetBEUI) is installed on the local computer and other computers on the network?

_____

_____

LAB 10.6 USE AT COMMANDS TO CONTROL A MODEM

OBJECTIVES

The goal of this lab is to help you use AT commands to initiate and receive modem calls. After completing this lab, you will be able to:

▲ Install HyperTerminal

▲ Use several modem commands to control a HyperTerminal session, dial a number, receive a call, and test your modem

MATERIALS REQUIRED

This lab requires the following:

▲ Windows 2000/XP or Windows 9x operating system

▲ Windows installation CD or installation files

▲ Access to a phone line that can send and receive calls

▲ The line's telephone number

▲ A lab partner to whom you can make modem calls

Notes

You might not have access to a phone line in a classroom lab environment. In this case, this lab might have to be completed at home.

LAB PREPARATION

Before the lab begins, the instructor or lab assistant needs to do the following:

▲ Verify that Windows starts with no errors.

▲ Verify that the Internet connection has been configured for HyperTerminal.

▲ Provide each student with access to the Windows installation files, if needed.

ACTIVITY BACKGROUND

The AT command set is used for controlling modems. When a modem receives commands, each command line is prefaced with AT for "attention." A modem stays in command mode any time it's not connected to another modem. When a modem is in command mode and bits and bytes are sent to it from a PC, the modem interprets the bytes as commands to be followed instead of data to be sent over a phone line. It leaves command mode when it receives an incoming call or dials out, and returns to command mode when a call is completed or the computer sends a special escape sequence. A modem responds to a command with "OK" or gives the results after carrying out the command. With AT commands, you can control almost every aspect of modem behavior; these commands are also useful in troubleshooting modem hardware and connections. Table 10-2 lists a few of the core AT commands that most modems understand.

You can type a command from a communications software window to run immediately or enter a command from a dialog box for the modem configuration to run later when the modem makes a call. HyperTerminal is an excellent utility you can use to make a quick and easy phone call from a Windows PC. HyperTerminal is installed by default in Windows 2000/XP but isn't installed automatically in Windows 9x. By using HyperTerminal, you can test a newly installed modem with AT commands. In this lab, you use AT commands to make and receive calls and to adjust modem settings.

ESTIMATED COMPLETION TIME: 45 minutes

 Activity

In Windows 9x, follow these steps to install HyperTerminal:

1. Open Control Panel, double-click the **Add/Remove Programs** icon, and then click the **Windows Setup** tab.

2. In the Components list box, double-click the **Communications** group. The Communications dialog box opens.

3. Click the **HyperTerminal** check box, and then click **OK**. The Communications dialog box closes, and you return to the Add/Remove Programs Properties dialog box.

4. Click **OK** to close the Add/Remove Programs Properties dialog box. Supply Windows installation files as necessary.

In Windows 9x and Windows 2000/XP, follow these steps to use AT commands in HyperTerminal:

1. Click **Start**, point to **All Programs** (in Windows 2000 and 9x, **Programs**), point to **Accessories**, point to **Communications**, and then click **HyperTerminal**. If a message box opens, asking whether you want to make HyperTerminal the default Telnet program, click **Yes.**

2. HyperTerminal starts, with the Connection Description dialog box open.

3. Type **Test 1** in the Name text box, and then click **OK**. The Connect To dialog box opens.

4. Click your modem in the drop-down list, and then click **Cancel** to close the Connect To dialog box. The Connect To dialog box closes, and the main HyperTerminal window is active.

5. Click in a blank area of the HyperTerminal window to position the cursor.

At this point, if you start typing AT commands, the commands run but you might not be able to see them as you type in the HyperTerminal window. To be able to see AT commands as you type them

Command	Description	Possible Values
AT	Get the modem's attention.	AT (Modem should respond with OK.)
*70	Disable call waiting.	ATDT*70,4045551212
+++	Escape sequence: Tells the modem to return to command mode. You should pause at least 1 second before you start typing the sequence. After you end the sequence, wait another second before you send another command. Don't begin this command with AT.	+++ (Follow each + with a short pause. Use this command when trying to unlock a hung modem; don't begin the command with AT.)
On	Go online: Tells the modem to return to online data mode. This is the reverse command for the escape sequence.	ATO0 (Return online.) ATO1 (Return online and retrain; perform training or handshaking again with the remote system.)
A/	Repeat last command: Repeat the last command the modem performed. Don't begin the command with AT, but do follow it with Enter. Useful when redialing a busy number.	
In	Identification: Instructs the modem to return to product identification information.	ATI0 (Return the product code.) ATI3 (Return the modem ROM version.)
Zn	Reset: Instructs the modem to reset and restore the configuration to what was defined at power on.	ATZ0 (Reset and return to user profile 0.) ATZ1 (Reset and return to user profile 1.)
&F	Factory default: Instructs the modem to reload the factory default profile. In most cases, use this command to reset the modem instead of using the Z command.	AT&F (This method is preferred to ATZ when trying to solve a modem problem.)
A	Answer the phone: Instructs the modem to answer the phone, transmit the answer tone, and wait for a carrier from the remote modem.	
Dn	Dial: Tells the modem to dial a number. Several parameters can be added to this command, as shown in the Possible Values column.	ATD5551212 (Dial the given number.) ATDD (Pause the dialing.) ATDP (Use pulse dialing.) ATDT (Use tone dialing.) ATDW (Wait for dial tone.) ATD& (Wait for the credit-card dialing tone before continuing with the remaining dial string.)
Hn	Hang up: Tells the modem to hang up.	ATH0 (Hang up.) ATH1 (Hang up and enter command mode.)
Mn	Speaker control: Instructs the modem on how to use the speaker.	ATM0 (Speaker always off.) ATM1 (Speaker on until carrier detect.) ATM2 (Speaker always on.)
Ln	Loudness: Sets the loudness of the modem's speaker.	ATL1 (Set to low volume.) ATL2 (Set to medium volume.) ATL3 (Set to high volume.)
Xn	Response: Tells the modem how to respond to a dial tone and busy signal.	ATX0 (Blind dialing; the modem doesn't need to hear the dial tone and won't hear a busy signal.) ATX4 (Default value; modem must first hear the dial tone, and it responds to a busy signal.)

Table 10-2   AT commands for Hayes-compatible modems

(if displaying commands hasn't already been enabled), you must begin with the AT echo command, ATE1. To practice using this command, follow these steps:

1. Type **ATE1** and press **Enter**. The modem's response (OK) appears under the cursor. Although you couldn't see the command ATE1 as you typed it, from now on, you should be able to see commands as you type.

2. Type **ATE0** and press **Enter**. (Be sure to type a zero, not the letter "O.") The command ATE0 appears on the screen as you type. OK appears below ATE0 after you press Enter.

3. Type **AT** and press **Enter**. The AT command issued by itself should always return an OK response, and, in fact, OK does appear on the screen. However, this time the command you typed is not displayed on the screen. Which command caused the text not to appear as you typed (that is, caused the text not to "echo")?

_____

4. Issue the ATE1 command again to echo the commands as you type.

Now that you know how to make commands appear as you type, you're ready to test your modem by using HyperTerminal. Follow these steps:

1. To verify that a working phone line is connected to the modem, type **ATD** followed by your computer's telephone number (for example, ATD5551212) and press **Enter**. You should hear the modem dial. What message does HyperTerminal return?

_____

2. Type **ATL3**, press **Enter**, and then use the ATD command to dial your computer's number again.

   ◢ What difference do you notice from the first time you dialed the number?

   _____

   _____

   ◢ What does the L in the ATL command stand for?

   _____

3. You can also control HyperTerminal by using menu commands. Click **Call, Wait for a Call** from the HyperTerminal menu.

4. Give your lab partner your computer's number and have him or her dial and connect to your computer. What messages does HyperTerminal display on your computer?

   _____

   _____

   _____

5. Click the **Disconnect** button (the button with a phone handset over a phone cradle), shown in Figure 10-2 for Windows 9x. Your modem disconnects.

6. Type **AT&T1** and press **Enter**. HyperTerminal runs a local analog loop to make sure the modem is working correctly. Record the results:

   _____

Figure 10-2 The HyperTerminal window

7. To end the test, type **AT&T0** and press **Enter**. (Ending the test might take a few moments.)

8. Click the **Disconnect** button again.

9. If you begin testing a working modem with AT commands and the modem begins to exhibit problems, you can use the AT&F command to reset the modem to factory settings. Type **AT&F** and press **Enter**. The modem's default settings are restored.

10. To close HyperTerminal, click **File, Exit** from the menu. When asked if you want to disconnect, click **Yes**. When asked if you want to save the session, click **No**.

REVIEW QUESTIONS

1. What Windows application is commonly used for working with AT commands?

2. What command turns on text echo so that you can see what you're typing?

3. What command dials a number?

4. What command returns the modem to its default settings?

5. Look in Table 10-2 for additional AT commands. What AT commands not used in this lab would you find useful in debugging a modem?

_____

_____

_____

LAB 10.7 SIMULATE MODEM PROBLEMS

OBJECTIVES

The goal of this lab is to help you simulate, diagnose, and remedy common modem problems. After completing this lab, you will be able to:

◢ Diagnose problems with a modem

◢ Remedy problems with a modem

MATERIALS REQUIRED

This lab requires the following:

◢ Windows 2000/XP or Windows 9x operating system

◢ A modem installed in a PC and connected to a phone line

◢ A PC toolkit with antistatic ground strap

◢ Modem installation drivers

◢ Windows installation CD or installation files

◢ A standard phone

◢ A lab partner with whom you can swap PCs

LAB PREPARATION

Before the lab begins, the instructor or lab assistant needs to do the following:

◢ Verify that Windows starts with no errors.

◢ Provide each student with access to the Windows installation files, if needed.

ACTIVITY BACKGROUND

Dial-up connections are notoriously unreliable. One of the challenges of troubleshooting these connections is determining whether a dial-up failure is related to a problem with the modem or the phone line. In this lab, you diagnose and remedy common modem problems. Mastering these skills makes it easier for you to determine when the modem is the source of trouble in a dial-up connection.

ESTIMATED COMPLETION TIME: 90 minutes

 Activity

1. To verify that your modem is working, start HyperTerminal, dial any reliable phone number, and listen for the sound of the modem dialing and attempting to connect. (The actual connection isn't necessary at this point.) Disconnect the call and close HyperTerminal.

2. Sabotage your modem by introducing one of these problems:

   ⏴ If your modem has jumpers or DIP switches, record the original settings on the following lines, and then change the settings.

   _____

   _____

   ⏴ In BIOS or Device Manager, disable the modem's COM port.

   ⏴ Loosen the modem card in the expansion slot so that it doesn't make good contact.

   ⏴ Unplug the phone cord from the wall.

   ⏴ Change the port the phone line connects to on the back of the modem.

   ⏴ Uninstall the modem in Device Manager.

   ⏴ Change or disable the IRQ for the modem.

   ⏴ Using Device Manager, disable the modem in the current hardware configuration.

3. Swap PCs with your partner, and then troubleshoot and repair your partner's PC.

4. Answer these questions:

   ⏴ What is the initial symptom of a problem as a user would describe it?

   _____

   _____

   ⏴ How did you discover the source of the problem?

   _____

   _____

   _____

   _____

   ⏴ What did you do to solve the problem?

   _____

   _____

   _____

   _____

5. Introduce another problem from the list in Step 2, and swap again. Continue this process until you have introduced and remedied all the problems listed in Step 2.

REVIEW QUESTIONS

1. What was the easiest problem to diagnose and why?

   _____

   _____

2. Which problems aren't apparent in Device Manager but would result in no dial tone when dialing?

_____

_____

3. Did all the problems listed in Step 2 actually prevent the modem from working? Which (if any) did not?

_____

_____

4. Which problem prevented the modem from being displayed in its Properties dialog box?

_____

_____

5. What was the simplest way to determine whether there was definitely a dial tone?

_____

_____

6. Suppose a user says, "I can't dial out using my modem." List the first three things you would check, in the order you would check them:

_____

_____

_____

LAB 11.1 EXAMINE NOTEBOOK DOCUMENTATION

OBJECTIVES

The goal of this lab is to help you find documentation for a notebook on a manufacturer's Web site and become familiar with it. After completing this lab, you will be able to:

▲ Locate documentation for specific notebook computer models

▲ Download the documentation

▲ Use the documentation to find critical information

MATERIALS REQUIRED

This lab requires the following:

▲ Internet access

LAB PREPARATION

Before the lab begins, the instructor or lab assistant needs to do the following:

▲ Verify that Internet access is available.

ACTIVITY BACKGROUND

Notebooks are designed for portability, compactness, and energy conservation, and their designs are often highly proprietary. Therefore, establishing general procedures for supporting notebooks is more difficult than for desktop computers. Often, consulting the documentation for a particular model is necessary to get information on technical specifications and support procedures. In this lab, you locate and download documentation for two different notebook computers, and then use that documentation to answer questions about each model.

> **ESTIMATED COMPLETION TIME: 30 minutes**

 Activity

Follow these steps to locate and download documentation:

1. Choose two notebook manufacturers listed in Table 11-1, go to their Web sites, and select one model from each to research. List your two choices here:

_____

_____

Manufacturer	Web Site
Acer America	*http://global.acer.com*
ARM Computer	*www.armcomputer.com*
Compaq Computer	*www.hp.com*
Dell Computer	*www.dell.com*
Gateway	*www.gateway.com*
Hewlett-Packard	*www.hp.com*

Table 11-1 Notebook manufacturers

Manufacturer	Web Site
IBM	*www.ibm.com*
Micron PC	*www.buympc.com*
PC Notebook	*www.pcnotebook.com*
Sony	*www.sonystyle.com/vaio*
Toshiba America	*www.csd.toshiba.com*
WinBook	*www.winbook.com*

Table 11-1 Notebook manufacturers (continued)

2. In the Support section of each Web site, search for documentation on both models you chose and follow the directions to download it. Were you able to find documentation for both models? If not, list the models for which you were unable to find documentation. Try other models until you have located documentation for two.

_____

_____

3. Using the documentation you found, answer the following questions for your first model. If you can't answer a question because the information isn't included in the documentation, write "information unavailable."

▲ What type of processor does the notebook use and how much RAM is installed?

_____

▲ What operating system does the notebook support?

_____

▲ Could you download or save the documentation locally, or did you have to view it on the company's Web site?

_____

▲ Does the notebook offer Quick Launch keys for commonly used applications? If so, can you customize them? How? If they can't be customized, what buttons are offered, and which applications do they launch?

_____

_____

_____

▲ List the functions assigned to keys F1 through F4:

_____

_____

_____

◢ Does the notebook have a sleep or hibernation mode? If so, how do you activate it? How does activating this mode differ from shutting down the computer?

_____

_____

_____

◢ What other types of downloads are offered besides the manual?

_____

_____

◢ What type of optical storage (CD, CD-RW, DVD, and so forth) does the notebook offer?

_____

◢ What type of networking (modem, NIC, infrared port, wireless LAN port, and so forth) comes built in?

_____

_____

4. Using the documentation you found, answer the following questions for your second model. If you can't answer a question because the information isn't included in the documentation, write "information unavailable."

◢ What type of processor does the notebook use and how much RAM is installed?

_____

◢ What operating system does the notebook support?

_____

◢ Could you download or save the documentation locally, or did you have to view it on the company's Web site?

_____

◢ Does the notebook offer Quick Launch keys for commonly used applications? If so, can you customize them? How? If they can't be customized, what buttons are offered, and which applications do they launch?

_____

_____

_____

◢ List the functions assigned to keys F1 through F4:

_____

_____

▲ Does the notebook have a sleep or hibernation mode? If so, how do you activate it? How does activating this mode differ from shutting down the computer?

_____

_____

_____

▲ What other types of downloads are offered besides the manual?

_____

_____

▲ What type of optical storage (CD, CD-RW, DVD, and so forth) does the notebook offer?

_____

▲ What type of networking (modem, NIC, infrared port, wireless LAN port, and so forth) comes built in?

_____

_____

Alternate Activity

If you have access to a notebook computer, do the following:

1. Go to the manufacturer's Web site for your notebook computer and download the user manual, if available. List other downloads that are available:

   _____

   _____

   _____

2. From the list of available downloads, choose a device driver or system update for your notebook. Download and install it following the instructions on the site. List the driver or update and the steps you took to install it on your notebook:

   _____

   _____

   _____

   _____

REVIEW QUESTIONS

1. On a manufacturer's Web site, where do you usually find support and documentation information?

   _____

2. For which model was it easiest to find documentation? Which manufacturer site did you think was most user friendly and, in general, offered the best support?

   _____

   _____

3. Besides the questions you researched in the lab, what other type of information is available in the manuals you reviewed?

   _____

   _____

4. Of the notebooks you researched, which one would you purchase? Explain your answer:

   _____

   _____

LAB 11.2 COMPARE NOTEBOOKS AND DESKTOPS

OBJECTIVES

The goal of this lab is to help you compare the specifications and costs for notebook and desktop computers. After completing this lab, you will be able to:

▲ Compile a list of specifications for a computer according to its purpose

▲ Locate a desktop computer and a notebook computer with similar specifications

▲ Compare the price of a desktop computer to a similar notebook computer and decide which you would purchase

MATERIALS REQUIRED

This lab requires the following:

▲ Internet access

LAB PREPARATION

Before the lab begins, the instructor or lab assistant needs to do the following:

▲ Verify that Internet access is available.

ACTIVITY BACKGROUND

When you shop for a computer, your purchasing decisions are generally driven by questions such as: What will the computer be used for? What features are required to accomplish your goals? What features would tebe nice to have but aren't essential? What features are you willing to compromise on to gain others?

One of the most basic decisions is whether to choose a notebook computer or a desktop. Unlike desktops, notebooks are portable; however, to make notebooks portable, manufacturers often sacrifice performance or other features. In addition, you usually pay more for a notebook than for a desktop computer with comparable features. In this lab, you compile a list of requirements for a computer, locate a notebook and desktop computer with those features, and compare the two systems.

ESTIMATED COMPLETION TIME: 30 minutes

Activity

1. Determine your requirements by answering the following questions:

   ◢ What will the computer mainly be used for? (Possible uses include office applications, graphics and multimedia, gaming, and software development.)

   _____

   ◢ Based on the purpose, what features are required? Include in your list the amount of memory and hard drive space you want. (Some features you might consider include wireless support, display or screen type, software packages supported, PC card support, and external device support.)

   _____

   _____

   _____

   _____

   _____

   ◢ List any additional features you would like but don't require:

   _____

   _____

   _____

   _____

2. Use computer manufacturer Web sites (such as the ones listed in Table 11-1) or comparison Web sites (such as *www.cnet.com* or *www.pricewatch.com*) to find one notebook and one desktop computer that fulfill as many of your requirements as possible and are as similar to each other as possible. Summarize your findings by filling in Table 11-2. Print the Web pages supporting this information.

Features	Desktop Computer	Notebook Computer
Manufacturer and model		
Processor type and frequency		
Memory installed		
Hard drive space		
Operating system		
Drive 1		
Drive 2		
Drive 3		
External ports		
Preinstalled applications		
Cost		

Table 11-2 Desktop and notebook computer specifications

3. Based on your research and the requirements you listed in Step 1, would you purchase a desktop computer or a notebook? Explain your answer:

_____

_____

_____

REVIEW QUESTIONS

1. Which computer was more expensive: the desktop or the notebook? What was the price difference?

_____

_____

2. What features, if any, were you unable to find information for?

_____

_____

3. What features, if any, were missing from the desktop and notebook? How did this information influence your purchasing decision?

_____

_____

4. Did you change your requirements or expectations based on the available products? Explain your answer:

_____

_____

5. Was it easier to find a comparable desktop and notebook from the same manufacturer or from a different manufacturer? Why or why not?

_____

_____

_____

LAB 11.3 REPLACE A NOTEBOOK HARD DRIVE

OBJECTIVES

The goal of this lab is to show you the process of replacing a hard drive in a notebook computer. After completing this lab, you will be able to:

◢ Locate the hard drive in a notebook computer

◢ Remove the hard drive from a notebook computer

◢ Replace the hard drive in a notebook computer

MATERIALS REQUIRED

This lab requires the following:

◢ A notebook computer or Internet access

◢ Printer access

◢ A PC toolkit with antistatic ground strap

◢ Additional smaller screwdrivers, if necessary

LAB PREPARATION

Before the lab begins, the instructor or lab assistant needs to do the following:

◢ Verify that Internet access is available.

ACTIVITY BACKGROUND

Hard disk drives are by nature delicate devices. Dropping one, even a few inches, can cause permanent damage to the read/write heads, platter surfaces, or both. Notebook systems are, of course, often moved and commonly subjected to forces that most other hard drives never encounter. Although drives intended for notebook systems are designed to be resistant to movement and shock, they are still more likely to fail than any other notebook component. In this lab, you remove a hard drive from a notebook computer, and then reinstall the same hard drive. If you don't have access to a notebook, skip to the alternate activity at the end of this lab.

Hard drives designed for notebook computers tend to be 75% to 100% more expensive than the standard 3.5-inch drives of comparable capacity for desktop computers. Also, the majority of newer notebooks support most 2.5-inch drives designed for notebooks, but sometimes a notebook computer requires a proprietary hard drive. For these reasons, researching your replacement options carefully is important. Read the documentation that came with your notebook to determine what drives it supports. If this information isn't available in the documentation, search the manufacturer's Web site. For the purpose of this lab, you remove the existing drive, and then reinstall the same drive. The steps for your notebook might be slightly different from the procedures in this lab, so make sure you study the documentation before you begin.

ESTIMATED COMPLETION TIME: 30 minutes

Activity

1. What are the manufacturer and model of your notebook computer?

   _____

2. Based on the notebook's documentation or information on the manufacturer's Web site, what type of hard drive can be used to replace the existing hard drive? Be as specific as the documentation or the Web site:

   _____

   _____

3. Search the Internet for a replacement hard drive that meets your notebook's requirements. Print the Web page showing the specifications and cost for the drive. How much space does the hard drive have?

   _____

4. Look for specific directions (in the documentation or on the Web site) for removing and replacing your notebook's hard drive. If you find any, summarize those directions here. (If you're using the Web site as your source of information, print any relevant Web pages.)

   _____

   _____

   _____

   _____

Follow these general steps to remove the hard drive from a notebook computer. Note that these directions might not list every step necessary for your model. Refer to specific directions in the documentation or the manufacturer's Web site, as needed.

1. Remove the main battery or batteries and, if necessary, unplug the computer from the AC adapter. Close the screen and turn the computer so that the bottom is facing up.
2. Locate and remove the access panel or component enclosing the drive bay. In many notebooks, the hard drive is located beneath a floppy drive or other removable device, as shown in Figure 11-1.

Bottom of notebook

Floppy drive

Hard drive

Figure 11-1 Remove the floppy drive first to reveal the hard drive cavity

3. After you have accessed the drive, determine how it's secured in the system. It's commonly attached to a frame or "cradle" with small screws, and the cradle is often attached directly to the system chassis. This cradle helps locate and support the drive inside the drive bay. Remove the screws securing the cradle.

4. In most notebooks, data cables don't connect the hard drive to the motherboard, as in desktop computers. Instead, a hard drive connects to the notebook's motherboard by way of an edge connector, similar to those on expansion cards in desktop computers. This type of direct connection has two advantages. First, it improves reliability because it reduces the total number of connection points; fewer connection points mean fewer connections that could shake loose as the notebook is moved around in daily use. The second advantage is that the lack of data cables reduces the notebook's overall size and weight. To remove the drive-cradle assembly, slide the cradle away from the connector. Slide the assembly back until all pins are clear of the connector. When the pins are clear, lift the assembly straight up out of the drive bay.

5. Note the orientation of the drive in the cradle so that when you reinstall the drive, you can mount it in the same direction. Remove the screws securing the drive in the cradle, and then remove the drive.

Follow these general steps to reinstall the hard drive in the notebook computer. Note that these directions might not list every step necessary for your model. Refer to specific directions in the documentation or the manufacturer's Web site, as needed.

1. If necessary, configure the jumper settings to indicate master or slave. Place the drive in the cradle so that the pins are oriented correctly, and then secure it with screws.

2. Set the drive-cradle assembly straight down into the drive bay. Gently slide the assembly to the connector, and verify that the pins are aligned correctly with the connector. Slide the assembly until the drive is fully seated in the connector. The cradle should now align with the holes in the chassis. If the holes don't align, you should remove the assembly, loosen the drive-retaining screws, and adjust the drive's position in the cradle. Repeat this process until the drive is fully seated so that there's no room for it to move after the cradle is secured. When the assembly is seated, secure it with screws.

3. Replace any drives or access covers you removed to get at the hard drive.

4. Reinstall any batteries and reconnect to AC power, if necessary. As with any other hard drive, a notebook drive must be recognized by BIOS correctly, and then partitioned and formatted before it can be used. This process isn't necessary in this lab because you haven't installed a new hard drive.

Alternate Activity

If you don't have access to a notebook computer, follow these steps:

1. Using the documentation for one of the notebooks you selected in Lab 11.1 as your source, what are its requirements for a replacement hard drive? Be as specific as the documentation:

   _____

   _____

2. Search the Internet for information on replacement hard drives, and print the Web page showing the correct specifications for a replacement hard drive. What is the cost of the drive? How much space does the drive have?

   _____

3. Locate the steps for replacing the hard drive. To find this information, use the manuals you downloaded in Lab 11.1, the manufacturers' Web sites, and other Internet resources (such as Web sites for manufacturers of replacement notebook hard drives).

4. How do the steps you found differ from the steps in this lab? Note the differences here:

   _____

   _____

   _____

   _____

   _____

   _____

   _____

   _____

REVIEW QUESTIONS

1. Why should you research hard drives thoroughly when replacing one in a notebook computer?

   _____

   _____

2. Why is cabling commonly not included in notebook systems?

   _____

   _____

3. How was the installation procedure for your computer different from the one in this lab?

_____

_____

_____

4. Suppose you need to install a hard drive in a notebook that doesn't include an access panel for the hard drive. Where should you look for the hard drive inside the notebook?

_____

_____

5. What do you have to do in CMOS setup before a new hard drive can be used?

_____

_____

LAB 11.4 RESEARCH SOFTWARE AVAILABLE FOR PDAS

OBJECTIVES

The goal of this lab is to help you research and compare personal digital assistants (PDAs). After completing this lab, you will be able to:

⊿ Locate and compare information on available PDAs

MATERIALS REQUIRED

This lab requires the following:

⊿ Internet access

LAB PREPARATION

Before the lab begins, the instructor or lab assistant needs to do the following:

⊿ Verify that Internet access is available.

ACTIVITY BACKGROUND

One common problem with PDAs is finding compatible software (in addition to preinstalled software). There are two basic choices for a PDA operating system: Windows Mobile and Palm OS. Earlier handheld OSs by Microsoft are PocketPC and Windows CE. Before you can install additional software, you must verify that the software is compatible with the PDA's operating system and with the specific PDA model. On some basic models, you can't add any software. You must also make sure the software is compatible with the desktop PC that you want to synchronize with the PDA. Finally, some business organizations don't allow certain PDAs to synchronize with the business network. You learn more about these issues in this lab as you research software availability for two different PDA models.

ESTIMATED COMPLETION TIME: 30 minutes

Activity

1. Using the manufacturer sites listed in Tables 11-3 and 11-4, select one Palm OS PDA and one Windows Mobile PDA. Record the name and model number of your choices here:

_____

_____

Manufacturer	Web Site
HandEra	*www.handera.com*
Handspring	*www.handspring.com*
IBM	*www.ibm.com*
Palm	*www.palm.com*
Sony	*www.sonystyle.com*

Table 11-3   Manufacturers of Palm OS PDAs

Manufacturer	Web Site
Casio	*www.casio.com*
Compaq	*www.hp.com*
Hewlett-Packard	*www.hp.com*
Toshiba	*www.toshiba.com*

Table 11-4   Manufacturers of Windows Mobile and PocketPC PDAs

2. On the manufacturers' Web sites, search for technical specifications and lists of installed software for the first model you selected. Then answer the following questions for this model. Download and search user manuals if necessary.

▲ What version of the operating system is installed?

_____

▲ What software comes installed on the PDA?

_____

_____

_____

_____

▲ Can you install other software? If so, list some available programs:

_____

_____

_____

_____

_____

_____

◢ Can the applications on the PDA synchronize with common office applications on a desktop PC or notebook? List the applications on the PDA and the applications on the desktop PC or notebook with which they can synchronize:

_____

_____

_____

_____

_____

◢ Does the PDA support upgrades to the OS? Why would you want to have this capability?

_____

_____

◢ What add-on devices are available for the PDA, such as recharger cradles, cameras, and so forth?

_____

_____

_____

3. Answer the following questions for the second model PDA:

   ◢ What version of the operating system is installed?

_____

   ◢ What software comes installed on the PDA?

_____

_____

_____

   ◢ Can you install other software? If so, list some available programs:

_____

_____

_____

_____

_____

_____

◢ Can the applications on the PDA synchronize with common office applications on a desktop PC or notebook? List the applications on the PDA and the applications on the desktop PC or notebook with which they can synchronize:

_____

_____

_____

_____

_____

_____

◢ Does the PDA support upgrades to the OS? Why would you want to have this capability?

_____

_____

◢ What add-on devices are available for the PDA, such as recharger cradles, cameras, and so forth?

_____

_____

_____

Alternate Activity

If you have access to a PDA, perform the research suggested in this lab for your model. Try to locate, download, and install a trial version of an add-on software program for your PDA. Record the steps and the name of the program you installed:

_____

_____

_____

_____

_____

_____

_____

_____

_____

REVIEW QUESTIONS

1. Was add-on software available for both PDA models you researched?

_____

2. How easy was it to find the information you needed? List the Web sites you visited, ranking them from most user friendly to least user friendly:

_____

_____

_____

_____

3. Which PDA OS supports the most PDA applications? Explain your answer:

_____

_____

_____

4. Are more or fewer software options available for the higher priced PDAs? Explain your answer:

_____

_____

_____

5. Would you consider purchasing either PDA you researched in this lab? Why or why not?

_____

_____

_____

_____

6. List three questions on software availability you should research carefully before selecting a PDA:

_____

_____

_____

LAB 11.5 BATTERY CALIBRATION AND POWER MANAGEMENT

OBJECTIVES

The goal of this lab is to demonstrate the effect battery calibration has on the power-management features of a notebook PC. After completing this lab, you will be able to:

⊿ Explain the calibration process

⊿ Discuss how a battery might drift from calibration

⊿ Explain how battery calibration affects some power-management features

MATERIALS REQUIRED

This lab requires the following:

⊿ A Windows desktop computer

⊿ A Windows notebook computer

⊿ Internet access

LAB PREPARATION

Before the lab begins, the instructor or lab assistant needs to do the following:

⊿ Verify that Windows starts with no errors.

⊿ Verify that Internet access is available.

ACTIVITY BACKGROUND

Many factors affect the battery life of a notebook PC. Two common types of notebook batteries are nickel metalhydride (NiMH) and lithium ion (LiION). Lithium batteries, the most common, are more expensive and last longer. A fully charged lithium battery in good condition can provide about 3 hours of normal use. By contrast, a healthy, fully charged NiMH battery can provide about 2 hours of normal use.

As you might expect, however, "normal use" is a subjective term. The actual way you use your notebook can affect battery life dramatically. For instance, editing text in a word processor doesn't require much power compared with playing a DVD. The word processor uses only a little processor time and occasionally reads or writes to the hard drive. Playing a DVD is processor intensive and requires powering the laser in the drive, thus requiring more power than the word processor.

What the notebook does when you stop using it for a time also affects battery life. For instance, if you don't use the notebook for 10 minutes, it might go into hibernation mode automatically to conserve power. Notebooks also have a few additional power-management features to extend battery life during inactivity and protect data when the battery charge becomes low. Some of these features depend on the notebook being able to accurately judge how much life is left in the battery. If the battery is calibrated accurately, the notebook can make better power-management decisions. In this lab, you explore how power management and battery life are related.

ESTIMATED COMPLETION TIME: 30 minutes

Activity

1. Examine your desktop computer's CMOS setup utility and the Power Management applet in Control Panel. Usually, a computer's BIOS offers a wider range of options for defining a power-management profile than in Windows. Fill in the following chart to compare the power-management options offered in BIOS and Windows:

Power-Management Options and Settings	In BIOS	In Windows

Although the two power-management systems might work together, to avoid possible conflict, Microsoft recommends using BIOS power management as the preferred method if BIOS power management conforms to ACPI standards. These standards have been set by a group of manufacturers, including Microsoft, Intel, and Compaq.

In addition to the BIOS features you just explored, notebooks often have features or settings that allow the computer to shut down or suspend activity if the battery is about to run out of power. But how does the computer know when power is about to run out? Electronically programmable read-only memory (EPROM) is often included in the battery assembly to inform the computer about remaining battery life. The following steps explain the basic procedure for calibrating a battery's EPROM. For specific steps for your notebook, consult its documentation or search the manufacturer's Web site.

1. Verify that your notebook has a fully charged battery attached to AC power.

2. Enter the CMOS setup utility and select the **Power Management** section.

3. In the Power Management section, disable the **Power Savings** option so that the computer doesn't attempt to save power during the calibration process.

4. In the Power Management section, disable any **Suspend on Low Battery** options to prevent interference with calibration.

5. In the Power Management section, select the **Battery Calibration** option. A warning message indicates that the calibration should be carried out only with a fully charged battery and prompts you to confirm that you want to continue.

6. Remove the AC power, and then immediately press **Y** or **Enter** to continue. A message displays the estimated remaining battery life. In a real-life situation, when you actually need to calibrate your notebook's battery, this information would likely be incorrect.

7. Wait for the battery to drain, which might take more than an hour.

8. The manufacturer might specify that the battery should be left to cool for a period after it's drained and the notebook switches off. When appropriate, reattach AC power, boot the laptop, and enter CMOS setup.

9. Select the **Power Management** section, and then select the **Battery Reset** option. This option tells the EPROM that the battery is at (or very near) zero charge and takes you back to the Power Management section of CMOS.

10. Reapply your preferred power management settings, and then save and exit CMOS setup. The battery is now calibrated so that the related power-management and suspend features will work correctly.

If you have access to a notebook and the permission of your instructor, do the following to calibrate the battery:

1. Locate documentation (in the user manual or on the Web) that explains how to calibrate the battery. Note how these steps differ from the ones listed previously:

_____

_____

_____

_____

_____

2. Follow the specific steps for your notebook to calibrate the battery. (Do *not* attempt this procedure unless you have the specific steps because you might do damage to the notebook or battery.)

Some factors can prevent power management from functioning as intended. For instance, word-processing programs often include an auto-save feature that continually saves changes to a document at specific intervals. This feature is intended to safeguard against lost work but tends to interfere with hard disk power-down settings. Many screen savers cause similar effects and can prevent a computer from entering or exiting standby or suspend modes.

REVIEW QUESTIONS

1. What types of activity might decrease the battery life of a fully charged battery more quickly than reading a document or spreadsheet? Give three examples:

_____

_____

_____

2. In your opinion, is aggressive power management more important on a desktop computer or a notebook computer? Explain why:

_____

_____

_____

3. Should BIOS power management always be used with Windows Power Management? Why or why not?

_____

_____

4. What types of programs might prevent a hard drive power-down setting from saving power as intended? Why?

_____

_____

_____

_____

5. What are two possible consequences of an incorrectly calibrated battery? Explain:

_____

_____

_____

_____

CHAPTER
12

Supporting Printers and Scanners

Labs included in this chapter:

- **Lab 12.1:** Install and Share a Printer
- **Lab 12.2:** Install a Network Printer
- **Lab 12.3:** Update Printer Drivers
- **Lab 12.4:** Install and Test a Scanner
- **Lab 12.5:** Printer Maintenance and Troubleshooting
- **Lab 12.6:** Critical Thinking: Sabotage and Repair a Network Printer

LAB 12.1 INSTALL AND SHARE A PRINTER

OBJECTIVES

The goal of this lab is to help you install and share a printer. After completing this lab, you will be able to:

⊿ Install a local printer on a computer

⊿ Share a local printer with other users on the network

⊿ Using another computer on the network, install and use the shared network printer

MATERIALS REQUIRED

This lab requires the following:

⊿ A printer and its printer drivers

⊿ Two or more Windows 2000/XP or Windows 9x computers connected to a network

⊿ Windows installation CD or installation files

⊿ A workgroup of 3 to 4 students

LAB PREPARATION

Before the lab begins, the instructor or lab assistant needs to do the following:

⊿ Verify that Windows starts with no errors.

⊿ Provide each student with access to the Windows installation files, if needed.

ACTIVITY BACKGROUND

A printer can be connected to and dedicated to one PC (called a local printer), or it can be shared with other PCs on the network (called a network printer). For a printer to be shared on a Windows operating system, it must be physically connected to and installed on one computer and then shared with others in the same Windows workgroup. The computer with the printer physically connected to it must have the File and Printer Sharing component installed, and computers on the network using this printer must have the Client for Microsoft Networks component installed. In most cases, installing both components on all computers is easier. In this lab, you install and share a printer in a workgroup, and then use the shared printer on the network.

> **ESTIMATED COMPLETION TIME: 45 minutes**

 Activity

First, you must install Client for Microsoft Networks and File and Printer Sharing (if they aren't already installed). Both components are installed on Windows 2000/XP computers by default. Client for Microsoft Networks is installed in Windows 9x by default. To install both components on Windows 9x computers (if necessary), use these steps:

1. Open Control Panel, and double-click the **Network** applet. The Network dialog box opens.

2. Click **Add**. The Select Network Component Type dialog box opens.

3. In the list box, click **Client**, and then click **Add**.

4. In the Select Network Client dialog box that opens, click **Microsoft** on the left and **Client for Microsoft Networks** on the right. Click **OK** twice, and then insert the Windows installation CD. Reboot the computer when prompted.

5. Return to the Network dialog box. Repeat Steps 2 and 3, this time clicking **Service** instead of Client. The Select Network Service dialog box opens.

6. Click **File and printer sharing for Microsoft Networks**, and then click **OK**. Click **OK** to close the Network dialog box, and then insert the Windows installation CD. Reboot the computer when prompted.

7. Return to the Network dialog box, and then click **File and Print Sharing**. The File and Print Sharing dialog box opens.

8. Verify that the **I want to be able to give others access to my files** and **I want to be able to allow others to print to my printer(s)** check boxes are selected, and then click **OK**. (You aren't practicing file sharing in this lab, but as a general rule, you usually set up file sharing and print sharing at the same time so that remote computers have access to printer drivers already installed on the host machine.) Click **OK** to close the Network dialog box.

Next, you need to verify that all computers that need to use the printer are in the same workgroup. Follow these steps:

1. Ask your instructor for the name of the workgroup you should use for this lab, and record the name here:

---

2. In Windows 9x, right-click the **Network Neighborhood** desktop icon and click **Properties** in the shortcut menu. The network's Properties dialog box opens. Click the **Identification** tab. In Windows 2000/XP, right-click **My Computer** and click **Properties** in the shortcut menu. In the Windows 2000 System Properties dialog box, click the **Network Identification** tab, and then click the **Properties** button. The Identification Changes dialog box opens. In the Windows XP System Properties dialog box, click the **Computer Name** tab and then click **Change**. The Computer Name Changes dialog box opens.

3. To what workgroup does this computer belong?

---

4. If necessary, change the workgroup assignment to match the one you wrote down in Step 1.

Now you're ready to install and share the printer. On a Windows 2000/XP computer that will be physically connected to the printer, follow these steps. The steps for Windows 9x differ slightly, but you can use these steps as a guide.

1. With the computer off, connect the printer cable to the parallel port or USB port on your computer, turn on the printer, and then boot the computer.

2. If the Add Printer Wizard starts, click **Next** and then skip to Step 4.

3. If the wizard doesn't start, in Windows XP, click **Start, Printers and Faxes**. In Windows 2000, click **Start**, point to **Settings**, and then click **Printers**. In the Printers and Faxes window (Printers in Windows 2000) that opens, click the **Add a printer** link (in Windows 2000, double-click the **Add Printer** icon). When the Add Printer Wizard starts, click **Next**.

4. Click **Local printer** (Windows 2000) or **Local printer attached to this computer** (Windows XP), verify that the **Automatically detect and install my Plug and Play printer** check box is selected, and then click **Next**.

5. If a warning dialog box is displayed, click **Next**. A list of ports is displayed. Click **Use the following port**, click **LPT1**, and then click **Next**.

6. A list of manufacturers and printer models is displayed. Select the manufacturer and the model from the list, and then click **Next**. If your printer isn't listed and you have the correct printer driver on disk or CD, click **Have Disk**. Keep in mind that drivers designed for one Windows operating system might not work for a later version of Windows, so you need to make sure you have the correct drivers for your computer's version of Windows. (You can download printer driver files from the printer manufacturer's Web site.) If you select a manufacturer and model from the Windows list, a dialog box might open where you can specify the location of the Windows setup files. In that case, insert the Windows setup CD or select another location for the files.

7. The next window in the Add Printer Wizard asks for a name for the printer. This name appears later in the list of available printers. Accept the default name Windows provides or enter your own, and then click **Next** to continue.

8. Click **Share as** (Windows 2000) or **Share name** (Windows XP) to indicate that this printer will be shared with others on a network, and then click **Next** to continue.

9. If the Location and Comment window is displayed, you can describe the location of the printer, or leave it blank and click **Next**. Click **Yes** to print the test page, and then click **Next**.

10. Windows displays the printer settings you selected. Click **Finish** to complete the installation.

After the printer is installed, you need to make it possible for other computers in the network to access it. Follow these directions to share the printer with other computers in the workgroup:

1. On the computer with a locally installed printer, in Windows 2000 click **Start**, point to **Settings**, and click **Printers**. In Windows XP, click **Start, Printers and Faxes**.

2. The Printers and Faxes window (Printers window in Windows 2000) opens, showing the printer you just installed. Right-click the printer and click **Sharing** in the shortcut menu.

3. The Properties dialog box for the printer opens with the Sharing tab selected. Click the **Shared as** option button (Windows 2000) or **Share this printer** option button (Windows XP), and type a share name for the printer.

4. For Windows 2000/XP computers, click **Additional Drivers**, and select the operating systems that remote computers use. Windows can then provide remote computers with the necessary driver files when they first attempt to connect to the shared printer. (Windows 9x doesn't provide this service.) Click **OK**, and then click **OK** to close the Properties dialog box, if necessary.

The printer is now listed in the My Network Places window (Network Neighborhood window in Windows 9x) on all other computers on the network. However, before a remote computer can use the printer, printer drivers must be installed on it.

There are two approaches to installing a shared network printer on a remote PC. You can perform the installation using the printer drivers installed on the host PC or using the drivers on CD (the Windows CD or printer manufacturer's CD). If you need to install the printer on several remote PCs, it's faster to use the drivers installed on the host PC. The disadvantage of this method is that you must share the C:\Windows folder on the host PC, which is considered a security risk. For this reason, as soon as the printer is installed on all remote PCs, you should unshare the C:\Windows folder on the host PC to protect that critical folder.

Follow these steps to install the shared printer on the other PCs:

1. On the computer with the printer connected locally, you need to share the C:\Windows folder so that the drivers in this folder are available to the other computers. To do this, right-click the **C:\Windows** folder in Windows Explorer, click **Properties** in the shortcut menu, click the **Sharing** tab, and click the **Shared as** (Windows 2000) or **Share this folder** (Windows XP) option to share the folder. Don't require a password to access the folder unless you want to prevent some users from accessing the printer. Click **OK**.

2. On remote PCs, open My Network Places or Network Neighborhood, and find the printer. Right-click the printer and click **Connect** (in Windows 2000/XP) or **Install** (in Windows 9x) on the shortcut menu.

3. Enter a name for the printer and print a test page to complete the installation.

4. After all remote computers have installed the printer, you should remove the shared option on the local computer's C:\Windows folder to protect this important folder. To do this, right-click the folder in Windows Explorer, click **Properties**, click the **Sharing** tab, and click **Not Shared** (Windows 2000) or **Do not share this folder** (Windows XP). Click **OK**.

REVIEW QUESTIONS

1. What two Windows components must be installed before you can share a printer in a workgroup?

_____

_____

2. What would happen if the C:\Windows folder on the host PC wasn't shared when you tried to install the printer on remote PCs? How could you have installed the printer on a remote computer if you didn't have access to the C:\Windows folder on the host computer?

_____

_____

3. Name an advantage of setting up file sharing at the same time as printer sharing:

_____

_____

4. Suppose you want to stop some people on the network from using a shared printer, but you still want the printer to be available to the local computer to which it's connected. What's the easiest way to do this?

_____

_____

LAB 12.2 INSTALL A NETWORK PRINTER

OBJECTIVES

The goal of this lab is to give you more practice installing a local printer on a computer, sharing it, and then printing to it from a remote computer on the network. After completing this lab, you will be able to:

◢ Install a local printer

◢ Share a printer on the network

◢ Test the printer across the network

MATERIALS REQUIRED

This lab requires the following:

- ◢ Windows 2000/XP or Windows 9x operating system
- ◢ Printer, printer cable, and printer driver files
- ◢ A functioning network
- ◢ A workgroup of 2 to 4 students

LAB PREPARATION

Before the lab begins, the instructor or lab assistant needs to do the following:

- ◢ Verify that Windows starts with no errors.

ACTIVITY BACKGROUND

A local printer is connected to a PC by way of a serial, parallel infrared, or USB connection. Usually, it's not available to the network for general printing jobs, but allowing other computers to print from your local printer can be useful sometimes. For example, if you have an expensive photo-quality printer installed locally on your computer, you might want to let users who need to print photos access your printer through the network. In this lab, you install a local printer and a network printer. Instructions in this lab are written for Windows XP/2000 but work much the same for Windows 9x if you substitute Network Neighborhood for My Network Places.

ESTIMATED COMPLETION TIME: 30 minutes

 Activity

The following steps describe the default method for installing a printer in Windows XP. (The steps differ slightly in Windows 2000 and 9x.) However, printer manufacturers often provide specialized steps for installing their devices. In that case, you should follow the steps your printer manufacturer prescribes rather than the steps listed here.

1. With the computer off, attach the printer cable to the computer and the printer. Attach the power cable to the printer, and then plug it in. Turn on the printer and then the computer. After the computer starts, insert the installation disk if you have one.

2. Click **Start, Printers and Faxes**. The Printers and Faxes window opens, displaying any installed printers.

3. Click the **Add a printer** link to open the Add Printer Wizard.

4. In the Add Printer Wizard, click **Next** to begin the installation process.

5. What two printer options do you see in the Add Printer Wizard?

_____

_____

6. In the Add Printer Wizard, click **Local printer attached to this computer**, and then click **Next** to continue.

7. Select the appropriate port, and then click **Next** to continue. If the New Printer Detection window opens with a warning that Windows couldn't detect the device, click **Next**.

8. In the left pane, click to select your printer manufacturer. A list of printers for that manufacturer is displayed in the right pane. Scroll down the list to locate your printer.

9. If you can locate your printer, click it in the right pane, click **Next**, and then skip to Step 12. If you can't locate your printer, click **Have Disk**. The Install From Disk dialog box opens.

10. Click **Browse**, and then locate and select the installation file for your operating system. This file has an .inf file extension and is most likely in a folder named after your operating system (such as \WinXP\install.inf, \WindowsXP\oem.inf, or something similar). Click **OK** to tell the wizard to use the selected file.

11. Click **OK** in the Install From Disk dialog box to close it. The Add Printer Wizard identifies your printer. Click **Next** to continue.

12. In the Printer name text box, type a name for the printer (or leave the default name).

13. When asked if you want this printer to be your Windows default printer, click **Yes**, and then click **Next**. When asked if you would like to print a test page, click **No**, and then click **Finish**. The necessary files are copied to your computer, and in some cases (if the printer has fax capabilities, for instance) a new wizard launches. If it does, complete the wizard or follow instructions from your instructor. When the installation process is finished, an icon for the newly installed printer appears in the Printers window.

Follow these steps to test the printer:

1. In the Printers and Faxes window, right-click the icon for your printer and click **Properties** in the shortcut menu. The printer's Properties dialog box opens.

2. Click the **General** tab, and then click **Print Test Page**. A test print job is sent to the printer, and a dialog box opens asking you whether the page printed correctly.

3. Verify that your test page printed correctly (without any gibberish), and then click **OK** to close the dialog box.

4. Open Windows Explorer and arrange it so that you can still see your printer's icon in the Printers window. In Windows Explorer, locate a .txt or .bat file and drag the file to the printer's icon in the Printers window. What happens?

_____

_____

Now that you have tested your printer, share it (using Lab 12.1 as a guide). Then go to the other computer and follow these steps to install a network printer:

1. Open the Printers and Faxes window and launch the Add Printer Wizard as you did previously. Click **Next** in the first wizard window.

2. Click **A network printer or a printer attached to another computer**, and then click **Next** to continue.

3. Click **Browse for a printer** and click **Next** to locate the printer you'll install. The Browse for Printer window appears, which displays the network in a similar way to Windows Explorer.

4. Locate your printer by expanding the computer on which you installed and shared it. When you have found the correct printer, click to select it, and then click **Next**.

5. In the Add Printer Wizard, verify that the path is correct, and then click **Next** to continue. If a warning dialog box opens, click **Yes** to continue.

6. If necessary, select the manufacturer and model or click **Have Disk**, depending on your printer and operating system.

7. Select whether to make this printer the default, and click **Next**. Complete the Add Printer Wizard.

8. Test your printer.

REVIEW QUESTIONS

1. A printer is connected to the parallel port on computer A but is shared on the network. Computer B installs the shared computer and connects to it. Computer A considers it a(n) ___ printer, and computer B considers it a(n) ___ printer.

2. If a manufacturer's prescribed method for installing its printer differs from the default Windows method, which method should you use?

_____

3. When installing a local printer attached through a parallel cable, what port should you specify?

_____

4. Is it possible for a single printer to be both a local and a network printer? Why or why not?

_____

_____

_____

5. Explain how to print a document without opening it:

_____

_____

LAB 12.3 UPDATE PRINTER DRIVERS

OBJECTIVES

The goal of this lab is to give you experience in upgrading printer drivers. After completing this lab, you will be able to:

▲ Identify driver information

▲ Locate new drivers

▲ Install new drivers

▲ Test printer drivers for functionality

MATERIALS REQUIRED

This lab requires the following:

▲ Windows 2000/XP or Windows 9x operating system

▲ Windows installation CD or installation files

▲ Administrator account and password, if applicable

▲ *Optional*: A file compression utility

▲ Internet access

▲ A local printer

LAB PREPARATION

Before the lab begins, the instructor or lab assistant needs to do the following:

- Verify that Windows starts with no errors.
- Provide each student with access to the Windows installation files, if needed.
- Verify that Internet access is available.

ACTIVITY BACKGROUND

Printer manufacturers often release new drivers for their existing printers to fix problems with earlier drivers, add new functions, support new applications, and accommodate new operating system features. A PC support technician needs to know how to update printer drivers as they become available. The process of updating printer drivers is similar to that for other devices. You must gather information about the device and the currently installed drivers, download the new drivers, and install them. Like other devices, after the drivers are installed, you should test the printer to be certain it's functioning correctly before turning it over to end users. Unlike many other devices, it's easy to verify that a printer is working correctly. You also learn that the process of updating printer drivers is similar across different Windows platforms and printer manufacturers. This lab gives you general instructions for updating printer drivers. Modify these instructions to fit your situation and printer.

ESTIMATED COMPLETION TIME: 30 minutes

 Activity

The first step in updating printer drivers is to gather information about your current printer and drivers. Use Printers and Faxes (Device Manager in Windows 9x) to research and answer the following questions:

1. How is your printer generally used (for example, text, photographs, or graphics)?

   _____

2. What operating system are you using?

   _____

3. Who is the printer manufacturer?

   _____

4. What is the model of the printer?

   _____

5. What is the printer interface (USB, parallel, other)?

   _____

6. Printers typically have many setup options that deal with print quality and paper handling. Right-click the printer in Printers and Faxes (Device Manager in Windows 9x) and click **Properties** in the shortcut menu. Note any important settings because you'll probably need to reapply them after the driver is updated:

   _____

   _____

   _____

In Windows 9x, follow these instructions to view driver details:

1. Open Device Manager, click the **+** (plus sign) next to the printer to expand the heading, and then right-click your printer in the list. Click **Properties**, and a dialog box with both General and Driver tabs should open.

2. Click the **Driver** tab, and then click the **Driver File Details** button to open the Driver File Details dialog box shown in Figure 12-1. List all drivers displayed in the Driver files section:

_____

_____

_____

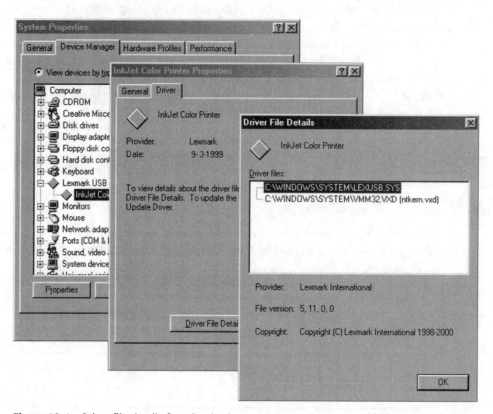

Figure 12-1   Driver file details for a local printer

3. In addition to the previous information, list all driver information shown in the dialog box that can help you identify the current driver later. Include the provider, file version, and copyright information. This information gives you a starting point in locating new drivers for your printer.

_____

_____

_____

In Windows 2000/XP, follow these instructions to identify the printer driver:

1. Open the Printers and Faxes (or Printers in Windows 2000) window.

2. Right-click your printer icon, and click **Properties** in the shortcut menu. The printer's Properties dialog box opens.

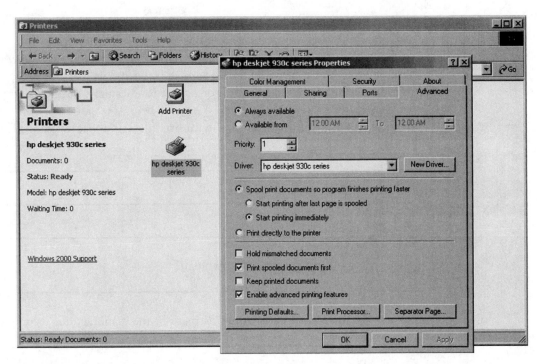

Figure 12-2   Identifying the printer driver in the printer's Properties dialog box

3. Click the **Advanced** tab (see Figure 12-2). Note that tabs might differ from one printer to another.

4. What's the name of the driver listed in the Driver text box?

_____

Follow these general directions to locate available driver updates:

1. Go to the printer manufacturer's Web site and locate the driver download section. Use Table 12-1 to help you find a Web site. What's the URL of the driver download page?

_____

Printer Manufacturer	Web Site
Brother	*www.brother.com*
Canon	*www.canon.com*
Hewlett-Packard	*www.hp.com*
IBM	*www.ibm.com*
Lexmark	*www.lexmark.com*
Okidata	*www.okidata.com*
SATO	*www.satoamerica.com*
Seiko Epson	*www.epson.com*
TallyGenicom	*www.tally.com*
Xerox	*www.xerox.com*

Table 12-1   Printer manufacturers

2. When you search for the correct driver on the Web site, you might find more than one driver that will work for your printer, operating system, or application. Generally, you should select the most recent version that matches your printer and operating system. There are exceptions, however. For instance, if a driver is listed as beta, it's still in development and has been released for evaluation. Usually, but not always, the manufacturer has most of the kinks worked out. To be on the safe side, don't download a beta release driver. List all drivers, with brief descriptions, for your printer and operating system:

_____

_____

_____

3. What driver have you selected to download?

_____

4. Find and list any special installation instructions the manufacturer recommends:

_____

_____

5. Create a folder on your C drive named **Downloads,** if necessary, and then create a subfolder named for the manufacturer, such as C:\Downloads\Lexmark. What's your folder name?

_____

6. Download the driver you intend to install to that folder.

With any device, it's best to follow the manufacturer's recommended method of installation instead of the Windows approach. A good manufacturer tests the driver as well as the installation process. The exception is when you have several printers installed on a system and you think one set of drivers might overwrite files another printer needs. In this case, use the Windows method to update the drivers. Do the following to install the new driver using the manufacturer's installation process:

1. Print an example—a document or a digital picture—of the printer's main use. This printout verifies that your printer is working before you make any changes and is used for comparison later to verify that the new drivers are working.

2. In Windows Explorer, double-click the file you downloaded. If it's a compressed file, it self-extracts files or uses file compression software on your PC to extract the files. If an installation wizard starts, exit it.

3. Were any files extracted? List them here:

_____

4. Locate any Readme.txt files for late-breaking information about installation.

5. Double-click the setup or install program. Document the process you used to install the new drivers:

_____

_____

_____

Do the following to test the printer and new drivers:

1. Open the Printers and Faxes (Windows XP) or Printers (Windows 2000) window.

2. Right-click the printer icon and click **Properties** in the shortcut menu. Click the **Print Test Page** button and verify that the test page is legible.

3. Apply the correct printer settings you recorded in Step 6 at the beginning of this lab.

4. Reprint the typical document or photograph and compare it to the one printed before the driver update. List any differences you see:

_____

REVIEW QUESTIONS

1. List four reasons you might want to update a printer's drivers:

_____

_____

_____

_____

2. List four things you should know before you start searching the Web for updated drivers:

_____

_____

_____

_____

3. What does a driver being in beta release indicate about that driver?

_____

4. List the steps to print a test page in Windows:

_____

_____

LAB 12.4 INSTALL AND TEST A SCANNER

OBJECTIVES

The goal of this lab is to give you experience installing and testing a scanner. After completing this lab, you will be able to:

◢ Install a scanner on a computer

◢ Test the scanner for functionality

MATERIALS REQUIRED

This lab requires the following:

- ◢ Windows 2000/XP operating system
- ◢ Windows installation CD or installation files
- ◢ An administrator account and password, if applicable
- ◢ A USB scanner
- ◢ Any necessary installation software or drivers for the scanner

LAB PREPARATION

Before the lab begins, the instructor or lab assistant needs to do the following:

- ◢ Verify that Windows starts with no errors.
- ◢ Provide each student with access to the Windows installation files, if needed.

ACTIVITY BACKGROUND

A scanner is a popular peripheral device used to digitize images, such as pages from a book or photographs. The images can be saved as an uncompressed bitmap or, because the files are often quite large, saved in a compressed file format, such as .jpg or .gif. Scanners can be purchased separately or combined with a printer in a single device that prints, scans, and copies. Most scanners use a USB connection, but other interface types, such as FireWire, parallel, and SCSI, are available. In this lab, you install and then test a scanner.

ESTIMATED COMPLETION TIME: 30 minutes

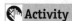 **Activity**

It's best to follow the manufacturer's directions when installing a scanner. You can get the directions and any required software from the CD that comes with the scanner or from the manufacturer's Web site. If the instructions tell you to use the Scanner and Camera Installation Wizard, you can use the following steps:

> **✎ Notes**
>
> Most USB scanners come bundled with their own installation software. It's important to run this software *before* attaching the scanner.

1. Log on to an administrative account in Windows, and make sure all unnecessary programs are closed.

2. Attach the scanner to your computer, and then power on the scanner.

3. Because most scanners are Plug and Play, the Scanner and Camera Installation Wizard should launch automatically. If it doesn't, click **Start, Control Panel, Printers and Other Hardware**, and **Scanners and Cameras**. In the Scanners and Cameras window, click the **Add an imaging device** link.

4. Click **Next** in the Scanner and Camera Installation Wizard.

5. Click to select the manufacturer and model of your scanner (or click **Have Disk** if your scanner came with separate drivers), and then click **Next**.

6. Click to select the correct port, and then click **Next**.

7. Enter a name for your scanner, and then click **Next**. Write the name of your scanner in the following space:

_____

8. Finally, click **Finish** to begin installing the drivers.

To test that your scanner is working correctly, do the following:

1. Click **Start, Control Panel, Printers and Other Hardware,** and **Scanners and Cameras.**

2. Right-click the scanner you want to test and click **Properties.**

3. Click the **General** tab and click the **Test Scanner** button.

4. What message did you get after the test was completed?

_____

_____

5. What message do you get if you turn off the scanner and then go through Steps 1 through 3 again?

_____

_____

REVIEW QUESTIONS

1. What are some advantages and disadvantages of combining your printer and scanner into a single device?

_____

_____

2. Why does the Scanner and Camera Installation Wizard usually launch automatically the first time a scanner is attached to a computer?

_____

_____

3. When might you want to save images as .jpg files?

_____

_____

4. What are some reasons that a scanner might not work correctly after it has been installed?

_____

_____

_____

LAB 12.5 PRINTER MAINTENANCE AND TROUBLESHOOTING

OBJECTIVES

The goal of this lab is to give you experience supporting printers. After completing this lab, you will be able to:

◢ Use the Web to help with printer maintenance

◢ Correct common printer problems

MATERIALS REQUIRED

This lab requires the following:

◢ Internet access

◢ A printer

LAB PREPARATION

Before the lab begins, the instructor or lab assistant needs to do the following:

◢ Verify that Internet access is available.

ACTIVITY BACKGROUND

Printers require more maintenance than most other peripheral devices. Paper gets jammed, the ink cartridge or toner runs out, and image or document quality is degraded by dust and misalignment. Most manufacturers and many models have specific instructions for maintaining ink and toner cartridges that apply exclusively to their printers, so you must rely on the printer manufacturer for instructions when maintaining a printer. In this lab, you investigate maintenance and troubleshooting instructions for several types of printers.

ESTIMATED COMPLETION TIME: 30 minutes

 Activity

Use the Internet to research how to solve the following problems. The printer is a high-end color laser printer by Hewlett-Packard (*www.hp.com*), the LaserJet 9500. Answer these questions about routine maintenance for this printer:

1. Everything needed for routine maintenance of the LaserJet 9500 can be purchased in a printer maintenance kit. List the printer components included in this kit:

   _____

   _____

   _____

2. On the HP Web site, find the instructions for using the kit to perform routine maintenance. What should you wear while you do the maintenance?

   _____

3. How many pages can be printed before maintenance should be performed?

   _____

The next printer is an inkjet printer, the HP Deskjet 930c. Answer these questions:

1. Your computer displays a message to replace the ink cartridge. You replace the cartridge, but the message is still displayed. Also, you notice that the resume light on the printer is blinking. Search the HP Web site and locate the troubleshooting steps to solve the problem.

2. What is the first thing HP suggests you do when you see these errors?

   _____

3. One thing HP suggests is that you clean the cartridge contacts. List the steps:

_____

_____

_____

_____

4. If the problem isn't fixed, HP suggests you reclean the cartridge contacts, this time using a cotton swab dipped in what?

_____

Next, follow these steps to learn how to perform routine maintenance or troubleshoot problems on your local printer:

1. List the following information to identify your local printer:

▲ Printer manufacturer:

_____

▲ Printer model:

_____

▲ Printer interface (parallel, USB, other):

_____

2. Search the manufacturer's Web site for troubleshooting and maintenance procedures and answer the following questions:

▲ What types of problems are addressed for your printer?

_____

_____

_____

▲ Does the manufacturer offer a printer maintenance kit? If so, what components are included and how much does the kit cost?

_____

_____

_____

▲ What maintenance tips for your printer can you find on the Web site?

_____

_____

REVIEW QUESTIONS

1. When a printer isn't working correctly, what are two ways the problem is communicated to users?

2. Why do printers require more maintenance than other peripherals?

3. How often should you perform printer maintenance using a maintenance kit purchased from the manufacturer?

4. After you replace an ink cartridge in an inkjet printer, an error message is displayed. What's the first thing you should do?

LAB 12.6 CRITICAL THINKING: SABOTAGE AND REPAIR A NETWORK PRINTER

OBJECTIVES

The goal of this lab is to learn how to troubleshoot problems with a network printer.

MATERIALS REQUIRED

This lab requires the following:

- Two or more computers connected to a network, one with a local printer attached
- Windows installation CD or installation files
- A workgroup of 2 to 4 students

LAB PREPARATION

Before the lab begins, the instructor or lab assistant needs to do the following:

- Verify that Windows starts with no errors.
- Provide each student with access to the Windows installation files, if needed.

ACTIVITY BACKGROUND

Problems with a network printer are common, and a PC support technician is often called on to solve them. This lab gives you practice solving these types of problems.

ESTIMATED COMPLETION TIME: 45 minutes

 Activity

1. Using the steps in Lab 12.1, verify that each computer in a workgroup is able to print to a network printer that's locally installed on one of the computers in the workgroup.

2. Trade systems with another group, and sabotage the other group's system while that group sabotages your system. The following list has some suggestions for preventing a computer from using the network printer. Do something in this list, or think of another option.

   ◢ On the host computer, remove the sharing option for the printer.

   ◢ Uninstall the printer on a remote computer.

   ◢ Pause printing on one or more computers.

   ◢ Turn the printer off or offline.

   ◢ Disconnect the printer cable from the host computer.

   ◢ Remove paper from the printer.

   ◢ Introduce an error in the printer configuration on the host computer or a remote computer.

3. What did you do to sabotage the other team's system?

   _____

   _____

   _____

4. Return to your system and troubleshoot it.

5. Describe the problem as a user would describe it to you if you were working at a help desk:

   _____

   _____

6. What is your first guess as to the source of the problem?

   _____

7. List the steps you took in the troubleshooting process:

   _____

   _____

   _____

   _____

8. How did you solve the problem and return the printing system to working order?

   _____

   _____

REVIEW QUESTIONS

1. What would you do differently the next time you encounter the same symptoms?

   _____

2. What are three easy things you could ask a user to check that don't require experience with Windows?

_____

_____

_____

3. What might cause this problem to happen? List three possible causes:

_____

_____

_____